Dancing with the Unconscious

Psychoanalysis in a New Key Book Series
Volume 14

PSYCHOANALYSIS IN A NEW KEY BOOK SERIES

DONNEL STERN
Series Editor

When music is played in a new key, the melody does not change, but the notes that make up the composition do change in the context of continuity, continuity that perseveres through change. "Psychoanalysis in a New Key" publishes books that share the aims psychoanalysts have always had, but that approach them differently. The books in the series are not expected to advance any particular theoretical agenda, although to this date most have been written by analysts from the Interpersonal and Relational orientations.

The most important contribution of a psychoanalytic book is the communication of something that nudges the reader's grasp of clinical theory and practice in an unexpected direction. "Psychoanalysis in a New Key" creates a deliberate focus on innovative and unsettling clinical thinking. Because that kind of thinking is encouraged by exploration of the sometimes surprising contributions to psychoanalysis of ideas and findings from other fields, "Psychoanalysis in a New Key" particularly encourages interdisciplinary studies. Books in the series have married psychoanalysis with dissociation, trauma theory, sociology, and criminology. The series is open to the consideration of studies examining the relationship between psychoanalysis and any other field—for instance, biology, literary and art criticism, philosophy, systems theory, anthropology, and political theory.

But innovation also takes place within the boundaries of psychoanalysis, and "Psychoanalysis in a New Key" therefore also presents work that reformulates thought and practice without leaving the precincts of the field. Books in the series focus, for example, on the significance of personal values in psychoanalytic practice, on the complex interrelationship between the analyst's clinical work and personal life, on the consequences for the clinical situation when patient and analyst are from different cultures, and on the need for psychoanalysts to accept the degree to which they knowingly satisfy their own wishes during treatment hours, often to the patient's detriment.

PSYCHOANALYSIS IN A NEW KEY BOOK SERIES

DONNEL STERN
Series Editor

Dancing with the Unconscious

The Art of Psychoanalysis and the Psychoanalysis of Art

DANIELLE KNAFO

Routledge
Taylor & Francis Group
New York   London

Cover Image: Oskar Kokoschka, *Two Nudes (Lovers)* (1913). Oil on canvas, 163.2 x 97.5 cm. Museum of Fine Arts, Boston; Bequest of Sarah Reed Platt 1973.196. Photograph © 2012 Museum of Fine Arts, Boston.

Routledge
Taylor & Francis Group
711 Third Avenue
New York, NY 10017

Routledge
Taylor & Francis Group
27 Church Road
Hove, East Sussex BN3 2FA

© 2012 by Taylor & Francis Group, LLC
Routledge is an imprint of Taylor & Francis Group, an Informa business

Version Date: 20120120

International Standard Book Number: 978-0-415-88100-5 (Hardback) 978-0-415-88101-2 (Paperback)

Library of Congress Cataloging-in-Publication Data

Knafo, Danielle.
    Dancing with the unconscious : the art of psychoanalysis and the psychoanalysis of art / Danielle Knafo.
        p. cm. -- (Psychoanalysis in a new key ; v. 14)
    Includes bibliographical references and index.
    ISBN 978-0-415-88100-5 (hbk. : alk. paper) -- ISBN 978-0-415-88101-2 (pbk. : alk. paper) -- ISBN 978-0-203-84886-9 (e-book)
    1. Psychoanalysis and art. 2. Psychoanalysis. I. Title. II. Series.

N72.P74K63 2012
150.19′5--dc23
                                         2011031861

Visit the Taylor & Francis Web site at
http://www.taylorandfrancis.com

and the Routledge Web site at
http://www.routledgementalhealth.com

In loving memory of my father, Maurice Knafo, who loved to dance

Contents

Acknowledgments

This book was made possible by the encouragement and support of my friends and family. You are too numerous to name, but I hope you know the important role you play in my life. I am also grateful to those who shared with me that most singular and creative encounter called psychoanalysis and who gave me permission to write about our clinical work together.

Special thanks are due to Rocco Lo Bosco, who not only co-wrote two chapters with me, but also generously edited numerous versions of the remaining chapters and contributed important ideas to them. His unwavering belief in this project helped sustain my own.

Seymour Moscovitz, my good friend and colleague, read early versions of several chapters, and his input always led to important improvements.

Others who offered thoughtful comments on early versions of select chapters are Ruth Setton, Irwin Hoffman, Stefanie Solow Glennon, and Jeanne Wolff Bernstein.

Maryellen Lo Bosco's careful editing was invaluable. It always amazes me how often language can be made clearer.

Jeremy Novich, my research assistant, was available throughout the writing and editing process and helped me find even the most obscure reference.

I am very grateful to Donnel Stern, the series editor, who had faith in this project from the start, and who read and returned the chapters I sent him in a timely manner. It was wonderful to discover our shared love of Bruno Schulz.

I could not have asked for a better editor than Kristopher Spring, who was always upbeat and responsive. Thanks, too, to my production editor, Susan Horwitz.

Finally, I thank all the people and institutions that provided me with images used to illustrate this book. In particular, thanks go to Art Resource, Artists Rights Society, Michal Heiman, Bracha L. Ettinger, Martha Posner, George Paichas, and Marek Podstolski; Galerie Lelong in New York; the

Jewish Historical Museum in Amsterdam; the Muzeum Literatury im Adama Mickiewicza in Warsaw; and the Museum of Fine Arts in Boston. Permission costs for these images have been supported by a grant from the Psychoanalytic Society of the Postdoctoral Program, Inc., which is the graduate society of the New York University Postdoctoral Program.

List of Illustrations

Cover: Oskar Kokoschka, *Two Nudes (Lovers)* (1913). Oil on canvas, 163.2 × 97.5 cm. Museum of Fine Arts, Boston; Bequest of Sarah Reed Platt 1973.196. Photograph © 2012 Museum of Fine Arts, Boston.

Plate 1: Martha Posner, *Dancers for Boscobel* (2011). Honeysuckle vine, bamboo, and jute. Photo: George Paichas.

Plate 2: Pablo Picasso, *Bust of a Woman in a Hat* (1970). Musee des Beaux-Arts, Rennes, France. Scala/White Images/Art Resource, New York.

Plate 3: Frida Kahlo, *My Nurse and I (Mi Nana y yo)* (1937). Fundacion Dolores Olmedo, Mexico City, D.F., Mexico. Schalkwijk/Art Resource, New York. © 2011 Banco de México Diego Rivera Frida Kahlo Museums Trust, Mexico, D.F./Artists Rights Society (ARS), New York.

Plate 4: Bracha L. Ettinger, *Autistwork, n. 1* (1993). Courtesy of the artist.

Plate 5: Bracha L. Ettinger, *Untitled* (1988–1989). Sketch. Courtesy of the artist.

Plate 6: Charlotte Salomon, *Self-Portrait* (1940). Jewish Historical Museum Collection, Amsterdam. © Charlotte Salomon Foundation.

Plate 7: Charlotte Salomon, from *Life? or Theater?* (1940–1942). Gouache, 13 × 10 in. Jewish Historical Museum Collection, Amsterdam. © Charlotte Salomon Foundation.

Plate 8: Charlotte Salomon, from *Life? or Theater?* (1940–1942). Gouache, 13 × 10 in. Jewish Historical Museum Collection, Amsterdam. © Charlotte Salomon Foundation.

Plate 9: Charlotte Salomon, from *Life? or Theater?* (1940–1942). Gouache, 13 × 10 in. Jewish Historical Museum Collection, Amsterdam. © Charlotte Salomon Foundation.

Plate 10: Charlotte Salomon, from *Life? or Theater?* (1940–1942). Gouache, 13 × 10 in. Jewish Historical Museum Collection, Amsterdam. © Charlotte Salomon Foundation.

Plate 11: Michal Heiman, *Mirror Test* (2001). Courtesy of the artist.

Plate 12: Michal Heiman, *Michal Heiman Test (M.H.T.)* (1997), with Plate 15S (4). Courtesy of the artist.

Introduction

Dance is the hidden language of the soul.

—Martha Graham

The unconscious is the true psychical reality; in its innermost nature it is as much unknown to us as the reality of the external world, and it is as incompletely presented by the data of consciousness as is the external world by the communications of our sense organs.

—Sigmund Freud

I have lived and worked at the junction of psychoanalysis and art for many years. The origin of my interest in these two disciplines, and especially in their connection, is rooted in my early childhood. I was a child when my family emigrated from French Morocco to Pennsylvania Dutch country in the United States, two worlds farther apart in culture than in miles. Whisked away from the bright, fiery colors of Morocco, baked by the sun and caressed by the sea, I was deposited in Pennsylvania, a land of cold, empty streets and hills coated with endless snow. In the country of my birth, people with olive-colored skin sang Andalusian melodies in passionate voices, the marketplace boomed with the raucous pyrotechnics of gritty commerce, and ghosts walked among the night trees. In my new home, pale Amish women quietly sold their produce, their hair pulled back so tightly that their faces seemed stretched upward, while their stone-faced men stood, inscrutable, behind unruly beards. Having gone from couscous and b'stilla to funnel cakes and shoo-fly pie, I had no choice but to creatively bridge those two worlds.

Watching my parents reinvent themselves also taught me about trauma and creativity, resilience and sublimation. My father had been at the top of the class ladder in the small coastal town of Safi, where he was both a mathematics teacher and the owner of a local department store. In the United States, he was humbled in his new position as clerk in a supermarket, but he slowly managed to create a new and prosperous life for himself and his family. My mother, a homemaker who learned English by watching *I Love Lucy* episodes on television, was more isolated. Having had a number of servants in Morocco, she now did everything herself. I learned from her how to use creativity and resourcefulness to survive in a strange land. She sewed haute couture clothing for me and my sister as well as our dolls. She cooked gourmet food and served up 10-course feasts on a daily basis. She helped us put on plays and created all the costumes for them. She was a gifted storyteller, a true Scheherazade who brought the dazzling tapestry of her Moroccan childhood to life in the stories she told us.

I learned from my parents' adaptation to trauma and my own bridging of worlds how creativity infuses everyday life. When I became a professional psychologist in Israel I learned how much creativity and resilience survivors of trauma must have in order to continue living a life that has betrayed them. Helping Holocaust survivors, combat veterans, and victims of terrorism create new lives after undergoing the worst human experiences reminded me of what Elie Wiesel once said: "When He created man, God gave him a secret and that secret was not how to begin but how to begin again" (1976, p. 32). No doubt beginning again is a creative act, and it is no coincidence that so many immigrants and exiles—persons who have suffered great loss and survived trauma—are often among the most creative. Art often becomes the new home for those displaced from the mainstream. Living outside the box becomes thinking outside the box. Theodor Adorno wrote that "For a man who no longer has a homeland, writing becomes a place to live" (1974, p. 87), and Saint Lucian poet Derek Walcott expressed the same notion in "The Schooner Fight," where he wrote, "I have no nation now but the imagination" (2007, p. 129).

Working with severely disturbed individuals, often diagnosed as psychotic, has taught me that there is no manual for entering the human mind and that one has to be creative to reach those deemed unreachable. While many of my colleagues found psychosis frightening or labeled it untreatable by psychoanalytic methods, I have always felt excited and privileged to encounter and treat a human being suffering extreme disturbance, because the psychosis itself is a creative response to some unbearable situation and holds the key to its own creative resolution. I additionally perceived similarities between psychotic experiences and the products of creative artists. Both involve fluid, even regressed, self states and access to unconscious processes; both create new worlds to deal with pain; both are attempts at healing what's broken; both offer alternative ways of viewing and experiencing reality.

The life of an immigrant, the work with trauma, and the treatment of psychosis all demanded of me a creative response. Just as I lived the double life so common to immigrants and traveled between cultures, I learned to move easily between the worlds of art and psychoanalysis. In addition, since my early childhood, I danced, played music, drew, and wrote. I have always loved the arts and felt that both art and psychology deal with the human condition and require many of the same skills. As a result, bringing worlds together and having them dialogue with and learn from each other have characterized my life's work, and that work is reflected in this volume, which contains many examples of creative transcendence precipitated by various forms of exile and loss.

Why the Dance?

Psychoanalysis has traditionally been thought to exist somewhere between the disciplines of science and art. John Bowlby (1979) distinguished the "art of psychoanalytic therapy" from the "science of psychoanalytic psychology." He explained that while the clinician deals with complexity, the scientist seeks to simplify, and while the clinician employs theory as a guide, the scientist challenges theory. Loewald (1974) similarly divided psychoanalytic technique into the art of applying psychoanalytic knowledge and methods to particular cases and the science of psychoanalytic observations and theory.

More recently, articles in *Psychological Science in the Public Interest* (Baker, McFall, & Shoham, 2008), *Newsweek* (Begley, 2009), and *Nature* (Abbott, 2009) harshly criticize psychotherapy—and especially psychoanalysis—for not being scientific enough. In contrast, Shedler (2010) has presented abundant empirical evidence to support the effectiveness of psychodynamic therapy. The debate rages on, although categorizing psychoanalysis as a science remains an elusive goal. Irwin Hoffman (2009) argues against the current ascendance of empiricism, saying that questions addressed in psychoanalysis, such as "What is a good way to be in this moment?" "Which human motives are most important?" and "What constitutes the good life?" "cannot and should not be adjudicated by ... 'science'"(p. 1049).

Although theorists of psychoanalysis are often influenced by empirical study, and many aspire to scientific validation, the practice of psychoanalysis possesses commonalities with many art forms. Analysis and dynamic therapy have been compared to the interpretation of literary texts, co-authorship, the construction of narratives (Lacan, 1959; Loewald, 1974; Schafer, 1992; Spence, 1982), and storytelling (Ferro, 1999/2006). Dreams, a frequent subject of analysis, are visual and depict scenes, like paintings or "moving pictures." They speak in code and demand access to unconscious revelation. The analyst "sculpts" the patient's material. The patient and analyst enact and reenact [psycho]dramas and, in many respects, they are both creative and performing artists, each fluidly (one hopes) moving from one role to the next (Loewald, 1974). Like artists, both therapist and patient enjoy sessions of white-hot creativity thrumming with possibility, as well as endure slow and seemingly unproductive fallow periods, where, nonetheless, some important change may be taking place within the unconscious. Many decisions made during therapeutic engagement rest upon intuition, hints, clues, associations, pregnant silences, and missteps. How much like the artist is the therapist who often may be at nearly a complete loss about how to proceed when, in the gloomy darkness of uncertainty, a door suddenly opens and fills the room with dazzling light.

Wilfred Bion, in his 1978 Paris seminar, stated, "One cannot afford to cast aside imaginative conjectures on the ground that they are not scientific enough." He compared the psychoanalyst to the artist and invited him to consider which type of atelier he works in: "What sort of artist are you? Are you a potter? A painter? A musician? A writer?" His interviewer opined that some analysts might not see themselves as artists, to which Bion replied, "Then they are in the wrong job" (1978). If Bion were to ask me that question, I would answer that my consulting room is a dance studio and my patients and I are partners in dance. The metaphor of dance appeals to me as a provocative representation of the dynamic aspect of the psychoanalytic process and relationship—the movement from past to present, the movement of defense and catharsis, the movement of containment and release, the movement between conscious and unconscious and, most of all, the movement created by analyst and analysand. Like the dance, psychoanalysis is an art in which we use ourselves as the medium; the dance and the dancer are one fabric. Steps are required, but they cannot be performed rigidly, without grace or fluidity; every passage must involve creativity. Theory guides me but cannot restrict my engagement with my partner; theory cannot be adhered to so closely that it binds the interaction, nor can it be loosened to the point that the embrace is broken. I must remain ever sensitive to the rhythms, alterations, and intensities of the dance in which I sometimes lead and sometimes am led. It is a dance of high purpose whose proper execution, though informed by theory, is nothing if not art.[1]

Dance was present at the beginning of psychoanalysis when Breuer and Freud filled *Studies on Hysteria* (1893–1895/1955) with stories of women's bodies that were stuck. Some of them literally could not move. Freud danced with his patients as he addressed the performative elaboration of their symptoms. He passed from hypnosis to the pressure technique to free association to dream analysis, as he tried to move his patients out of emotional and "physical" paralyses. (See Plate 1.)

What Freud grasped early on is that dance is about the mind and body working together and that dance and health are about movement. Mitchell (1988), too, referred to a patient's dance as either restrictive or expansive:

---

[1] After I wrote this introduction, I came across a paper by Wilma Bucci (2011) comparing psychoanalysis to the choreography of Argentine tango.

I do not propose going to the dance and complaining about the music, but enjoying the dance as offered, together with questioning the singularity of style. How did it come about that the analysand learned no other steps? Why does the analysand believe that this is the only desirable dance there is? Most analysands need to feel that their own dance style is appreciated in order to be open to expanding their repertoire. (p. 212)

Movement contains a symbolic function; it gives evidence of the dissemination of unconscious processes and mental health. It has its own pulse, heartbeat, and breathing cycle—the enfolding of experience and the unfolding of knowledge and action that heals. Pathology is about being stuck, repeating the same patterns of behavior again and again, even when such repetition deepens restriction and despair. Any movement can be viewed as dance, and any dance—physical or emotional—has its own vocabulary. Think of the sexuality and aggression expressed in the tango, the relaxed, rhythmic movement of a waltz, or the lively, flowing feel of a samba. Psychologically speaking, we dance through life and change partners throughout. There are developmental dances, beginning with that of the mother and child, whose choreography is so beautifully demonstrated in the microanalysis of Beatrice Beebe's films. There is the dance of children playing together. There is ebb and flow of friendships and the excitement in the dance that is part of courtship and lovemaking. Finally, there is the dance of old age, as one begins to dance with loss and death.

And then there is the dance of psychoanalysis, offering freedom for personal expression and intuitive, spontaneous invention. Of course the dance of psychoanalysis is more than a dance, certainly even more than an art. Hoffman (2009) writes that "the reality of the ambiguity of human experience requires a creative dimension in the process of 'making something' of that experience" (p. 1048). Bollas (2009) likens the analytic session to "an act of creation" (p. 12), and Ringstrom (2011) speaks of the "ensemble work" and "spontaneous gesture" involved in playful analytic improvizations, which he likens to jazz (p. 469). That one human being works with another for the purpose of personal transformation is both a therapeutic and artistic endeavor. But the artistic component of psychoanalytic treatment (that is, the creative engagement with the analysand) might be the most significant in effecting positive change. If this is so, why has so little been written about the artistic elements of the therapeutic process itself? Perhaps it is because creating art is messy, full of false starts, interruptions, repeat attempts, punctuations of despair, flashes of inspiration, and long-awaited breakthroughs. The artistic process does not lend itself to linear descriptions. The inspired artist relies on the covert and spontaneous activity of the unconscious, never quite sure of, exactly, what she is doing or what she will do next. This is no less true of analysis. Even if the whole process were filmed, every word recorded, and every event analyzed from multiple perspectives, still something vital would remain hidden. The resonant, pregnant silences, the complex and subtle layers of cognitive, affective, and expressive patterns of embodiment, and the hidden radiances of the underground all remain elusively beyond capture through formula and theory.

To be sure, the deep work of psychoanalysis is not readily recognized in every session. This is because psychoanalysis is messy and because, like artistic production, it has periods of incubation. Just as an artist does not write or paint every day, so too, psychoanalytic work is not always visibly productive or creative. There are long days, weeks, months, and even years that prepare the way for breakthroughs, those dazzling moments when the rhythm of change beats the air. This period of incubation is a necessary prelude to the illumination that accompanies creative and emotional transformation and synthesis (Arieti, 1976). Stillness is also a part of the dance and beautiful in its own way.

Why the Unconscious?

The unconscious stands as the central pillar in psychoanalytic thought. Although Freud did not discover the unconscious, as many believe, he did bring our attention to its primacy in human life. LaPlanche and Pontalis (1973) claim that "if Freud's discovery had to be summed up in a single word, that word would without doubt have to be 'unconscious'" (p. 474). Freud emphasized that unconscious processes played a much larger role in human experience than conscious processes, comparing them to the greater portion of an iceberg submerged and hidden from view.

Freud's unconscious was influenced by his observations with hypnosis (Breuer & Freud, 1893–1895/1955). He theorized that a splitting of consciousness occurred when one is confronted with trauma, "incompatible ideas," or unacceptable wishes. Undoing repression was for Freud a major therapeutic goal related to that of making the unconscious conscious (Knafo, 2009a).

Over 100 years later, there is widespread agreement that most mental processing is unconscious (Bargh & Chartan, 1999; Velmanns, 1991; Wegner, 2002; Wilson, 2002). Nonetheless, theorists, researchers, and clinicians have different definitions of the unconscious mind. Pierre Janet (1919/1976) wrote of dissociation as a congenital weakness in synthesis that, when coupled with trauma, results in a separate state of consciousness. Interpersonal and relational schools of psychoanalysis have preferred to speak of dissociation rather than repression. Davies and Frawley (1992) and Bromberg (1998) have continued Janet's emphasis on dissociation to address the discontinuity of self states that takes place in trauma. Stern's "unformulated experience" is not restricted to trauma—"thoughts not yet thought, connections not yet made, memories one does not yet have the resources or willingness to construct" (1989, p. 12)—but can be correlated with research on trauma that shows how such experiences are not symbolized (van der Kolk, 1997).

Current ideas about the unconscious mind among cognitive psychologists (Greenwald, 1992; Hassin, Uleman, & Bargh, 2005; Kihlstrom, 1987; Kihlstrom, Barnhardt, & Tataryn, 1992; Wilson, 2002) and neuroscientists share common ground. Neuroscientific research on implicit memory, vision without awareness, critically injured patients, subliminal perception and the "adaptive unconscious" (Pierce & Jastrow, 1884; Silverman, 1983; Weinberger & Hardaway, 1990; Wilson, 2002) all point to the consensus that the unconscious directs thoughts, feelings, and behaviors (Banaji & Greenwald, 1994; Bargh, 1994; Higgins, 1989), and that we can learn without consciousness (de Gelder, de Haan, & Heywood, 2002; Kandel, 1999; LeDoux, 1996). Kihlstrom (1987) claims that "the unconscious of contemporary psychology is kinder and gentler" (p. 789) than Freud's (1933/1964) "cauldron full of seething excitations" (p. 73) in which sexual and aggressive drives needed to be banished from consciousness or socialized.

Eagle (2011) notes that within psychoanalysis there has been a shift from an unconscious of infantile wishes to an unconscious of learned cognitive structures and interactional representations. Regardless of the way in which the unconscious is viewed, it remains one of the primary constructs that distinguishes the interests of psychoanalysis from other therapeutic approaches. Both artists and psychoanalysts intentionally seek special access to the unconscious, a territory without full and accurate maps, a place where one thing may become another in the wink of an eye, where meaning itself originates not as a monolith, but as a deeply layered matrix of possibility, and where every action is multi-determined.

Indeed, what can we name that is more complex than the human mind? When Lacan (1953/2004) wrote that the unconscious must be structured like a language, surely he could not have been referring to language in any ordinary sense of the word. Language and conscious thought are essentially serial in nature; yet they spring from a subterranean world comprised of complex parallel processes that function simultaneously and result in a thinker, a thought, and a feeling about what is happening. If the unconscious is structured like a language, it must be a language that also keeps us alive—for instance, in the autonomic control of heartbeat, respiration, and fight–flight chemistry. It must be a language that creates a sense of time while remaining steeped in timelessness, a language that fashions limits through limitless vision, a language that denies nothing while embracing everything. It must be a multidimensional language capable of infinite representation and remarkable connectivity. It must be a language that dreams and from whose dreams emerge the forms of knowledge and expression that apprehend and expand the scope of human possibility. The unconscious makes possible the whole of the epistemological universe, encompassing the known and the as-yet undiscovered and unrevealed. Though all human disciplines must rely upon it for their existence, both psychoanalysis and art talk to and about it most obviously, the former rather directly, the latter in nuanced code, each discipline enhancing and clarifying the other.

This book focuses on the interrelatedness of psychoanalysis and art, and how the operations of both utilize the unconscious in the quest for creation, transformation, and healing. It has become important of late to position psychoanalysis as a science, but this view seems to minimize the creativity involved in both analytic and scientific endeavors. Similarly, artists obviously use unconscious processes in their creative work, yet many of them are unaware of the therapeutic aspects of art. This volume uncovers the creative structures common to both psychoanalysis and art and demonstrates how each can illuminate the processes of the other through a unique and valuable partnership.

The first section of this volume examines the artistic components in psychoanalytic theory and work. Case studies and commentary demonstrate how free association, transference, dreamwork, regression, altered states of consciousness, trauma, and solitude form a braid of creative elements in psychoanalysis. The first section also describes how the analytic couple functions as an artistic couple (dance partners) in the service of growth. Rather than tout the therapeutic action of psychoanalysis, this section emphasizes the artistry and profound creativity that exists at the heart of the psychoanalytic dance. I call this the *creative action of psychoanalysis*. In fact, the quest for transformation sought in psychoanalysis or psychodynamic psychotherapy is itself a creative endeavor, one best served by allowing the unconscious to speak to the analytic couple through the artistry of the analyst. Like the dedicated artist and his or her object of art, the analytic couple must be willing to endure the fallow times, where the unconscious slowly toils in the depths of the subterrain before a breakthrough occurs. For me this moment of breakthrough, creation, and discovery is the jewel in the crown of psychoanalysis.

The second section of this volume presents in-depth studies of a number of artists and their works. Just as Freud studied psychopathology in order to learn about the psyche, these chapters will look at creative artists and thinkers to understand psychological processes that exist in all of us. The artistic project can serve and illustrate many psychological needs: the creation of a self; the establishment of connections with the world; affect regulation; the working through of conflict and processing of trauma; myth and meaning making; and the symbolic search for immortality. For this reason, creativity is at the heart of self-transformation. The bridge between psychoanalysis and art does not need to be built; it has existed all along. Following is a synopsis of the individual chapters.

Part I: The Art of Psychoanalysis

Chapter 1, "Dancing with the Unconscious: The Art of Psychoanalysis," looks at psychoanalytic work as an art form and uses the metaphor of dance to describe the rich creativity of mental life and analytic work. The creative dimensions of free association, transference–countertransference, and dreamwork are each discussed, along with their coupling in the service of a "cure." A compelling session with a transsexual patient that used dream analysis is presented verbatim, supplemented by transient reflections and subsequent analysis. The case study illustrates the creative collaboration that occurs between analyst and analysand.

Chapter 2, "One Step Back, Two Steps Forward: Regression in the Service of Art and Psychoanalysis," develops a critical reexamination of the usefulness of Ernst Kris's concept of "regression in the service of the ego" and shows how regression is at the heart of creativity. It is argued that one must depathologize the concept of regression as well as expand its terminology to reflect advances in object relations theory. Creative regression is facilitated by the artistic setting and relationship to one's craft, just as therapeutic regression is facilitated by the analytic frame and the transference relationship. Case material is presented.

Chapter 3, "The Senses Grow Skilled in Their Craving: Thoughts on Creativity and Substance Abuse," explores the frequent connection between artistic creativity (and success) and the use of substances. Many artists use alcohol and drugs to aid in creative regression as well as ease personal sensitivity, deal with the pressures of fame and the fear of failure, and lessen the sense of isolation that accompanies the lone pursuit of art. The danger is of course addiction, degeneration, and destruction. A case is presented.

Chapter 4, "Creative Transformations of Trauma: Private Pain in the Public Domain and the Clinical Setting," examines two artists' lives and works. German born Charlotte Salomon, killed in Auschwitz at 26, engaged with personal and political turmoil and atrocity in her art, while Michal Heiman, a contemporary Israeli artist, deals with terrorism and its effects in her art. Additionally, a case of an artist who is the child of a Holocaust survivor is presented to demonstrate the creativity needed in the analytic relationship to deal with intensely destructive trauma. This chapter argues that no horror is off limits to the making of art, which can act on the destructive event to attenuate its impact, promote healing, and generate a meaning that better contains it.

Chapter 5, "Alone Together: Solitude and the Creative Encounter in Art and Psychoanalysis," examines the central role of solitude in the creative process, particularly in relationship to the female artist. Artistic creation in essence is a solitary endeavor, and artists seek solitude to create and to work out their issues. Women, for the most part, are and have been expected to be more social, communicative, and nurturing; by retreating to create, they relinquish their leading roles in social engagement, a difficult and tricky affair. A clinical case is presented to describe the treatment of a woman who could not bear being alone until she began writing her memoir in solitude.

Part II: The Psychoanalysis of Art

Chapter 6, "Dreams of Genius: Sigmund Freud and C. G. Jung," illustrates the manner in which two dreams—one of Freud's and one of Jung's—inform the minds of these two giants, as well as their respective constructions of psychoanalytic theory. From the viewpoint of the unconscious, each man dreamed his theory before he wrote it. Dream analysis allows us to glimpse the dazzling complexity of the human mind.

Chapter 7, "Egon Schiele: A Self in Creation," describes the psychological processes underpinning the haunting work of Austrian *fin-de-siècle* Expressionist artist, Egon Schiele. Schiele's countless anguished self-images represent attempts at mastery over traumatic childhood events: the death of his father and three siblings and the lack of mirroring from his mother. The spectators' experiences in viewing the personal and emotional turmoil in Schiele's art are also examined.

Chapter 8, "At the Limits of the Primal Scene: Revisiting *Blue Velvet*," reveals the primal scene elements that infuse the cult classic film and help create its power. Director David Lynch plays with questions of looking and being looked at as well as revelation and concealment. His film incites and gratifies the viewer's curiosity, while also invoking feelings of helpless inadequacy and anxious guilt— all part of the primal scene. The primal scene is shown to be a guiding fantasy of the unconscious as well as a primary human reality that deals with exclusion, uncertainty, mystery, and the search for truth and meaning.

Chapter 9, "Ana Mendieta: Goddess in Exile," looks at Cuban American artist Ana Mendieta, known for her earth and body art. Mendieta was separated from her mother and her motherland at a young age and later created art from the earth to express the suffering of exile, the ephemeral quality of existence, and the need to merge with the mother archetype and grow beyond her personal loss. Mendieta's art, born in the gap between loss and longing, conveys the fragility of human bonds as well as the process of reunion and recovery.

Chapter 10, "Bruno Schulz: Desire's Impossible Object," examines the sadomasochistic vision of Polish artist Bruno Schulz, shot by a Nazi at the age of 50. Schulz, one of the 20th century's most enigmatic artists, mastered both the visual and textual medium. He wrote between the dream and the waking state, with an evocative language that uses mechanisms of fantasy, regression, condensation, and the spatiotemporal plasticity of the unconscious. Schulz positions nature and women as sadists and men as masochists. Though Schulz's role is one of a castrated and powerless masochist, he stuns us with his mastery as an artist; though he found life very difficult, he was able to see into its depths and eloquently render its brutal and beautiful vision.

Creativity generally involves something new, something fresh, something with an original perspective. It can entail bringing things together or taking them apart, reformulating questions, sniffing out novel connections, or taking leaps of imagination that take the mind into a new territory. It involves bracketing what one feels sure of in order to welcome and see what may appear when we put certainty aside.

Creativity in the service of life, art, and psychoanalysis is an open-ended, ongoing process of discovery, revelation, and construction. It is one of our greatest and most elegant adaptations, seated in the very heart of human possibility. Everything made by human beings begins as an act of imagination, an adaptation not merely in the service of survival but also of growth. It is not enough for us to merely survive. We must also thrive, and our growth is assisted by our creativity. Psychoanalysis at its best is a life-serving enterprise that can unlock the creative potential in ourselves and in others.

Part I

The Art of Psychoanalysis

Chapter 1

Dancing with the Unconscious
The Art of Psychoanalysis[1]

> Those who danced were thought to be quite insane by those who could
> not hear the music.
>
> —Angela Monet

Begin with a room, its four walls displaying a few choice prints, evocative images that perhaps speak with artistic subtlety to the room's singular
purpose. It is a room with a view, less to the outside than the inside, a
room prepared for a human encounter like no other. Within this room
two people will dance, not with hands and feet, but with voice and soul.
Moving with faith through the ballroom of the unknown, they will make
up the steps as they go along, guided by currents of unconscious thought
that ebb and flow between them. As the dance unfolds in imagery and
sound, in memory and meaning, in desire and suffering, their aim is to
suspend disbelief, judgment, and censorship in order to invite life to speak
from its deepest recesses. Ideally, this dance will not end in stillness but in
self-awareness and transformation.

This dance will employ three forms of unconscious expression unique
to analytic work: free association, transference–countertransference, and
dreams. All bear an important relationship to art, and all require a creative
response on the part of the analyst. In the course of our discussion we will
see how all three function creatively and how the analyst employs them in
the art of the psychoanalytic dance.

FREE ASSOCIATION

When a patient speaks to the analyst in an atmosphere of safety and trust
about "whatever comes to mind" in a stream of free associations, he or
she is expressing thought and meaning that is largely woven together and
determined unconsciously. Such content, against which the patient may be

---

[1] A revised version of this chapter appeared in *Psychoanalytic Inquiry*, 32(3), 2012.

defended, is the hidden narrative that nurtures the dialogue, keeping it alive and moving it forward. Bollas (2009) calls the "momentum" gained from free association's serial logic, "an intrinsic connective reasoning" (p. 4). In turn, the analyst listens to the patient with an "evenly hovering attention" or, as Freud (1912/1958b) said, the analyst "should withhold all conscious influences from his capacity to attend, and give himself over completely to his 'unconscious memory' ... He should simply listen, and not bother about whether he is keeping anything in mind" (p. 112). The analyst's rarified, nongrasping listening puts consciousness in brackets while heightening unconscious receptivity to the secluded, disguised, or inaccessible dimension of the patient's communications. The analyst listens for what thus far has remained silent. It is listening for the voice of the other who is denied; who has been rendered silent; and who can speak only in the language of the body, affect, symbol, or action.

Theodor Reik (1948) called this receptivity "listening with the third ear," or "perceiving what has not yet been said" (p. 17). Anton Ehrenzweig (1967) referred to a similar "apperception" when he spoke of being able to grasp "the hidden order" of things. Such listening establishes the basis for connectivity, not only among the disparate thoughts of the analysand, but also between the analytic couple. Ogden (1997) has written about the analyst's states of reverie as corollaries to the patient's free associations. In his reveries Ogden believes he taps into something crucial occurring between him and his patients as well as into his ability to use what emerges to guide him in the treatment. This bidirectional connectivity thus allows transmission and reception while encouraging continued and deepening exploration. The analyst is often *right there* with the patient in a state of openness and unknowing, and she allows links to form on their own without yet applying the shaping force of analysis. Both the analyst and the analysand are like the artist who, in the act of creation, *always stands on the threshold of the unknown.*

Partnered with the listening analyst, the patient speaks about whatever comes to mind. As the analyst suspends the urge to listen with the aim of immediate construction and analysis, the patient suspends the need to adhere to an agenda, or tell an interesting story, or make a point, or follow any specific logical form ordinarily found in ordinary speech. The patient *freely associates*; that is, he allows one thought to follow another in a stream of internal monologue, speaking unreservedly about the reflections and feelings that demand voice. This partnership ideally allows the unconscious to become known. What is hidden and yet driving what is apparent can now begin to permeate the dialogue. This movement is itself the transformation of understanding in both parties. At its best, it is the literal and gradual integration of disparate and cut off aspects of embodiment.

The sequential, yet nonlinear and sometimes seemingly contradictory thinking that characterizes free associations is a central component of creative thought. Albert Rothenberg (1990) names this "Janusian thinking" and explains how it shapes the ability to perceive relations among things where such connections might not otherwise be perceived. The content of free association, like the content of creative thought, emerges from the multiple meanings and affective perspectives embodied as memory, trauma, and knowledge. Of course, theory guides the linear and logical interpretation and reconstruction of the deeper and continuous meanings that tie together seemingly discontinuous and disparate associations. Surrealist artists were quick to notice the creative potential of associative thinking, and they incorporated its methodology into specific artistic techniques, such as automatic writing. James Joyce is an early example of a writer who replaced linear storytelling with stream of consciousness as form and content of the novel. Today, it is well known that creative thinking entails at least partial withdrawal of judgment and censorship, as well as the ability to make links not immediately apparent to reason or logic (Arieti, 1976). In working associatively and teaching the patient to do so, the analyst invites creativity into the sessions, the kind that creates personal movement and "new being."

TRANSFERENCE–COUNTERTRANSFERENCE

If free association functions as a highly compact creative language that contains multiple perspectives and meanings within the patient's unconscious, transference unconsciously expresses that embodiment in action and within the relationship. The patient will naturally enact and repeat (early) relational patterns within the therapeutic context, and the analyst will function as a living screen and a dynamic container for the issues or wrongs the patient needs to redress. At the same time the analyst will help the patient apply a therapeutic and transformative perspective to what occurs. In doing this, the analyst naturally comes into the relationship with her own transferences. Because the transference relationship is bidirectional and co-created, it functions as a malleable context within which layers of identifications, projections, enactments, and symbolizations can come to light and be explored and worked through. What this means is that the relationship itself becomes the means by which the patient and analyst grow and are transformed.

Transference–countertransference is the unknown, delimiting factor in the therapeutic relationship. As with any relationship, it is what ultimately determines the quality of the work. But here the analyst is very much in the dark. No one can know the extent of her own transference with regard to a specific individual. Because transference–countertransference involves the relationship between two unconscious minds, it is the most unknown and exciting aspect of the work. "It is a very remarkable thing," wrote Freud in 1915, "that the unconscious of one human being can react upon that of another, without passing through the conscious" (p. 194).

The transference is creatively handled by allowing the relationship to flow and change, by guiding, through free and spontaneous dialogue, the growing insight of the patient, and by becoming aware of the multiple transference dimensions arising in oneself. This process requires that the analyst engage multiple meanings while taking on multiple identities—a highly fluid process fraught with potential difficulty and requiring a loosening of boundaries between the self and the other, between what is inside and what is outside. Such boundary fluidity (though often not smooth) is a hallmark of creativity, where the artist extends his notion of self to take on other identities, and explore and step into alternate realities. Ogden (1994b) speaks of the third analytic space that is created between the analyst and analysand, a space that moves them both beyond the boundaries of their limited selves and experiences. Winnicott (1971a) introduced the concept of play in analytic encounters that takes place in this third, potential, space—the space of creativity.

DREAMS

Dreams are perhaps the most direct communications of the unconscious mind. Freud (1900/1953b) used the dream as the model for all unconscious mental experience. Like graphic artworks, dreams employ an economy of visual expression to articulate our inner lives. Dreams occur prior to the intervention of conscious thought and frequently present themselves as riddles to consciousness. Often the more incoherent dreams appear, the greater their revelatory value, for the condensation of their symbolism contains a world of meaning. Clearly, creative processes underlie both dreams and art. The creative aspect of working with dreams involves the art of interpretation, which includes asking the questions that will lead the analytic couple deeper into the dream's hidden meanings.

When working with dreams the analytic couple interprets an intimate and mysterious language, because buried in the dream may be the repressed memory, the hidden fear, the gnawing anxiety, the destructive assumption, or the quivering hope, the silent courage, the astonishing insight, the unseen solution. The dream is less governed by theory, censorship, or convention than by conscious thought. But more than a site of repressed content, the dream unites layers of memory, imagination, and desire, and crucial elements of our psychic life are encrypted in its architecture. Freud (1900/1953b) famously stated that "the interpretation of dreams is the royal road to a knowledge of the unconscious activities of the mind" (p. 608).

Dreams, like free associations and transference, are bidirectional in nature. They express unconscious thoughts as well as our attempts to modify and understand them. When dreams engage the analysis—and, among other things, dreams reported while in analysis are doing just that—analytic work gains the power to counteract or undo repression, to expand the limitations of our conscious minds, and to unite with the other in a profound and multidimensional encounter.

Following is a session that illustrates the raw, creative power of the dream as well as the creativity needed to mine some of its meanings. Additionally, the session incorporates free association and transference. In this case, we bear witness to the dance between two (conscious and unconscious) minds. Although many (e.g., Fenichel, 1939; Loewald, 1960/1980) have written about the therapeutic action of psychoanalysis, it is also important to attend to the *creative action* that takes place in analytic work. As demonstrated here, *creative action is therapeutic action.* Part of the artistry involves the ways in which the dream's meaning and context are brought into being. It may look simple, but it is often a subtle, quiet aspect of technique.

By including minimal information about the patient I aim to focus on the session itself. (For more on this case, see Knafo, 2006.)

DANCING WITH DEATH

Ana was a 29-year-old male-to-female transsexual when she sought help for the first time. Significantly, Ana's birth was the result of a rape. At the beginning of treatment Ana physically appeared as a man and was married to a woman. She claimed to utterly hate her maleness and felt that she was a lesbian trapped in the body of a man. By the end of her 4-year treatment, Ana was a woman living with a man, referring to herself as an "omnisexual." The following session was the third in Anna's treatment and the first dream she shared with me. Consciously Ana was wholly resolved about going through the transition from male to female and claimed to have no conflict about her decision, as she simply wished to rid herself of everything male. The dream work that took place in the session reveals the many layers of unconscious meaning regarding this life-altering decision. The session is interspersed with an amalgam of my initial reactions and later analysis, in italics.

ANA: [*Enters and approaches my office window*] So you do have a view! It is difficult coming here with the gym across the street. My body will never be as pretty as a woman's ... I had a dream fragment. It came at the end of a series of dreams.

I already sense this session will be profound. What tells me this? She begins with her hope for a view as well as her despair. I have a view. She believes I have a view. Perhaps in this room she, too, will have a view.

The opening lines of a session are like the opening theme in a concert; they will be repeated with variation throughout this session and those that follow it. I have a perspective that she lacks. Like the women in the gym, I also have the woman's body that she lacks. I feel the gentle urge to move with her, to let her lead me inwardly as I lead her outwardly. The dream yet unspoken electrifies the air between us.

DK: Tell me what you remember.

ANA: There was a group of people. I was with a school group. We went to see … It wasn't clear where we were going. We went to one place where they were going to have a public execution. I've never seen one.

I listen to her and allow my associations to flow with her narrative. She has come to see something she has never seen before. Again she uses the language of vision. She dreams to see. She has brought me a dream to see, and she has perhaps brought me a dream that sees. Someone will be executed. We will see who and how and perhaps even why.

ANA: It's strange, but it's as though I thought, society does this, takes kids to see a public execution. There was a woman there, sitting in a chair. You could see her face. She is as far as you are from me. She is thin, with thin features, forlorn, long, dishwater grayish-brunette hair, and very sad eyes.

Ah, we dance now in the embrace of the transference. She is saying something about us, about the distance between us, the distance we are closing: "as far as you are from me." The dream incorporates the analysis. It refers to the analysis. It is meant at least partly as a communication to the analyst.

ANA: And she sat there and the group came around. And the executioner people were fitting her, taking a noose and adjusting it. I couldn't figure out how this process would work, taking vital signs.

How does this process of treatment work? What is its execution? What is happening here, and how does it correspond to what is happening within her? I let go and trust the movement.

ANA: No one was talking to this woman. She was there all alone with no one to comfort her, only to watch her die. It became clear that she wasn't going to get executed at that spot. They were going to move her, and the group wouldn't see it. So, the group that came with me moved, went for coffee. But I felt that wasn't appropriate to just let a person die and no one make contact with her. I felt empathy for that person. So, I went up to her, looked at her. She was troubled.

As she speaks I begin to see and feel her loneliness. The woman is being moved from "that spot" and will be executed elsewhere. A position must be relinquished in order for the execution to occur. This may refer to the future surgery and the therapy as well. Ana is with the group and yet is uncomfortable with it. Ana is separating from the group, feeling empathy for the woman, moving closer to what is so hard to face. As she does so I am called to enter her dream more deeply, to dream with her.

ANA: I asked, "How are you?" She didn't say a lot. She was depressed.

Ana does not yet know that it is perhaps she who is depressed. She believes she is just fine with her decision.

ANA: She knew she was going to be killed and wasn't going to say anything. But she looked at me and felt comforted and cared for. Someone from this world condemning her cared enough to talk to her, knowing this person was condemned.

I savor that image of comfort and care, feeling she is talking about the therapy. We are joined to witness an execution. We are joined in being executed ourselves. Together we are executing a process of revelation.

ANA: She looked at me knowingly. She knew I knew she'd be killed. [*Ana looks at me knowingly.*]

Sometimes the dance moves so beautifully the two become as one. Where does the dream end and where do we begin? I deeply sense but do not yet fully know what is here to see. As I dance with Ana she dances with that figure who seems not to dance at all but sits trapped in a chair awaiting execution.

ANA: This is what a person feels at the end of their life. There's nothing more that they can do. There's a recognition they have, and they can look at your life and think: you're so young and won't be anymore. She looked at me and said something like, "I feel cold."

I quiver at this insight. She is leading me into my own fear, the fear of annihilation, the radical solitude which results from the awareness "I will die," an awareness that leaves us with nothing except the feeling of cold.

ANA: Nothing more expressive. I noticed she was holding something in her hand. She looked at me and handed it to me. It was an empty cassette, a tape box. There was a liner on it, but no tape. It was as though they grabbed her and this was the last thing she could hold onto. So this was it. And she realized what she held was nothing. But she handed it to me and I said, thank you.

How the dream speaks of Ana's dilemma. The dream figure hands her an empty tape cassette. She will change her body into that of a woman. But will she be a woman inside or just an empty container, a box without content, a form without substance? Will she become nothing by doing this? Will nothing change? Is her sex change an empty gesture after all? How profound is the image of the empty tape box! Connections buzz through my mind too rapidly to analyze. My ears drink her words, and I am touched by the beauty and complexity of her dream.

ANA: She asked, "Why do you have such long hair?" I answered, "Well, I am a transsexual." She looked at me very disappointed, as if to say, "Another crazy … it figures." The only person who would care for her is an outcast. She may have glanced at me one more time but that was it. Then they came—one person in a white coat—took both her arms, took her to a room, and closed the door. I knew that was the execution chamber. I knew that I was the last person she had seen and that she was going to be killed. That was the end of her life and the end of the dream.

Again I am struck with the depth of Ana's conflict over her decision, though she consciously felt little if any conflict. Part of her feels that she is "crazy" for making this choice. I know that the dream she has brought me is profound. I encouraged Ana to free associate to the various elements of the dream, and the dance continued to unfold.

DK: Can you tell me about the group?

Why this question? It feels right, but why? Because she begins here, being part of a group, then breaks away to encounter the condemned woman, and, of course, this encounter is with herself, with her choices, with her analysis, and with me. She is an outcast, and so the group holds clues to her identifications.

ANA: I am not sure. I see myself as I am, but they were sixth graders. But I am among them. It's a cross between a sixth-grade population of boys and girls and a postgraduate population of men and women. The whole thing was a field trip—amusement.

So it was a good question. She condenses two time periods. I recall that Ana was 11 when she dressed in her mother's clothing for the first time.

Gazing defiantly in the mirror, the little boy told himself that once he wore a woman's clothes—mother's clothes—there would be no turning back. Mixed with this is the postgraduate population, an age where one completes the launch into adulthood, having made most of the decisions that will shape the rest of one's life. I note her use of both genders—"boys and girls," "men and women"—since she herself is still very much of both genders. I feel the two of us are really beginning to move, to dance.

DK: Was anyone in the group recognizable to you?

I want Ana to show me who she carries within herself, the characters of her embodiment. I want her to focus here and connect us to her reality.

ANA: No. We just met. It makes me think of the group TA [Transgendered Anonymous]. You walk in and they already have relationships with one another, not to you. I knew of them but had no close association with them.

Like her dream, she speaks of her isolation. Excluded from the group from the first time she donned her mother's clothing; now, ironically, she has attained the ultimate exclusion—from a group that is itself extremely marginalized: Transgendered Anonymous.

DK: And the execution?

Her body shifts back in her chair, away from this question. I've made my first leading move, avoiding it until now, by choosing to step around the periphery of the dream's roiling center, its compression of conflict, terror, and hope. Will she pull away or step deeper into her own unknown territory? How to describe this dance? When do I stay back, attend to the edges, listen for the echoes of hidden meaning? When do I advance? How do I follow Ana as she leaves a thin trail of intent through the tangled brush of dialogue? When and how do I open a new path, engage a new question, move to a stronger and more insistent rhythm? Her body shift warns me not to advance too quickly. How we wish to know and not know the truth at the same time! How each of us plays the blind king or queen in our own drama!

ANA: I would be curious.

Strange wording indeed. Not "I am" or "I was" curious about the execution. But "I would be" curious, the conditional "would" indicating a defense against knowing and especially against feeling.

ANA: It was a medieval image, a Civil War image, and a 1930s image. Someone is sitting in—taken from a black-and-white B movie made in the '50s—a chamber, an electric chair, someone taped and tied to the chair. There are windows and around are reporters. And the person is all alone, in the room of course. They pull the big switch and, of course, the person jolts and jumps. The silver of the metal has a glistening aura of cold. I can't relate to that person. It's probably some ugly criminal, but it is the spectacle of death. And there are Crimean War images with people on the gallows—dangling, with hoods over their heads. It is ghastly. The crowds. It is as though people don't exist and life wasn't worth a lot then. And a medieval image. There is a fair around an execution and everyone brings their kids. It's a cross between public humiliation and public entertainment. Ultimately, it's a combination. It's why people come to a public execution—the festival, celebrity, morality. But I don't relate to any of the people getting executed.

Ana's narration is flowing easily now, in a quickened, excited voice. Her eyes are closed and her head is tilted back. As she speaks to me, past me, through me, meanings and connections arise in my mind without the need for reflection: war, circus, the pulling of the big switch, the black-and-white scenes. These images whirl through my mind, and I know she is telling me about her fear and terror, and its connection to what she is and what she may become. The multiple images of war and death and the public circus that surrounds them condense the horror of the spectacle she herself is enacting. One image by itself will not suffice, though the horror is implied in the odd phrase of "pulling the big switch"—pulling it off, switching genders—the literal castration that must occur, the execution of the man and the execution of the woman. The graphic quality of castration demands the harshness of black and white. The scene is too extreme for color, even if the one to be executed is little more than an "ugly criminal." The dream suggests that, at least for a part of her, the act of self-castration mocks the self built from biology's foundations. She is terrified and guilty. But she must negate the connection to the "ghastly," overwhelming terror she faces and so, even in her dream, she cannot relate to anyone being executed. She denies connection twice within a single paragraph. She must keep dreaming, and so must distance herself from the condemned; otherwise her dream will become a nightmare and she will awaken. Even in the depths of sleep the unconscious defends us from what we cannot yet handle. What a marvelous movement of revelation, what an uncanny masquerade.

ANA: To me, the issue of execution is peculiar. I don't think the state is wrong in dealing with execution. So, I don't feel execution is so awful.

This happens. You're more likely to get killed by an accidental shooting. So I was curious.

Her strange construction is haunting: The state is not wrong in dealing with execution. This avoidant, awkward construction suggests she may be speaking not only of the state at large but also of her state of mind. Her state of mind is not in error in wanting to change genders—in executing the surgery. If only her need were fully acceptable—to others and to herself. But Freud's concept of negation (1925/1961c) instructs us to remove negatives from dream reports. Thus, the state is also wrong for allowing executions. Still execution is less likely to occur than an "accidental shooting." Note that the "state" chooses the "execution" while death by "shooting" is "accidental." She chooses to execute the procedure; her biological gender, however, is arbitrary, an accident. What rage she must feel at being born wrong by accident (an accident of gender and an accident of rape), an accident that may not even be properly corrected by a proper "execution." But now she has moved from the conditional "I would be curious," to the admission that she "was curious."

DK: Tell me about the woman.

The flow of the dance is now carrying us along. I move back to the dream. I step lightly from the group/context to the action/execution to the woman/person being executed.

ANA: Yes. She was sitting in a chair, probably like this, a chair not uncomfortable. She was in the position to contemplate, but without anyone paying attention to her—except her neck size, weight—the best way to dispose of her body. It was impersonal.

The chair holding the one to be executed is like the chair in therapy. The negation of discomfort suggests that, at least to some extent, she experiences therapy as uncomfortable. Concern for the one to be executed only involves impersonal physical aspects.

DK: What did she look like?

Why do I ask this question? Is this a misstep? I seem to be colluding with the others in her dream who concern themselves solely with the physical. Am I proving her right? Is this what people are primarily interested in?

ANA: She looked like a woman I know from church. We go to a church in Harlem, mostly Black and Hispanic. This woman—she's White—has a Black husband or boyfriend. She always seems sad. She has more streaky gray hair than the woman in the dream. I don't expect a cheery outlook from the woman I know in church. In the dream too, I don't expect it. Also, the body type doesn't apply to me—5′2″ and 100 pounds. I don't feel it's me or someone I know.

The woman to be executed resembles a White woman in a Black church, a "sad" outsider. Her hair is "streaky gray" or in between black and white as Ana is in between male and female. The woman in the church and the woman in the dream bring no cheer. But again this is not Ana, she makes sure to tell me twice. "Dance with me Doctor, but let us not yet stare too directly in the magic mirror as we pass it." She cannot yet admit the questions her dream is asking: Why does my decision to change my sex fill me with sadness and pain? She is asking, too, for me to lead her lightly on. I must connect her with this figure at the heart of her dream, this phantasm composed of her terror and doubt that interrogates both the meaning of her act and the meaning of her life. Perhaps I stepped on her toes, but now I will take her whirling into the next series of movements. I am excited because I sense the dance beginning to quicken, bearing us both toward that inner flight that makes this thing we do so special. My next question seems simple, but it is meant to deepen our knowledge of the meaning the dream woman has to her.

DK: Can you tell me about this woman?
ANA: I talk to her once in a while. Some people have the appearance that indicates there's something more to them—mysterious—you can tell this woman in church has been through a lot and you don't know what it is. It's the same thing in the dream.

She is asking, "What is it about myself that I do not understand? What is the nature of my mystery—the mystery of who I am and where I fit in?" Naturally, she is also wondering about me, this woman who sits opposite her, reflecting her to herself—who am I, and what role will I play in her life?

DK: And you're curious and approach her.

Together we are cautiously approaching the woman to be executed, the forbidden signifier that both conceals and reveals. I am leading her closer to the truth she circles but does not directly encounter. The woman in the church—a sacred figure—has brought us nearer.

ANA: Right. I was there to hear what she has to say—not to express something myself—but I had a sense she might've had last words, some sense of what life is about, even her sadness or anger or hopes, heaven forbid!

Note the condensation of the church woman with the dream woman. This moment is a beautiful example of unconscious connection. We wonder together: Are there any "last words," any final "view" that will save her situation? Can she dare (heaven forbid!) to hope? And if so, what might she hope for?

DK: And you get from her an empty tape cassette?

ANA: Well, there's something precious about it ... and something unprecious. The precious is that she felt some grasp on life. It's the last thing she could grab, a security blanket. Seeing the empty tape box, maybe you could read the title, what's important. But I had a sense that it was on the table and she grabbed it, so there was no significance except that she held it. It's the last thing she expressed caring for. It is precious and, therefore, she clings to it. It is unprecious because there is no meaning to this life.

I'm struck by the poignancy of the contradiction of the precious and the unprecious. I want to obtain a pure association, thus my next question.

DK: Can you associate to the empty tape cassette outside of the dream?

ANA: It's a simple metaphor. It's obvious; a tape unfolds. You only listen to one moment at a time. You look at it, or you could take it out and spread it. It's tangled stuff, but when you play it, it makes sense. Even if it's not quality, it records human life over time. I was a recording engineer and a musician. There are all sorts of things you have on tape. You can't make it perfect. And people I like to listen to the most are people who leave space for mistakes in humanity—Brian Eno—where imagination is allowed to be there in the mistakes. But this tape box has no tape in it. It was discarded or left out. So I could never listen to or hear those glitches. I could only have the empty shell and not come close to hearing it. In the end, she was executed and I still have the tape box, the vague idea of who she is.

I am so moved by what she has said that I am close to tears. This is the moment of flight when our feet leave the floor and we sail through the air, assured of a precious instant of truth, a beautiful revelation. A simple metaphor indeed! Yes, the tape is a metaphor for her life, a moment-by-moment record, and once exposed a tangled mass of moments to be understood and analyzed. This is why she is here. Over time memory revisits its tangled events and makes meaning, orders them into a story of some kind, a song, a dance—a unique creation. It may be more fiction than fact and more music than text, but still it is a life—both precious and unprecious. I did not know she was a recording engineer until just now. The cassette has a real historical significance. It is the dream's central issue. The tape can't be perfect of course; there must be space for "mistakes in humanity." There must be room for the mistake she feels herself to be. There must be space for the creative possibilities of imagination. There must be a space for healing. I am reminded of Leonard Cohen's lyrics in his song "Anthem": "There is a crack in everything. That's how the light gets in." Realizing all this as I recount and analyze the session, I am in awe of the profundity and aching beauty of Ana's thoughts. This dance with her feels visionary. In it she envisions despair and hope. But the box is empty, its tape, its (and her) meaning and substance "discarded and left out." She holds in her hand the blank tape, "the empty shell"—the shell of the man who will be eliminated, the shell of the woman who will live out the rest of this life. We have come full circle, back to the session's beginning. She will never be a real woman, she fears, not in body and not in mind. How much different does she feel than the figure of execution, the ghost destined for extinction in her dream? Not very much at all. Finally I manage to speak, moving her back to the dream.

DK: But before that, she asks about your hair.

Why this question? I'm not sure. I wanted to move from the existential to the concrete and try to balance the two extremes. I felt the hair was significant but didn't know why.

ANA: She says, "Why is your hair so long?" I was touched she'd ask. She's being killed and she's making pleasantries. It was touching she'd ask someone who was to live a question about their life minutes before she'd be killed.

Again she refers to the therapy, to hope. There is always hope in life that one can gain insight and understanding by asking questions.

ANA: When I had a beard, I wondered about myself. I grew up Christian. It struck me funny that Christ was around 30 years old and didn't do anything. He was a carpenter; he hung around with rabbis. When God—excuse me, Jesus—was 30—my age practically—he suddenly was called by God to be this different thing. You had a sense that Jesus didn't know about it until then. Even historically, Jesus was a person, a character until 30. And then he changed and became a messianic figure. It's as though he had been called to something he didn't realize. And before Jesus was crucified, he asked God, "Take this cup if it is your will because I don't want to taste this poison." Life is sweet, and you don't have to feel pain. Funny, I'd grown a beard so I wouldn't look to myself like a woman. At the same time, with the beard, people saw Jesus's face from postcards and velvet paintings.

This next movement is almost predictable. Opposed to the possibility that (her) life is without meaning is that it means everything. Her identification with Christ transforms the execution into a crucifixion, the castration into a sacrifice. Executions are performed on those who sin; the crucifixion is the sacrifice that God makes for humanity to expiate sin. God's sacrifice bears the burden of human existence. This sacrifice of Ana's will crucify the man and resurrect the woman. And here is Ana, now, standing at the threshold of her execution, which might also be a crucifixion, both a sinner and a saint, a figure of infinite emptiness and infinite fullness, asking me, asking God, "Take this cup from me." If only life were "sweet and you don't have to feel pain." If only she knew what she was—a phony Jesus, pious-faced on a postcard or a velvet painting, or something else altogether, something with sufficient meaning to live on with hope— someone precious enough to merit life, recognition, and most of all love.

DK: People said that to you?

ANA: Sometimes. God forbid, the first time I put on a wig and I looked like Jesus. I looked ridiculous. I did look weird. In a roundabout way, I had a sense that this woman was asking: "Who are you?" Like Jesus, I was in a group of spiritualists who had their hair long and didn't shave their beards. It was the only way we know what Jesus looked like. So, this person was asking about my hair, as though it's a messianic thing, or I came to save her. So, there was some hope in her. But when I told her I'm a transsexual, there goes that hope. I wrote a poem, "Jesus Had a Sex Change," three months ago. It made fun of my peculiarities and I wondered, what is spirituality? Who is Jesus? What does it mean to me to have this feeling in me? Is it like a calling people feel? Does it have a purpose?

"Who are you?" is the central question her dream is asking her and me, and it is the nexus of all of her other questions, equally important. The woman to be executed is asking to be saved. Can she be saved by the one she inhabits, Ana? And she is also Ana asking to be saved by me. Can her life mean something? Is she good or bad? Is she worthy? Can she again belong to some group? Will she love and be loved? Is she like Jesus, or is she ridiculous? Hope and hopelessness exist simultaneously in the unconscious. The hopelessness is symbolized by the empty tape cassette. The hope is symbolized by the quest to understand what she is doing, her needs and her longings. Her hope is symbolized by the dance we two are engaged in, for what we represent as we move together is the possibility of a creation that reconciles hopelessness and hope. What we strive for in the dance between two minds is the protection and nurturing of her life.

DK: Or does it just lead to death?

I was bringing back the execution, the duality and ambivalence, but I went too far. I stepped on her toes, as her reaction demonstrates.

ANA: [*She flushes*] I didn't think—or it's just an inconvenience to make my life difficult.

Ana becomes flustered and reduces the entire affair to an inconvenience. I know our time is ending. It is my move. Especially because of my misstep, I try to wrap up in a way that embraces the dualities and layers explored in the dreamwork. I especially want to say something about the transference level.

DK: Perhaps the dream is telling us about the crossroad at which you find yourself in coming here—between male and female, life and death, your hopes about what you might get from me, as your therapist and as a woman—the "tape of life" that reveals the mystery of what it means to be a woman or the empty shell, like the women's bodies you saw at the gym on your way here today.

I try to develop and bring to the surface the latent meanings in all of Ana's verbal and nonverbal productions, from opening commentary about the women, the view (perspective) and body that I have as a woman, and the dream itself. The interpretation is a creative synthesis that I hope will resonate with her experience.

ANA: [*She begins to cry*] I only feel positive when I feel pain. I like coming here. And, yes, I know it isn't all pleasure; that there's pain.

I led, she followed; she led, I followed. The dance can be graceful or clumsy. Ana embraces both pleasure and pain. It doesn't have to be black or white, life or death. There is a pleasure in looking, even if what she sees is painful.
On her way out of my office, Ana walks over to me, takes my hand, and holds it warmly for a long moment. I experience this as a repetition of what had transpired in the dream, the gift handed to Ana by the woman to be executed. Here Ana needs to show me concretely that I have given her something, she needs to get that something through touch, not only through mind-to-mind communication. It is an enactment that was never repeated in the remainder of the treatment. In this ending, Ana's dream literally dances with reality.

DANCING WITH LIFE

Freud (1915/1957d) believed that the unconscious was capable of development. Thanks to the associations, transference expressions, enactments, and dreamwork that took place in this session and the sessions that followed, Ana was positioned in a new relationship not only with me, but with her unconscious life. In the beginning she was aware only of being resolved about her upcoming sexual reassignment surgery, but that position was limited and reflected only a small part of her story. In fact, the possibility of not having "a view" that would save her situation and allow her to face the hard work of recreating herself as a woman, not merely from the outside but from the inside as well, made it impossible for her to realize her conflicts and fears. And that was where she was stuck. Thus, her dream brought to life her dilemma and a path to resolution.

Ana began the session telling me I had "a view." She could not yet know what it would mean to be a woman. But by the end of the session, despair is paired with hope, death with the prospect of a new life, and, most important, meaninglessness with the possibility of meaning. Through the dream work, Ana opened the possibility of "seeing" the complexity of her decision and the feelings she had about it. She began to develop a view of her own. Although this required more work to sort matters out, it also meant that she could become engaged with various parts of herself and open her world to new possibilities.

The nature of psychoanalytic interpretation is that it is riddled with subjectivity, highly malleable, readily supplemented by additional interpretation, incomplete, and even undecidable in many cases. No absolute answer exists for such questions as: "How shall one live?" or "How shall I save my situation?" or "What does my dream really mean?" But the very limitations of psychoanalysis also encompass its beauty, for we must remember that its purpose is not to nail down reality, but to open a new path on which reality can travel. However grounded in empirical knowledge are its theories, the practice of psychoanalysis is an art whose goal is to lessen human suffering and create personal options. This art takes the form of an intimate and rarified dialogue and enactment. This art is a dance toward and for freedom.

The image of the dream woman is actually quite brilliant, a creative contrivance of Ana's unconscious. Until the time they "pull the big switch," Ana as a woman had been merely potential; the woman is within her as a possibility, an aspiration, an object of desire, and an act of imagination. Part of Ana feels she is a mistake—the product of a rape and the wrong gender. Yet, she can imagine, and correct through imagination, the mistakes in the "tape," the mistakes in her life, and the mistake of her gender. She can bring forth the woman hidden within her. But in doing that she will lose the *causa sui* that has driven her life for nearly 20 years. She will no longer be the man who wants to be a woman; she will be a woman who must then perform as a woman. She fears she will be a woman who will be born empty, without true content. The woman within will be sacrificed, executed, and destroyed so the woman outside can be born. And she, the woman within, is represented by the dream figure. No wonder Ana aches for a "view."

The dream figure also represents me, and the ambivalence Ana feels about attaining a "view." She has come to me to help her make the transition from male to female, to surface the conflict she feels about her decision, and to realize a vision that will save her situation by giving her hope for meaning and love. Yet she is terrified of what she might find: that not ever being a real man, she will also never be a real woman; that the sacrifice she is making has as much sanctity and meaning as a velvet Christ; that her act of imagination will result in spiritual and emotional bankruptcy; that she will never fit in with any group or family; that she will never be worthy of love; that she will float for the rest of her life in a twilight zone of non-identity.

She has good reason to be frightened: her entire life is at stake, and her decision is momentous. Sexual reassignment could make everything worse than it already is. At best she may never look like the women in the gym, but she may learn how to live as a woman and align her life more fully with her hopes and aspirations. At worst she will have left her manhood behind forever to inhabit a female simulacrum, transmogrified into a spectral figure stranded in a dream of death. I stand with her on the threshold of both possibilities, one hopeful and the other utterly terrifying and hopeless. Small wonder that I too must be executed, for I am the executioner, the one bringing Ana to a truth that might save her or slay her.

Highly illustrative of the immense creativity of unconscious communication is the nested structure of Ana's dream. The richest and most poignant symbol at the dream's core is, of course, the cassette that represents Ana's decision in the mode of resulting in the worst possible outcome for her. Encompassing this cassette is the dream figure to be executed, a representation of Ana facing the surgery. Encompassing the figure to be executed is the dark and ominous atmosphere of carnival conveyed by the war and execution scenes; the voyeuristic engagement of the onlookers who pass the time by entertaining themselves with Ana's spectacle; and the indifferent attitude of the team handling the physical aspects of the execution. Finally, the entire dream is encompassed by the therapy, because Ana's unconscious prepared this dream specifically for her therapy. That such a complex set of relations can be depicted with such economy is indicative of the power of creation and the depth of art and neatly illustrates why free association, transference, and dreamwork are such potent analytic tools.

And yet the walls of the therapy room are not the last horizon of the dream. The nest of meaning transcends Ana's personal situation, just as a work of art transcends the personal issues of its creator. Ana's personal situation is rather unique and seems to have little to do with the problems most people face. She is a man who is utterly miserable being a man and wants to be a woman. Not many find themselves in this situation; surely, her case appears to fall outside the margins of ordinary concerns. However, her dream tells a different story. She is wrestling with issues common to all human beings—issues of identity, place, meaning, limitation, and mortality. Who among us has truly secured an identity? And what a fragile and temporary fabrication is identity, how easily damaged and vulnerable to assault by betrayal, loss, illness, and trauma. Who would not want to read or hear some last words of truth that would definitively convey life's meaning, for meaning is even more fragile than identity. Who does not long to belong? Who does not fear exclusion? Who does not repress the terror of death in order to live, and who does not wish to love and be loved? How poignant is Ana's plight, especially poignant because her situation places her farther outside the circle of life than most. Indeed, her pain is existential, and it is the problem of human existence itself that forms the ultimate boundary of her dream's concentric circles of significance.

Ana did go through with sexual reassignment surgery 4 years after she reported this dream. She claimed that, after the surgery, she was able to observe her body with relief for the first time. Although she had originally regarded the surgery as a terminal juncture in her life, an execution for an unspoken crime, she was surprised to find that from the "other side" there existed a continuity that had not been broken. She and I both knew that the work we had done in her analysis—the dance we had danced—helped to prepare her for the change. She had obtained a view—deep insight into the complexity of who she was and who she could be—so that by the time she faced the challenge, the cassette had been filled with a tape made by her creative mind and profound emotions. She had internalized me as a woman and as her partner in this most singular dance of life.

I also learned much from my work with Ana. I learned to question my female identity, something I had never done before. I learned to broaden my view of what comprises gender. I learned that gender is neither purely biological nor purely socially conditioned, but something that exists between reality and imagination. Most important, I learned about the resourcefulness and inventiveness of unconscious life and about the ultimate creativity that can take place in analysis: the creation of a self.

I've presented a narrative and a dream that highlight the rich possibilities open to the analytic dyad. The techniques of free association and dream analysis offer creative ways for the analytic couple to understand what is happening and how to further incorporate it into the work. The transference and countertransference represent the living context in which meaning is formed. Like the creativity of the artist, the creativity of the analytic pair translates unconscious possibilities into visible or lived actualities. As with art making, the art of psychoanalysis both reveals what exists and makes something new. But psychoanalysis does more; it functions in the service of personal repair and human freedom.

Working with a patient is a highly creative process. There is no formula, no algorithm that calculates an answer. Though science will guide us and provide evidence for the efficacy of what we do, it is the art of what we do that addresses the age-old questions of who we are and how we shall save our circumstance.

The human heart houses many dancers and dances. After all these years, I still love to dance that dance we do, the one that always must end in continued dancing.

Chapter 2

One Step Back, Two Steps Forward

Regression in the Service of Art and Psychoanalysis[1]

> What a distressing contrast there is between the radiant intelligence of the child and the feeble mentality of the average adult.
>
> —Sigmund Freud

When Picasso exclaimed that he used to draw like Raphael, but that it took him an entire lifetime to learn to draw like a child, he was referring to his hard-earned capacity to retrieve and employ a perspective marked by simplicity, freshness, and even "primitiveness" in creating his art (see Plate 2). Taking our lead from Ernst Kris, we might call Picasso's capacity "regression in the service of art." Kris (1952) called regression functioning to support the ongoing development of psychological growth "regression in the service of the ego." Indeed, there is a link between the two.

Originally regression in the service of the ego met with hearty approval, especially from psychologists seeking evidence of it in projective test protocols (e.g., Bellak, 1954/1973; Schafer, 1958), and also by those who wanted to further clarify the popular mythology of the mad artist. Eventually it became viewed as problematic by some and even dismissed by others. In recent years, one rarely sees it mentioned in the literature.

This chapter revisits Kris's important idea in light of recent knowledge about the artist, the creative process, and developments in object relations theory. I view regression through three distinct yet overlapping perspectives: temporal regression, which returns one to earlier (childhood) stages of psychological development; domain regression, which risks decompensation by subverting and playing with self-world boundaries; and topographical and structural regression, which allows freer access to visual and primary-process modes of thought. If we assume that regression remains under the control of the individual's ego for all three perspectives, then the backward and inward movement marks a deeper and fuller expression of

---

[1] An earlier version of this chapter appeared in *Psychoanalytic Psychology*, 19(1), 2002, pp. 24–49.

earlier forms of cognition and embodiment. In other words, more connection, invention, and vision may then be available to one through the process of regression.

Regression in art will be compared to and contrasted with the regression that takes place in psychoanalysis. Especially relevant is Loewald's claim, in his classic paper "The Therapeutic Action of Psychoanalysis" (1960/1980), that movement in treatment is achieved by "the promotion and utilization of [controlled] regression" (p. 224).

Because of my work in the psychology of creativity, many patients in the arts have been referred to me for treatment, and thus I've been afforded the opportunity to examine the complexities of the creative mind. I also teach the psychology of the artist at various academic institutions and invite artists who work in a variety of media to speak about themselves and their art. Over the years I have conducted over one hundred interviews with artists. My findings are, therefore, based on three types of data obtained over 20 years of research: firsthand communication with artists via classroom interviews or therapy; study of artists and their works; and personal interviews with artists. This chapter uses quotations from artist-patients, some well known, and artist-interviewees to illustrate its major points.

I begin with a review of Kris's concept of regression in the service of the ego and summarize the major criticism this concept has received. I then discuss regression in art and offer several illustrations, after which I present an object relations approach to the understanding of regression in the service of the ego. A short case is also presented to demonstrate the creative and therapeutic possibilities in regression. Finally, I briefly discuss the regression that takes place in observers of art.

ERNST KRIS'S THEORY OF REGRESSION IN THE SERVICE OF THE EGO

In 1936, Ernst Kris first introduced the concept of "regression in the service of the ego" in "The Psychology of Caricature":

> We have now to elucidate in greater detail relations of wit and caricature and dreams: in dreams, the ego abandons its supremacy and the primary process obtains control, whereas in wit and caricature the process remains in the service of the ego. This formulation alone suffices to show that the problem involved is a more general one; the contrast between an ego overwhelmed by regression and a "regression in the service of the ego"—*si licet venia verbo*—covers a vast and imposing range of mental experience. (p. 177)

In *Psychoanalytic Explorations in Art* (1952), Kris published his theory of creativity, in which regression in the service of the ego assumed a pivotal position. He relied on three separate sources for his elaboration of the concept: first, Freud's theory of wit (1905/1960), in which he explains how a preconscious thought is "given over for a moment to unconscious revision" (p. 166); second, Freud's statement that artists are endowed with a "flexibility [looseness or *Lockerheit*] of repression" (1917/1963, p. 376); and third, ego psychology's emphasis on the adaptive functions of the ego. The major focus of Kris's formulations on creativity, therefore, deals with shifts in psychic levels (primary–secondary processes) and cathexes of ego functions (inspiration–elaboration). The assumption here initially appears paradoxical; while the ego suspends its control, temporarily withdrawing cathexis, it simultaneously controls and regulates the regressive retreat. The control of ego functions, however, is one that Kris believed varies with regard to "the organizational functions of the ego, its capacity of self-regulation of regression and particularly to its capacity of control over the primary process" (1952, p. 28).

Kris depicted the creative process as composed of two phases, each of which involves a shift in psychic level and a corresponding shift in the cathexis of certain ego functions. During the first "inspirational" phase, the artist is passively receptive to id impulses or their derivatives. Kris described this phase as having much in common with regressive processes, in that id impulses and drives, otherwise hidden and unavailable, emerge to communicate with the ego. During this phase, the artist experiences rapture and a feeling of being driven by powerful external forces (e.g., writers frequently describe a feeling of being taken over by their characters who then dictate their aims and actions to the writer). The second "elaborational" phase calls for the artist's active use of such ego functions as reality testing, formulation, and communication. This phase resembles work or problem solving in that it entails concentration and purposeful organization. What was originally communicated to the passively receptive ego is now actively elaborated, shaped, reorganized, edited, and communicated to others. According to Kris, the inspirational phase donates the content to an artwork, whereas the elaboration phase is primarily responsible for the transformation of that content into communicable form, communication being the primary purpose of art. These phases may follow each other in swift or slow succession or may be interwoven with each other.

A continual interplay between inspiration (regression) and elaboration (criticism) informs the creative process, and the degree to which an artist's work balances these activities constitutes the major difference, in Kris's view, between normal and psychotic art. For instance, if regression predominates, the symbols employed in the artwork will be egocentric and take on private meaning; however, if there is too much control, the work of art will appear "cold, mechanical and uninspired" (1952, p. 254). Whereas Kris viewed art as having developed from magical ritual into a form of communication, he believed psychotic art deteriorates from communication back to sorcery. Since the ego plays a minimal part in psychotic creations, such an artist, like the dreamer, does not control his or her regression but, rather, becomes overwhelmed by it. And, like a dream, the psychotic product becomes partially intelligible, and only with the aid of interpretative translation. Kris believed psychotic art serves a primarily restitutive function rather than a communicative one, a view challenged by Kleinians (Fuller, 1980; Segal, 1991) who postulate that the purpose of all art, not merely psychotic art, is reparative. The point is that psychotic art is too solipsistic to speak directly to an audience and does not ordinarily presuppose communication.

CLARIFYING REGRESSION THEORY

Kris's theory of art has been widely criticized for the central position it attributes to the regressive function in creative activity (Arieti, 1976; Ehrenzweig, 1967; Gedo, 1983; Weissman, 1971). The critics maintain that regressive processes in adults imply pathological mental functioning. Regression, even when it is in the service of the ego, claims Rose (1980), has a depreciative connotation. Weissman (1971) also argues that Kris's use of the term *regression*, when speaking of creativity, produces a "terminological disadvantage" which "detracts from an evaluation of the positive and strong developmental aspects of ego functioning in creative activity" (p. 402). He proposes a desynthesizing or "dissociative function of the ego," which he claims more accurately describes the ego's functioning during creative activity. It can be argued that Weissman's alternative term, involving a dissociative ego, implies no less pathology than does Kris's. Furthermore, if the ego is dissociated from the creative process, how could its contents be communicated? Noy (1969) simply calls regression in the service of the ego a misnomer, and Nass (1984) maintains that the capacity to experience and tolerate early modes of functioning requires a strong ego rather than a regressed one. Again, one could reason that a strong ego is, in fact, one that is partly defined by the flexibility of its various functions. For example, the ego must be able to relax its controls to allow sufficient regression necessary for sleep.

I agree with Anna Freud's (1970) claim that the concept of regression needs to be disassociated not only from pathology, but also must be appreciated as a necessary component of normal development. In fact, Sigmund Freud (1900/1953b) originally referred to the regressive movement from motor to visual sensations, which takes place in dream life, as a universal phenomenon. Peter Blos (1962, 1967) called attention to the "normative" regression in the service of development that takes place ubiquitously in adolescence. Geleerd (1964) also wrote of adaptive regression in adolescence. It is no coincidence that dreams and adolescence have often been linked to creativity. These phenomena involve normative regressive trends that simultaneously result in expanded creative potential. From Freud (1900/1953b) onward, we know to distinguish dreams from creative products, even though they have many elements in common (e.g., use of symbols, condensation) and are at times employed as sources of creative inspiration (see Chapter 6 for examples). And though the large majority of adolescent art does not achieve public recognition, adolescents are nevertheless well known for their romantic predilections and creative productivity. Therefore, it is best to assume that at least part of the creative process, like that found in dreams and adolescence, involves regression not necessarily accompanied by, or the result of, pathology.

Borrowing Kris's term, Darwinian psychologist Keith Simonton convincingly argues, in his *Origins of Genius* (1999), that regression in the service of the ego is common to the creative process in the arts and the sciences. He identifies regression within a spectrum ranging from the far end as psychosis to the near end as everyday thinking. I agree with Simonton that the concept of regression in the service of the ego has not outlived its usefulness, particularly as it applies to the arts and to the psychoanalytic process.

All the artists I have studied or had in treatment have readily discussed regressive forces at work, to a greater or lesser degree, in their creativity. I am obliged to conclude, therefore, that much of the reluctance to recognize regression as an integral force in creativity derives not so much from artists but, rather, from psychoanalysts. It is possible that these fears date back to the time when Freud was fiercely criticized for comparing the artist with the neurotic and the creative product with a neurotic symptom (Bell, 1925; Fry, 1924). In any case, it is interesting that these hesitations are not present in papers on regression that takes place in psychoanalysis, papers in which many authors (e.g., Galler, 1981; Loewald, 1981; Tuttman, 1979) recognize the dual quality of regression and its potential for both pathological deterioration and reorganization or integration.

Although I am in favor of retaining Kris's term, I agree that there exists a lack of clarity and specificity with which his concept is sometimes employed. Furthermore, most descriptions of regression in the service of the ego originate in ego psychological theory, a theory whose popularity has waned since 1970 (Blum, 1998) and whose terminology, focusing on energic and structural formulations, is perceived as experience distant.

I propose to move beyond the descriptive nature of regression in the service of the ego to specify the particular dynamic factors responsible for the existence and development of such a capacity. I also wish to update the term by expanding its usage beyond that belonging solely to drive and ego psychology. Regression in the service of the ego, therefore, will be considered as the ability to maintain contact with early body and self states and with early forms of object relationships, as well as with different modes of thinking. It is the act of achieving fuller access to one's embodiment—or the totality of experiential and epistemological inscription within the human body–brain system—without being overwhelmed or possessed by such activity. Artists seem to be especially skilled at being able to do this. Additionally, the relationship artists have with their work is a form of object relationship, and creative work allows for reenactments with early objects. Regression then indirectly serves a psychoanalytic function: artists employ their art as vehicles for transformation and change, both within themselves (their egos) and without (the art product). These points will be elaborated further next.

REGRESSION IN ART

In 1895 Paul Gauguin wrote: "I wielded the ax furiously and my hands were covered with blood as I cut with the pleasure of brutality appeased, of the destruction of I know not what ... All the old residue of my civilized emotions utterly destroyed" (Kuspit, 1993, p. 3). Gauguin is, indeed, the prototypical artist who not only adopted a primitive form of art, but also left behind his bourgeois life in Paris to live among "primitives" in Tahiti. He wrote:

> I am leaving in order to have peace and quiet, to be rid of the influence of civilization. I only want to do simple, very simple art, and to be able to do that, I have to immerse myself in virgin nature, see no one but savages, live their life, with no other thought in mind but to render, the way a child would, the concepts formed in my brain and to do this with the aid of nothing but the primitive means of art, the only means that are good and true. (Kuspit, 1993, p. 8)

To be sure, 20th century artists like Gauguin, Picasso, Dubuffet (champion of "Art Brut"), Modigliani, Klee, Miró, and those belonging to the Surrealist, Dada, Neoprimitivism, and Naïve movements, purposefully used childhood perspectives in art, perspectives that, in most of us, have become eroded by time. These sophisticated artists consciously adopted species of primitive or childhood art to achieve a spontaneity and connectivity unaffected by the constraints of reason and convention. One such artist, Paul Klee, expressed this desire when he claimed, "I want to be as though newborn, knowing nothing" (Fleming, 1968, p. 522). Indeed, whereas Klee's playful art possesses the casual quality of doodles or impulsive improvisations, it also demonstrates mastery of line and color. Unpretentiousness should not be confused with carelessness or lack of control. Klee's art is filled with humor and wit, as is that of Juan Miró. The whimsically creative side of life is presented in Miró's titles, such as in *Persons Magnetized by the Stars Walking on the Music of a Furrowed Landscape*. Furthermore, both Klee and Kirchner are known to have included samples of their childhood drawings alongside mature ones to demonstrate the link between the two (Douglas, 1996).

Whereas these artists adopt childlike modes in their art, others represent regression in the content and form of their work. Frida Kahlo not only painted herself nursing at the breast of her wet nurse (*My Nurse and I*, 1937; see Plate 3); she depicted the scene of her own birth—in her words, "the way I imagine I was born"—in which she emerges from between her mother's spread legs (*My Birth*, 1932). Ana Mendieta, a Cuban-American artist, longed for the undifferentiated state between mother and self, and created earth works that use her own body or its silhouette. As we will see in a later chapter, the impermanence of most of the materials she used—soil, sand, gunpowder, flame, fiber—reflects the transient nature of the primary subject of her work: the ephemeral bonding with the mother (see Plates 28–36).

Why do some artists represent regression to childhood modes of expression and experience? Often the artist wishes to recapture the ability to look at the world with awe and a sense of wonder, what Baudelaire calls the "animally ecstatic gaze of the child confronted with something new" (1964/1995, p. 8). The world of the infant and young child is imbued with a dynamic sense of physical and emotional involvement; knowing and feeling are not yet differentiated, and even inanimate objects are experienced as vital and alive. André Breton (1924/1972) perhaps said it best when he wrote in his Surrealist Manifesto:

> The mind which plunges into Surrealism relives with glowing excitement the best part of its childhood … From childhood memories, and from a few others, there emanates a sentiment of being unintegrated, and then later of *having gone astray*, which I hold to be the most fertile that exists. It is perhaps childhood that comes closest to one's "real life"; childhood beyond which man has at his disposal, aside from his laissez passer, only a few complimentary tickets; childhood where everything nevertheless conspires to bring about the effective, risk-free possession of oneself. Thanks to Surrealism, it seems that opportunity knocks a second time. (pp. 39–40)

It is noteworthy that virtually all the theorists who have written about creativity, regardless of their theoretical orientation, compare creative activity to aspects of childhood—for childhood is a time when temporal and spatial boundaries are soft, and perception and thinking numinous and magical. Beginning with Freud's paper, "Creative Writers and

Daydreaming (1908/1959)," there is the claim that both the child at play and the creative writer have in common the desire to create a new reality or to alter the present one. Kleinians (Segal, 1991) proposed that unconscious fantasy, related to the depressive position, motivates the creation of artworks in its attempt to restore and recreate the lost harmony of infancy. Winnicott (1971a) wrote of the "potential space," discovered in childhood, as the location for future creative endeavors. Anton Ehrenzweig (1967), who combined psychoanalytic and Gestalt perspectives, discussed the syncretistic vision of the young child who perceives an object in all its myriad forms. This ability diminishes at a later age (eight), but is retained by artists. Ehrenzweig argued that object identification, or "thing perception," develops prior to "form identification," or Gestalt perception.

An example distinguishing the two types of perception is illustrated in an anecdote conveyed to me by a colleague. He and his five-year-old daughter were looking at a book on modern art together. He was puzzled by the titles of the art works and their correspondence to the works themselves. His daughter, however, had no trouble making connections and at once explained them to her father. Ehrenzweig would say that the girl had grasped "the hidden order of art," an ability lost to the father but retained by the artist. She instantly identified the man reading a paper, smoking a pipe, or playing an instrument in several of Picasso's cubist works, while the father searched the paintings for a long while before "seeing" a recognizable object.

Cognitive psychologists like Howard Gardner (1982) have also written of the "golden age" of creativity, which Gardner's research shows lasts only until age eight. The child's creative period is believed to come to an end at a time that coincides with the latency stage during which, on the one hand, libidinal yearnings are generally repressed and, on the other, abstract reasoning (for which attention to details and focus on external reality is necessary) becomes of paramount importance. Furthermore, it is generally believed that with maturation, the boundaries between primary and secondary process thinking become increasingly firm and less flexible (Noy, 1969).

At this point I must hasten to point out the obvious: artists who regress do not become children. Rather, they invoke earlier modes of functioning and experience, making original but adaptive connections and combinations rooted in primary process thinking. Or, as Sandler and Sandler (1994) write, there is a "release or disinhibition of past modes of functioning" (p. 431) that continue to exist underneath the superimposition of later modes of functioning. These early modes of functioning involve experiences dominated by primary process thinking: hallucinatory wish-fulfillment, fantasy, raw instinct, object alterations, combinations and superimpositions, affective animation of the object realm, fusion with the external world, and the absence of an observing ego (the capacity for self-reflection and distance from experience). Though artists may lose themselves in the creative process, they are usually able to maintain their observing capacity and to distance themselves from the experience. Indeed, sometimes the artist operates exclusively from this distant mode. Israeli author Yoram Kaniuk, for instance, once described to me how he sits at a café with a beautiful woman all the while contemplating how he will rush home in order to write about how he sat at the café with a beautiful woman.

The child's experience is one of heightened sensitivity to external stimuli and exquisite vulnerability to primal fears and anxieties frequently experienced in terms of life or death (e.g., separation). Marion Milner, in her 1957 book, *On Not Being Able to Paint*, describes her conflicts around uncovering inhibitions to produce free drawings. Her attempts required her to succumb to regression and to risk feelings of anxiety, terror, and rage. For instance, she recounts her endeavors to free herself from the tyranny of outline: "I noticed that the effort needed in order to see the edges of objects stirred a dim fear, a fear of what might happen if one let go of one's mental hold on the outline which kept everything separate and in its place" (p. 16).

Confronting the tyranny of the conventional, the artist must offer something original and run the risk of failure and breakdown. The result of Milner's self-analysis through her art clearly supports Kris's claim that "passive receptiveness" with all its attendant dangers is a necessary precondition for the achievement of freedom of expression. The artist sustains the threat of loss of self, loss of reality, loss of control, and reactivation of trauma (Bush, 1969, p. 165). One artist-patient who described the regression that takes place in her work stated that "the loss of self can happen at any time during the process, no warning: suddenly I'm *there*, no longer here—yet simultaneously here and there. During these times, as I'm coming out, I'm often trembling, blue with cold, sometimes my eyes are wet."

Bracha L. Ettinger, a contemporary Israeli-French artist-psychoanalyst, informed me that she chose the title *Autistworks* for a series of works "because this was my state in painting them. The autist in me" (see Plate 4). She claims to experience regression during creativity as

> a kind of fragilization that happens, together with a loosening of the ties between the thoughts, a wild attention which is the opposite of concentration; and what is usually nonsignificant sounds or color get full of sense and things become full of some kind of life, and fragments of memories hang in the air, and then you enter a zone without memories. (Personal communication, October 25, 1998)

Indeed, many of Ettinger's works depict indistinct figures with blurred boundaries suggesting layers of thought, emotion, and memory (see

Plate 5).[1] Plates 4 and 5 show "traces of traces of traces" from fragments of a photograph of a group of women and children about to be shot by German soldiers in Mizcocz, in the Rovno region of Ukraine in 1942. Plate 5 combines that same photograph with one of Ettinger's parents in Lodz in 1937.

Ettinger's description of her creative process attests to a disinhibition that takes place during the inspirational phase of her work. For her, and many other artists, this disinhibition allows for low levels of arousal, defocused attention, and primary process thinking that makes unlikely connections and engages simultaneous representations. Past, present, and future merge and become undifferentiated. Self and other, as well as inner and outer reality, conflate. Kris's hypotheses about what takes place during the inspirational phase of creativity have been confirmed by neurophysiological research. Colin Martindale (1998, 1999), having conducted a number of studies comparing neurophysiological functioning in creative and non-creative activity, found that individuals involved in creative immersion display lower levels of cortical arousal (creative activity requires defocused attention associated with low cortical activation), more right- than left-hemispheric activation (right hemisphere activity is responsible for global, parallel, and holistic processes associated with primary process thinking), and lower levels of frontal lobe activation (low frontal lobe activity is related to less cognitive inhibition allowing for unlikely connections).

WHEN REGRESSION SAVES OR DAMNS

But where does one draw the line between safe and dangerous regression? This important question is vividly addressed in author Amos Oz's judicious description of how he experienced regression while writing his novel *The Same Sea*:

> This is a book that I despaired over more than anything else I've ever written. And it also frightened me while I was writing it. I had the feeling that I was getting all fouled up … I had the feeling that maybe it

---

[1] Most of the artists I have referred to are associated primarily with the modern and postmodern age and thus it may be argued that my assumptions concerning regression in art apply only to later art. Although my case does appear strong in reference to visual art in the modern and postmodern age, I believe it applies equally to other forms of art as well as other eras. Goya (1746–1828) succumbed to deafness and became withdrawn and isolated, painting *Disasters of War* and *Black Paintings* while he feared for his sanity. Nonvisual artists have long described the angst they experience in the creation of their works. English poet Gerard Manley Hopkins, for instance, explained that his "Dark Sonnets" were "written in blood." Because regression is a universal and spectral phenomenon, indeed a part of our evolutionary heritage, and is needed to generate variation in associative connections, it is inherent in human creativity.

wouldn't end well. Not in terms of how the book would be received. But in terms of its implications for my identity. Sometimes I was afraid that something happened to me. Something in my mind went awry. Something wrong. Sometimes when I did other things, like shaving or standing in line at the bank ... the characters of the book would flow in and out of me ... as if it wasn't me writing them, but them writing me. And I was beset by the fear that I was losing my own identity. Maybe I was going insane. Wondering if there was any way back from this washing away of the borders between me and not me. I had the feeling that I was in the middle of the sea, that I might not be able to reach the coast, to get back to myself. That I would never again set my feet down on *terra firma*. (1998, p. 16)

Naturally there is a difference between pathological and healthy regression, similar to Kohut's distinction between pathological and healthy narcissism (1971, 1977). Moving backward need not imply any more negative connotation attached to it than moving forward. If the move backward can open doors, why should it be viewed in pejorative terms? Yet, as Oz tells us, it is risky, but new and original ideas are not born without risk. Salvador Dali once wrote: "The only difference between a madman and myself is that I am not mad!" (1964, p. 21). This seeming absurdity beautifully illustrates Kris's distinction between the psychotic and nonpsychotic artist. The artist may sometimes visit the neighborhood of madness and disassemble, but he does not make his home there. Interestingly, Dali referred to his statement as his "first motto" and the "theme" of his life.

The line between regression that saves and regression that damns is not always easily or clearly drawn. But here are some questions that may help us decide on the nature of regression: Is the artist or the artistic product overwhelmed or destroyed by the regression that takes place or not? Is it controlled and adaptive regression? Can the artist shut it off when necessary in order to attend to other reality demands? Van Gogh's *Wheat Field with Crows* (1890), with its sad road leading nowhere beneath a cobalt blue sky, clearly illustrates his regressive decline and desperation. In a letter to his brother Theo, he wrote, "There are vast fields of wheat under troubled skies, and I did not need to go out of my way to express sadness and extreme loneliness" (Van Gogh, 1937, p. 478). He took his life shortly thereafter. On the other hand, author David Grossman (1998) has described living in two worlds: the world of his writing, in which boundaries are blurred and experiences are regressive and emotionally overwhelming, and the world of everyday life, in which he attends to his family and daily chores.

What is it that allows an artist not only to risk regression but also to return from it? The answer to this question is where much of the controversy surrounding the concept of regression in the service of the ego lies. Ego psychologists as well as their opponents have long claimed that only someone with a strong ego can regress in its service (Bellak, 1954/1973; Noy, 1969; Schafer, 1958). However, this view fails to explain why a considerable number of artists live dysfunctional lives, a fact that can be indicative of a weak ego and poor reality ties. Clearly, postulating a strong (or a weak) ego does not account for the uneven development in ego functions witnessed in many creative individuals. A theory like Winnicott's (1958/1968), on the other hand, claims that a good enough mother allows for the internalization of benign introjects which in turn fosters the capacity to tolerate ambiguity and accept paradox. But this approach fails to explain why numerous artists experience early parental losses, or poor, neglectful, and even abusive parenting (Eisenstadt, Haynal, Rentchnick, & De Senarclens, 1989; Pollock, 1975). In fact, many artists are consciously aware of their attempts to enlist their creativity to repair defective early upbringing.

This leads to a question that may clarify the problem at hand: Does art-making possess therapeutic powers? Some believe that art merely repeats and cannot repair, whereas others, myself included, are convinced that art is potentially therapeutic. Therefore, I do not see the necessity to postulate that artists' strong egos or healthy early object relations hold the key to creative regression. On the contrary, I believe that artists employ their art as a means of strengthening their egos or building their self-esteem. Many artists whom I have interviewed over the years have stated, in one manner or another, that if they had experienced a happy childhood, adequate parenting, or high self-esteem, they would not have had to choose the tortuous path of artistic creativity.

CLOWNING AROUND

Some time ago I treated a young female artist, Debbie, whose childhood had been greatly troubled, particularly by an oppressive father who was either distant or hypercritical and emotionally abusive. A heavy woman who claimed she became fat as a child to discourage her father from looking at her, Debbie turned to art at a young age and had experienced moderate success with her paintings and drawings. At the time she entered therapy she was fully blocked, unable to create anything "even worth the paint on the canvas." She claimed that if she couldn't create art, "life seemed flat and dead, nothing but routine and responsibility."

After several months of treatment, Debbie had still not lifted a brush to paint and greatly feared she might never paint again. She had two people on her mind: her young son, Ryan, and her husband, Bill, who suffered from such severe back problems that he had to stop working. He mostly moped around the house and drank wine.

The resentment Debbie felt toward her husband since he became an invalid was entirely unconscious. She knew he needed her constant attention and intruded on her private artistic space. But she remained unaware of her fury at him, which seemed to grow daily. Instead, she talked obsessively about how puzzled she was at not being able to paint. I danced gently around the subject of her relationship with Bill, while she held on to her role of "good wife" who took excellent care of an increasingly drunk and dependent spouse. Here is a portion of a pivotal session in which Debbie came to my office with a wine bottle sticking out of her purse. After she failed to mention it for 15 minutes, I brought up the elephant in the room.

DK: I notice you have a wine bottle in your pocketbook.
DEBBIE: Yes. Bill stuck it there for spite because I was telling him we need money for food.
DK: What are you going to do with it?
DEBBIE: I don't know.
DK: What would you like to do with it?
DEBBIE: I'd like to smash him over the head with it.
DK: Wow. You're very angry at him.
DEBBIE: He's not the person I married. Since he hurt his back, another man came out. And now he drinks all the time and we don't have enough money to live. Do you have any idea how many bottles of wine there are in my house?
DK: How many?
DEBBIE: Dozens!
DK: Where are they?
DEBBIE: They're in my garage. Where I used to paint. He's even taken over my studio. He drinks out there and looks at old porn magazines. He should be in therapy, but he'd never come.
DK: Then these bottles are very symbolic. They're in your studio. They're in your pocketbook. They've come into your therapy.
DEBBIE: Yeah, I know. We don't have sex anymore, but he sticks a bottle in my purse! [*Nervous laugh.*]
DK: Maybe he wants to be here too. [*Debbie removes the bottle from her bag and places it on the table.*] No, he'd never come. He's much too committed to being an idiot.
DK: So what does he want to say?
DEBBIE: I don't know … but, maybe he needs a head …
DK: You want to give him a head?
DEBBIE: Yeah, he needs a new head. I'm gonna give him a head.

That evening, after she ate dinner with her husband and son, Debbie gazed at an empty wine bottle standing on the windowsill. Using bits of colored paper and string, a burned out light bulb and various buttons and bits of junk, she enlisted her young son in creating a glass clown out of the wine bottle. In her next session, she said she had great fun making the clown and she had actually laughed "for the first time in months. I was a kid again without a care in the world, flying with my little boy through the world of childhood imagination. Sitting with Jimmy and making that clown made me feel like we were two children. I had that same feeling I had when I was a kid: the feeling that anything could be changed into something else, and made even more beautiful."

This one event led Debbie to begin a series of bottle artworks, progressively more sophisticated and intricate, which she eventually sold at a local art fair. From the bottle works she eventually turned back to her canvas and resurrected her artistic project.

Later when we discussed her original set of bottle clowns she claimed they were connected to her father, her husband, and herself. "My Dad's stiff and rigid, hard to the touch, like glass. My husband always drinks wine. He's dark like wine, often intoxicated, but no longer intoxicating. Me, I'm shaped like a wine bottle, way too thick at the hips. I turned us all into one clown after another." She realized that releasing her anger allowed her to channel it into her creativity rather than have it block it. "I made us funny and beautiful," she said. "I lifted myself up."

In this connection, I once gave a lecture to a group of art therapists who brought up an interesting problem. They regularly encounter regression in patients who are not artists and who are not particularly talented in the arts. They described to me the difficulties they face in fostering therapeutic regression in people who lack the ability to take pleasure in the creative process or its final product. This matter confirmed my hunch that part of what allows artists to regress is the confidence they have in their abilities or, to quote George Klein (1976), a pleasure of "effectance," a joy in the sense of competence. John Gedo (1996) has also applied Klein's notion of effectance to creative individuals and believes that the competence produced by creativity serves to heighten the artist's self-esteem. One artist described the agony and ecstasy of her creativity in this way: "Yesterday I read a version of a chapter I wrote last year, and I just sat and wept. Why? Because it was so good—and I had created so many universes, so many alternate realities that it was torture to pick one to stand for all of them."

REGRESSION AND RELATIONSHIP TO CRAFT

When Kris wrote of the artist's regression, he referred to a one-person, intrapsychic act. In recent years, psychoanalysis has moved from a one-person to a two-person psychology (Greenberg & Mitchell, 1983; Mitchell, 1988; Mitchell & Aron, 1999). I propose that a similar transition takes place with regard to the relationship between the artist and the creative product. For Balint (1968), therapeutic regression occurs within a dyadic relationship. He conceived of regression as benign and beneficial to the therapy on condition that the analyst provides an accepting environment in which the patient can feel safe to regress. Loewald (1981) also recognized the analyst's role in validating the patient's regressive experience so that the patient is not left alone with it. Blum (1994) too notes that therapeutic regression is dependent upon and influenced by the object relationship with the analyst both inside and outside the transference.

In a similar vein, I am suggesting that artists' regression is enabled by a relationship, the relationship to their craft. The structure of art, like the analytic setting, establishes parameters within which artists must work (Knafo, 1993). It functions as a holding, containing, and validating environment that allows artists' psychic organization to fluctuate with relative safety. And just as analysts may intervene with an interpretation to regressed patients in order to prevent their becoming overwhelmed by regressive forces, so too artists can move from what Kris called inspiration (regression) to elaboration (editing, criticism) in order to attain a higher level of organization and meaning.

Indeed, although some artists possess relatively weak egos and poor ties to reality, their relationship to their work is strong, and it is this relationship that sustains them and allows them to regress in its service. In fact, many artists live for years with no close relationships in the outside world and no external validation for what they do (see Chapter 5). In spite of this situation, they continue to create, and their drive is not weakened. I believe this is because the work of art embodies containing (Bion, 1959/1984) and self-object properties (Kohut, 1971, 1977), and functions in mirroring or idealizing capacities. Furthermore, art making creates meaning for the artist, allowing the dissemination of experience and personal history. Kris's concept of regression in the service of the ego is, therefore, exactly what it says: The regression feeds the ego, not just the art product.

I am not the first to recognize the transferred object relationships artists have with their art (Greenacre, 1957/1971a; Jacobson, 1964: Weissman, 1971). Jacobson (1964) compared artists' hypercathexis of their created product with the child's exclusive oral investment in his or her single primary love object. Weissman (1971) also perceived the created object as "derivative of the early infantile analge [sic] of object relationships" (p. 401). Adrian Stokes, himself a painter and writer about art, has said, "The work of art is esteemed for its otherness, as a self-sufficient object, no less than an ego-figure" (Fuller, 1980, p. 116).

I agree with these views yet wish to take them a step further. The work of art functions not only as a type of object relationship but can provide a site for transformation and change. Clearly, Debbie was changed by her glass clowns. In them she expressed her conflict and its transformation;

something cold, dark, and brittle in her became fluid and beautiful. And I have seen transformation through art happen with many artist-patients. One poet and fiction writer recently confessed to me:

> I don't have a choice about whether or not I write. Publication is truly secondary. I write not only to keep my life together, to give it an organizing and meaningful center, but to further my growth—not merely as a writer but as a human being. Believe me when I tell you, I have created characters based on people I despised and have come to feel compassion for those very same people based on what happens to them as characters in my stories! For me, fiction is a way of imagining and feeling the other, a way of getting beyond my petty resentments and brooding sense of injury. It is revenge and reconciliation all in one. It grows me because it forces me to expand the boundaries of imagination and the intelligence of my sensibilities.

Indeed, creative activity produces a locale wherein the artist seeks objects and reenacts reunion with them. (Ana Mendieta's work is an excellent example.) It is true that some artists' relationship to their work has the quality of compulsive repetition and thus does not allow for development beyond an unsatisfactory early relationship. Artists like Arshille Gorky or Mark Rothko, great artists in their own right, were nonetheless psychically stuck and, as a result, their art reflects an almost addictive use of repetitive patterns. In Gorky's case, there are endless variations on a theme based on a photograph of his mother (whom he lost in childhood) and him as a boy. In Rothko's oeuvre, numerous reproductions exist of two or three stacked, colored rectangles. Fuller (1980) claims that Rothko's work serves as an excellent example of the absent mother. The fact that both artists eventually took their lives may be related to their inability to employ their art in order to fully express an otherwise inarticulate relationship as well as transform it.

I am suggesting that many artists reunite and identify with their original objects in the creative process, thereby embodying maternal generativity (Knafo, 1996). At the same time, artworks are like babies that result from this symbolic reunion (McDougall, 1980; Segal, 1991). Through their work artists give life to objects of their own. Byron, in his poem, "Childe Harold's Pilgrimage," describes this relationship between the artist and his creation (1812–1818/1886, p. 78):

> Tis to create, and in creating live
> A being more intense, that we endow
> With form our fancy, gaining as we give
> The life we image, even as I do now.
> What am I? Nothing; but not so art thou,

Soul of my thought! With whom I traverse earth,
Invisible but gazing, as I glow
Mix'd with thy spirit, blending with thy birth,
And feeling still with thee in my crush'd feeling's dearth.

REGRESSION IN THE VIEWER

I would like to add a few words about the audience's reaction to works of art as involving regressive processes analogous to those experienced by the artist. Cezanne described the aesthetic response as follows:

> [A painting is] an abyss in which the eye is lost. All these tones circulate in the blood. One is revivified, born into the real world, one finds oneself, one becomes the painting. To love a painting, one must first have drunk deeply of it in long draughts. Lose consciousness. Descend with the painter into the dim tangled roots of things, and rise again from them in colors, be steeped in the light of them. (Milner, 1957, p. 25)

Cezanne's oral imagery of intoxication, as well as his description of the viewer's eschewing of ego boundaries and hold on oneself, recall the drink from a mother's breast, the pull of symbiosis. It is particularly striking that Cezanne did not leave his viewer in this state of regression, blissful though it may be. He described how the viewer, after he or she has drunk, must "rise again."

Some modern art, and much postmodern art, is experienced as much more disturbing than the description given by Cezanne (although it must be remembered that Cezanne's work caused quite a stir when it first appeared in France). Such strong reactions may well be related to the regressive pull of the art. Additionally, many postmodern artists manipulate their audience and abuse their trust. Viewers are attacked, exposed to things they would rather not see, and forced to take part in an experience not of their choosing. For example, French multimedia artist Orlan has viewers watch her undergo surgery on her face while she reads from philosophical and psychoanalytic texts; American performance artist Chris Burden masturbates from a hidden place while talking to gallery or museum goers; Yugoslavian artist Marina Abromoviç invites her audience to choose from a number of objects, including a knife and gun, to do whatever they want to her. The setting or boundaries between art and life are often dissolved (e.g., literal frames have disappeared in much contemporary art, and the viewer often becomes part of the artwork itself), leaving the spectator feeling exposed, manipulated, and vulnerable. Audiences often recoil from or avoid art that requires such risks. They may feel that the regression demanded of them is not compensated for by the aesthetic pleasure offered by the work of art.

It is this notion that Kleinians like Segal, Fuller, and Rickman have explored in their writings on the aesthetic response. Segal (1991), for instance, claims that the viewer identifies with the artist's creative process, a process that involves the balancing of destructive and reparative forces. If one is unable to tolerate one's own aggression, then one will encounter difficulty with art products that contain such affects and acts. Peter Fuller, in his book *Art and Psychoanalysis* (1980), devotes a chapter to the aesthetic response to *Venus de Milo* as a recreation, in fantasy, of the damaged image of the mother. Because viewers observe a statue that has sustained damage and fragmentation, they are invited and compelled to complete (i.e., repair) it internally. It is this admission of original destruction à la Klein that has the potential to enhance the aesthetic experience. Whereas we tend to think of destructiveness in art as exemplified in Cubist, abstract, or sensationalist postmodern art, Rickman (1940) has emphasized the aesthetic delight experienced by many who view mutilated Greek and Roman statues. For Rickman "the whole psychic mechanism of frustration, retaliation, compensation, guilt, and anxiety for restitution ... becomes operative and creative in art" (Fuller, 1980, p. 127).

Thus, regressive forces in the viewer function in two ways. They have the potential to arouse fear and anxiety because of the aggressive and destructive forces they unleash and because of the loss of boundaries they represent. They can also be reassuring and developmentally constructive, since they invite us to achieve, at least in fantasy, the experience of feelings and situations otherwise rarely had in adulthood. It is this dialectic between destruction and construction, and between fusion and separation that exists in every work of art and that creates its own unique aesthetic response. Just as the analyst is called upon to temporarily regress along with his or her patients (Blum, 1994; Loewald, 1981; Searles, 1959/1965), so too viewers are invited to participate in regressive processes parallel to those the artist experienced during creation, as well as the regression depicted in the artwork itself. These regressive forces ultimately belong to a dynamic, two-way relationship between artist and viewer. Those who allow themselves to regress as part of their aesthetic response to artworks become not only art viewers, but also re- and co-creators.

I have endeavored to bring Ernst Kris's concept of regression in the service of the ego up to date by expanding the terminology beyond that of libidinal energy cathexes and ego psychology. I have illustrated the relevance of this concept when viewed through the lens of developmental theory, neuroscience, and object relations. The creative process as well as the aesthetic response involve a willingness to engage in nonpathological regressive operations. Regressive forces exist in creativity, and these forces allow artists to frequently experience levels of consciousness usually not accessible to most adults. Although these processes resemble childlike states or characteristics generally associated with madness, they are under the artist's control in the sense that he or she has the capacity to make the transition from these states to others requiring observation, discipline, and criticism. Creative regression is facilitated by the artistic setting and relationship to one's craft, just as therapeutic regression is by the analytic frame and transference relationship. The artist's relationship to his or her art is a type of object relationship, imbued with reality and fantasy, comparable to that between patient and analyst. In its self-object capacity, the work of art validates the artist's sense of effectance. It also has the potential to repair defective early object relations and to strengthen ego and self-esteem. According to this view, it does not matter whether artists had good or bad mothers, or mothers who were present or absent. The domain of art allows for playful engagement with one's mother of the past, one's fantasy mother, and one's newly created mother, the transformational object of art. Regression is integral to both creative activity and personal growth.

Chapter 3

The Senses Grow Skilled in Their Craving

Thoughts on Creativity and Substance Abuse[1]

For art to exist, for any sort of aesthetic activity to exist, a certain physiological precondition is indispensable: intoxication.

—Friedrich Nietzsche

The connection between creativity and addiction is nearly as legendary as that between creativity and madness. Many people expect creative individuals to abuse substances and are hardly surprised to discover that yet another famous artist has checked into a rehabilitation facility or died from a drug overdose. A *New York Times* op-ed piece (Mehlman, 2005) commenting on Philip Roth's remarkable late-age productivity marveled at the fact that the author has retained freedom from "performance-enhancing drugs." The implication is that if Roth is not "juiced," like O'Neill or Capote, how could he write some of his best novels after the age of 60?

It is often assumed that artists live in the romantic tradition. John Cheever said that self-destruction is expected of the writer (Cheever, 1984). Indeed, the list of creative individuals who are or were famous addicts is remarkably long. The history of this connection dates back at least to the 19th century, when opium and opium-based products were widely used and sometimes abused by writers and poets. Along with Balzac, Dumas, and Flaubert, Baudelaire belonged to an elite group of French artists called The Hashish Club, led by novelist Pierre Jules Theophile. Although the club's members met on a monthly basis to study the drug's effect on creativity, little is known about what they actually discovered. What remains extant are Baudelaire's (1859/1996) poetic renderings about the effects of wine and hashish:

---

[1] An earlier version of this chapter appeared in *Psychoanalytic Review*, 95(4), 2008, pp. 571–595. That the senses grow skilled in their craving is a key idea in Eastern traditions, especially yoga philosophy and Buddhist philosophy. Ancient teachers of renunciation explained the psychology of craving as an escalating cycle in which the desire for the object becomes more intense the more that the pleasure is satisfied or indulged.

What man has never known the profound joys of wine? Whoever has had a grief to appease, a memory to evoke, a sorrow to drown, a castle in Spain to build—all have at one time invoked the mysterious god who lies concealed in the fibers of the grapevine. How radiant are those wine-induced visions, brilliantly illuminated by the inner sun! How true and burning this second youth which man calls wine. But how dangerous, too, are its fierce pleasures and debilitating enchantments. (p. 5)

For Baudelaire (1860/1998, p. 381), intoxication clearly entailed a corporeal sublime state in which "we flutter towards infinity," with drunkenness leading to the "hypersublime."

In England, some Romantic poets matched the French in their use of opiates to foster creative inspiration. Shelley, Coleridge, Keats, and Byron used opium. John De Quincy's descriptions of opium's ability to enhance and even induce dream states in *Confessions of an English Opium-Eater* (1821/1950) are perhaps the most frequently cited in literature after those of Baudelaire. "The opium-eater," writes De Quincy, "feels that the diviner part of his nature is paramount; that is, the moral affections are in a state of cloudless serenity, and overall is the great light of the majestic intellect" (p. 37).

In the early 20th century many American writers took to the bottle. A list of these alcoholic writers includes such luminaries as Edgar Allen Poe, Theodore Dreiser, Hart Crane, Eugene O'Neill, Edna St. Vincent Millay, Dorothy Parker, Carson McCullers, F. Scott Fitzgerald, Dashiell Hammett, Wallace Stevens, e. e. cummings, Theodore Roethke, Edmund Wilson, James Thurber, Jack London, Tennessee Williams, Truman Capote, Jack Kerouac, O. Henry, John Cheever, Conrad Aiken, Stephen Crane, William Saroyan, Irwin Shaw, Delmore Schwartz, Robert Lowell, Jean Stafford, James Agee, and Raymond Chandler. Nobel Prize-winning American writers who are alcoholics account for 70% of the American winners. Sinclair Lewis, William Faulkner, Ernest Hemingway, and John Steinbeck are among this elite cadre (Goodwin, 1988). In *Alcohol and the Writer* (1988), Donald Goodwin claims that alcoholism among writers reached epidemic proportions in America during the first half of last century.

Why only the first half? Speculation tempts the reply that drugs trumped alcohol in the latter half of the century. In "The Rhetoric of Drugs," Jacques Derrida (2003) moves beyond the definition of addiction as the disease of modernity; he claims that the birth of "narcotic modernity" is itself a cultural formation shaped by drugs. In the second half of the century, both jazz and rock musicians became tied to drug addiction. Reggae music, too, is associated with Bob Marley, Rastafarianism—and marijuana. Louis Armstrong was reputed to have smoked three huge joints every day of his life. Ray Charles is alleged to have written his best music during his 40-year heroin habit. Despite the notable accomplishments of drug-addicted artists, terrible casualties from drug overdoses unavoidably come to mind: Jimi Hendrix, Jim Morrison, Janis Joplin, Judy Garland, Billie Holiday, Elvis Presley, Kurt Cobain, and Amy Winehouse all died before their time due to drug and alcohol addiction. Jazz great Charlie Parker was said to have looked 30 years older than his age when he died from his well-known heroin habit.

Clearly, alcohol and drug addiction is not limited to writers and musicians. Many in the entertainment industry, among them comedians and actors, have also succumbed to the allure of alcohol and other drugs. W. C. Fields, Buster Keaton, Bing Crosby, John Barrymore, Humphrey Bogart, Spencer Tracy, Ava Gardner, Marilyn Monroe, Elizabeth Taylor, John Belushi, and Robert Downey, Jr. are a few names that spring to mind. Beat generation writers, including Aldous Huxley, Allen Ginsberg, William Burroughs, and Henri Michaux experimented with LSD and mescaline. Elaine de Kooning (artist and wife of Willem de Kooning) reported that in 1950 "booze flooded the New York art scene" and "the whole art world became alcoholic" (Schildkraut, Hirshfield, & Murphy, 1994, p. 485).

Despite this impressive list of famous artists/addicts, there are far more artists who were never addicts. Nevertheless, for some, writing has become synonymous with alcoholism and music with narcotics addiction—with chemicals playing the role of both muse and demon. How is it that the relationship between artists and substance abuse is now taken as a given? Is such a tie justified or merely part of the popular myth of the unstable artist? And, if there is a strong bond between creativity and addiction, is the creative process helped or hindered by drugs? What meager literature exists on this rich subject consists of a few empirical studies, many of them from abroad. In this chapter, using theoretical research and clinical material, I explore the connection between substance abuse and the arts, between chemically-induced, altered states of consciousness and the work created under its influence, and the relationship of those dyads to psychological sensitivity and the problem of fame.

THE PURSUIT OF ALTERED STATES

> In Xanadu did Kubla Khan
> A stately pleasure dome decree:
> Where Alph, the sacred river, ran
> Through caverns measureless to man
> Down to the sunless sea.
>
> —Samuel Coleridge

Like Coleridge, the archetypal Romantic poet and addict who claimed to have written these opening lines to his famous poem "Kubla Khan" (1899, p. 35) upon waking from an opium-induced dream state, other artists often sense that they are being guided by forces outside their conscious control. Jung (1952) addresses this phenomenon when he wrote about the artist as visionary, a passive instrument of his work, which has an agency and energy of its own. *The Strange Case of Dr. Jekyll and Mr. Hyde* (1886/2002), similarly inspired by drug-induced dreams, apparently spilled from the pen of Robert Louis Stevenson during his 6-day cocaine marathon. The author's proper and conscientious Edwardian physician, Dr. Jekyll, transmogrifying into the demonic Mr. Hyde, perfectly illustrates the capacity of substances to induce altered and uninhibited states of consciousness as well as overwhelm and even destroy the user.

The power of chemical substances to dramatically modify sensation and perception, to steep consciousness in trance and phantasmagoria, is both frightening and fascinating. One patient who is a writer described the way marijuana affects him:

> It loosens the glue that holds ordinary reality together. The associations arising in my mind become unusual and get connected in strange ways. Bubbles of light climb up my spine and pop in my brain, making everything shimmer with an odd luminescence. Sounds echo in my body and smells become acute. Ordinary concerns fall to the background, and a sense of intense immediacy and wonder ensues. I get the feeling of being a receiver, like I'm some kind of radio tuned to a different station. In the spectrum of perception and imagination, the dial shifts, and suddenly I'm listening to new voices and new music.

Common expressions, such as "it is the alcohol/drug speaking" or being "under the influence" of a "mind-altering" or "mind-expanding" substance, refer to the transformative power chemicals possess to modify one's state of being—the body–mind, perception, affects, and behavior.

Depersonalization, the disconnect between the observing and experiencing aspects of the self, is often assumed to occur in states of mental illness. Yet, under certain circumstances, depersonalization is a welcomed rather than aversive condition. For example, those practicing meditation or mindfulness are not necessarily frightened or disoriented by states of depersonalization. Substance abusers, too, seek experiences that intentionally invoke depersonalization and that may be liberating (Ten Berge, 2002) as well as uncanny or terrifying. Writing about the effects of mescaline, poet Henri Michaux describes his familiarity with depersonalization: "There isn't one me. There aren't ten me's. There is no me. ME is only a position of equilibrium. An average of me's, a movement in the crowd" (LaCharité, 1977, p. 56). *Derealization*, the alienation in one's experience of reality, is often thought to go hand-in-hand with depersonalization and is also a common consequence of hallucinogenic drug use. William Burroughs described how hallucinogenics "shift the scanning pattern of 'reality' so that we see a different 'reality'—There is no true or real 'reality'—'Reality' is simply a more or less constant scanning pattern" (1964, p. 53).

The multiple self-states revealed in both depersonalization and derealization may culminate in dissociation. *Dissociation* refers to the existence of several self-states, each presented in exclusion of the presence and consciousness of the others. The notorious "black out" of memories in alcoholics who awaken from drunken binges epitomizes classical dissociation caused by a substance. In our postmodern age, it is often argued that we all dissociate to a greater or lesser degree, depending on how much our self-states converge with or diverge from one another. Multiple Personality Disorder (or Dissociative Identity Disorder) is located at the extreme pole of dissociation. Stevenson's Hyde, a callous and murderous man totally distinct from Jekyll, the respectable doctor, perhaps best illustrates the process of extreme dissociation created by drugs. Jekyll, aware of the double life he wishes to lead, expounds on the dissociative process at hand:

> If each, I told myself, could be housed in separate identities, life would be relieved of all that was unbearable; the unjust might go his way, delivered from the aspirations and remorse of his upright twin; and the just could walk steadfastly and securely on his upward path, doing the good things in which he found his pleasure, and no longer exposed to disgrace and penitence by the hands of this extraneous evil. It was the curse of mankind that these incongruous faggots were thus bound together—that in the agonized womb of consciousness, these polar twins should be continuously struggling. How, then, were they dissociated? (1909, p. 375)

Later, Jekyll depicts the temporary success of his dissociation: "Think of it. I did not even exist! Let me but escape into my laboratory door, give me but a second or two to mix and swallow the draught that I had always standing ready; and, whatever he had done, Edward Hyde would pass away like a stain upon a mirror" (pp. 380–381). At first, Jekyll seems to be able to get away with it, but ultimately, the dissociation fails.

To a much lesser degree, Freud, too, describes how cocaine produced a new man, one more "silly," "daring and fearless," and even more "simply normal" than his usual "wretched self" (Jones, 1953).

Considering the question of why many artists rely on drugs, F. Scott Fitzgerald declared that creative vitality demands stimulation (Goodwin, 1988, p. 187). Getting started is often deemed the most challenging aspect of creative work. "Before I start to write," explains E. B. White, "I always treat myself to a nice dry martini. Just one, to give me the courage to get started. After that, I am on my own" (cited in Goodwin, 1988, p. 189). Indeed, many creative geniuses are convinced that the disinhibiting effect of alcohol helps them to break through their blocks and fears.

Artists also use substances to perceive life through a new, fresher, or deeper lens, one difficult to come by naturally. Hallucinogens, or psychedelic drugs, allow the user to explore strange inner and outer worlds and their associated possibilities. The word *psychedelic* literally means "to make the soul visible." Two Beatles albums, written at a time they experimented with psychedelic drugs, are listed at the top of the influential Rolling Stone's "500 Greatest Albums of all Time" list. Number 1 is *Sgt. Pepper's Lonely Heart's Club Band* (1967), with its song, "Lucy in the Sky with Diamonds," and number 3 is *Revolver* (1966), whose most innovative track, "Tomorrow Never Knows," was written by John Lennon as an atempt at distilling an LSD trip into a three-minute song. Creative genius and visionary, Steve Jobs, was known to have said that taking LSD was one of the two or three most important things he had done in his life (Markoff, 2005, p. xix). Indeed, Markoff argues that psychedelic drugs propelled the computer and Internet revolutions forward by altering reality through unconventional and highly intuitive thinking. In *Alternating Current*, Octavio Paz writes of the heightened emotional responsiveness and susceptibility inspired by drugs: "Drugs arouse the powers of analogy, set objects in motion, make the world a vast poem shaped by rhymes and rhythms" (1983, p. 76).

In the words of Stephen King, "The main effect of the grain or the grape on the creative personality is that it provides the necessary sense of newness and freshness, without which creative writing does not occur" (cited in Goodwin, 1988, p. 187). Ten Berge (1999) employs the term *gaucherie* to describe the disinhibition frequently sought by creative artists. For example, some right-handed artists might deliberately work with their left hands. Some artists turn to substances to have their senses reinvigorated. John Cheever, who struggled with alcoholism, lamented that getting old dulls the senses. We saw in Chapter 2 on regression how artists try to recapture a youthful—that is, wondrous, immediate, and full of possibility—way of encountering the world. When artists like Cheever experience the loss of this faculty, they may turn to substances in order to revive earlier states of knowing and feeling.

A common effect of many drugs is an overacuteness of the senses known as *hyperaesthesia*. William James, cognizant of this effect, alleged that alcohol's charms lay in the "deepening sense of reality and truth. In whatever light things may then appear to us, they seem more utterly what they are, more 'utterly utter' than when we are sober" (1890, p. 284). In his "Tale of the Ragged Mountains," Edgar Allen Poe likewise describes the way morphine imbued the external world with a heightened intensity:

> In the quivering of a leaf—in the hue of a blade of glass—in the shape of a trefoil—in the humming of a bee—in the gleaming of a dew drop—in the breathing of the wind—in the faint odors that came from the forest—there came a whole universe of suggestion—a gay and motley train of rhapsodies and immethodical thought. (1992, p. 681)

In 1859, Baudelaire wrote *Artificial Paradises*, a monograph that traces the transformations in thoughts and sensations that arise from smoking cannabis. He mentions both euphoric and dysphoric reactions and elaborates on drug-induced *synesthesia*, a conflation of the senses (e.g., he describes the sound of color and the color of sound). In *Les Fleurs du Mal* (*Flowers of Evil*, 1982), he delineates the deleterious effects of hashish. Anaïs Nin, in her famous diary, conveys the hyperanasthetic and the synesthetic responses she had to LSD:

> The music vibrated through my body as if I were one of the instruments and I felt myself becoming a full percussion orchestra, becoming green, blue, orange. The waves of the sounds ran through my hair like a caress. The music ran down my back and came out of my fingertips. I was a cascade of red-blue rainfall, a rainbow, I was small, light, mobile. (1974, p. 256)

The artist's pursuit of altered states can be understood partially in terms of regressive phenomena covered in the last chapter—regressive in a creative and nonpathological sense, with the goal of resurrecting early body states and object relations, and inducing unconventional and unexpected modes of cognition. But now these earlier self-states and cognitive shifts arise within the frame of an induced alteration of consciousness that carries the intent to create. The regression is brought on and exists in symbiosis with the desire to fashion art. There is risk and danger in doing this, associated in particular with the dark side of addiction.

As explained earlier (Chapter 2), Ernst Kris saw the creative process as involving the phases of inspiration and elaboration. Inspiration engulfs the artist in a rapturous feeling that enables visionary insight and creates new constellations of meaning. In this state even ontic and epistemological barriers are sometimes transcended. These altered states of consciousness created by regression return the artist to visceral possibilities and ways of thinking present in early life. Yet, such states can exist once the world is known from a mature perspective, possibly only after one experiences the world as unpredictable and potentially disappointing. Furthermore, artists, like mystics, may be receptive to something not reducible to theory, a mystery neither inside nor outside that cannot be objectified. In some Eastern philosophical traditions, for instance, drug usage is seen as allowing a taste of the beyond, a kind of storming the temple of the All, necessitated by the desire for transcendence (Feuerstein, 2001). Tribal people used drugs to enter into a state of spiritual ecstasy. Soma (an intoxicating juice) was drunk by the Vedic seers to write the sacred poems of the Rg Veda (De Nicholas, 1998; Feuerstein, 2001).

Kris's elaboration phase shapes the givens of the first phase. In this second phase the raw product of the regression or altered state of mind is transformed into a recognizable and communicable form. It is at this point that the private gift of the muse is transformed into a public offering. One writer described it like this: "I write my first rough drafts while high on pot. The next day I read what I wrote and find mostly garbage, but also a few beautiful gems among the banana peels. I take those precious jewels, those resonant revelations, and then I connect them in a coherent way." Illustrating the two phases of creativity is a recurring motif on Grecian urns depicting Apollo, god of form and reason, holding the hand of Dionysius, god of intoxication, ecstasy, and intuition.

The sparse research that has been conducted on the effects chemicals (mostly alcohol) have on the creative process suggests that they may facilitate Kris's inspiration phase because they help to reduce blocks and censors, lessen inhibition, and induce relaxation after sustained effort (Koski-Jännes, 1985; Norlander, 1999). The saying in vino veritas reflects the longstanding belief that alcohol can be used to establish contact with deeper levels of the psyche (Ten Berge, 1999). On the other hand, alcohol appears more likely to hinder the second, elaboration phase of the creative process because it relaxes the artist's focus and concentration, as well as reflective and critical faculties, all essential for the problem solving and reality testing facets of creativity. It has been found, for instance, that alcohol contributes to a weakening of secondary process thinking (Gustafson & Källmén, 1989a, 1989b; Kalin, McClelland, & Kahn, 1965), damaging those skills responsible for the concrete, physical formation of an art product and its communication with the outside world. Hajcak's (1976) findings that alcohol enhances originality but lowers creative problem-solving abilities further support the uneven effects alcohol has on the creative process. Norlander (1999) sums up the studies on alcohol and phases of the creative process as follows: "A moderate intake of alcohol obstructs those phases of creativity that are mainly based on the secondary process (preparation, certain phases of illumination, verification), but facilitates those phases mainly based on the primary process (incubation, certain parts of illumination, restitution)" (p. 40).

Since these studies refer primarily to the influence of alcohol on creativity, it is possible that different drugs might have different effects. For instance, amphetamines or cocaine sustain attention, a function of the secondary process. Freud describes this effect during the period he used cocaine: "You perceive an increase of self-control and possess more vitality and capacity for work ... Long intensive mental or physical work is performed without any fatigue" (Jones, 1953, p. 82). Philip Dick, a wildly prolific science fiction author, confessed to producing most of his writing while under the influence of amphetamines. He wrote an incredible 68 pages a day, published 40 novels, over 120 short stories, and many essays (Anton & Fuchs, 1996, pp. 37–46). On the other hand, Storr (1976) claimed that marijuana inspired captivating melodies from his unconscious, which he was regrettably incapable of writing down.

Using drugs or alcohol can also help some artists deal with specific anxieties that are aroused by the creative process itself. As one artist-patient once told me, "Art is a put up or shut up proposition. You jump off a cliff in the dark and pray your parachute opens." The risk of failure is great, and the stakes are very high because the intensity of serious creation, within and outside of art, requires one to be totally engaged and fully committed. Failure can bring deep despair. Furthermore, accessing preconscious and unconscious material can be frightening and so deeply upsetting that it threatens ego integrity and the project itself. The same artist-patient also said, "I love to roam the cosmic junkyard looking for new stuff, but it gets really dark out there, and the place is guarded by a pack of vicious hounds." Anxieties generated from the creative process may become crippling, and some artists use substances to bring them down to a level that permits the continuation of creative work.

THE ROLE OF ARTISTIC SENSITIVITY

The creative person is a sensitive person. You see, I was so different from everyone, so much more intelligent and sensitive and perceptive. I was having fifty perceptions a minute to everyone else's five. I always felt that nobody was going to understand me, going to understand what I felt about things. I guess that is why I started writing. At least on paper I could put down what I thought.

—Truman Capote

The sensitivity of the artist is nearly a cliché. When she wrote about the childhood of artists, Phyllis Greenacre (1957/1971a) emphasized their enhanced sensitivity to and perceptivity of their surroundings. Though the exquisitely attuned temperament may power creativity, it can also foster unbearable vulnerability, self-consciousness, sorrow, and a sense of meaninglessness (Jamison, 1993). Poet, playwright, drug addict, and quintessential madman of the modern avant-garde, Antonin Artaud recounts the excruciating quality of such an existence in *Lettres a Genica Athasiou*: "State of nerves, states of mind, state of the world. There are moments when the universe seems to resemble most closely a scalp quivering with electric jolts" (Weiss, 2003, p. 161). Expanding on Artaud's poignant description, editor William McIlwain says that "a writer perhaps can't stand all the things he sees clearly and … must take the white glare out of the clarity" (Goodwin, 1988, p. 169). Some artists remove the "white glare" by seeking substances that dull the pain of extreme sensitivity. Canadian author Malcolm Lowry seems to agree with McIlwain when he professes that he lacked the usual filters. In fact, Lowry felt that he'd been born without a skin, alleging his drinking prevented a "nervous breakdown" (1996, p. 174). Like Lowry, Robert Lowell wrote of "seeing too much and feeling it with one skin layer missing" (1988, p. 307).

Capote, Artaud, Lowry, Lowell, and many other creative individuals are painfully sensitive and attend too minutely to their environments and suffer sensory overload as a result. Artists often use substances to emancipate them from sensorial tyranny, haunting memories, and current stressors. Furthermore, the insecurity inherent in living a creative life derives from a number of sources, not the least of which is the constant confrontation with one's own limitations in previously untested arenas, only to have those limits scrutinized and evaluated on a constant basis. Such insecurity in artists' lives combines with an already sensitive nature. Jazz musician Stan Kenton (1960) maintains that "It's hard for the average person who isn't in creative work to know what a terrible insecurity exists within someone who dared to be different, and you have to dare to be different if you're going to create anything fresh" (p. 38).

Andy, a novelist, betrayed his exquisite sensitivity during a session when he told me, "One of the earliest memories I have is crying because the yoke of my egg ran out, while there was still plenty of white left. I know it sounds silly, but it wasn't the yoke running out in itself that set me off. It was the first time I realized that *stuff runs out*. Things break and get lost. People get old and sick. Everything changes. All the forms of life are finite. That's why I cried, and even though at the time I didn't clearly entirely realize such formulations, I sensed at a deep level that life gives way to change, loss, and death."

Sensitivity, shyness, insecurity, and isolation are bound to coexist in the lives of many, if not most, creative individuals. Creativity is a solitary occupation; time spent alone is needed to generate and implement ideas. Such requisite isolation offers an escape from the stress of social situations, but it also produces loneliness and requires the creative person to labor for extended periods of time with little or no emotional support from others (see Chapter 5). Substances like alcohol are known to provide courage for those who lack it and companionship for those who seek it. Writers are loners and alcohol is a loner's disease, says Goodwin (1988, p. 180). Writing and drugs are two forms of companionship. "It's my life, it's my wife," sang Lou Reed of his heroin; William Burroughs referred to his "old friend

Opium Jones" (Burroughs & Odier, 1989, p. 151). To convey this relational component, Lisa Director (2002) claims that underlying most compulsive substance abuse is "a relational impasse that finds concrete expression in the act of drug use, that, in turn, sustains it" (p. 551). Indeed, Baudelaire (1859/1996) is known to have compared opium to a woman, an old and terrible friend, full of caresses and deceptions. In her poem "The Addict," Anne Sexton writes, "The pills are a mother, but better ... I like them more than I like me. It's a kind of marriage. It's a kind of war" (1981, p. 165).

Sensitivity involves a greater capacity for feeling, emotional reactions, and tolerance of extreme affective states. Ironically, it is the artists' inordinate sensitivity that provides the link between creativity and mood disorder. In 1921, Emil Kraeplin delineated the positive aspects of manic-depressive illness by mentioning its connection to creativity:

> The volitional excitement which accompanies the disease may under certain circumstances set free powers which otherwise are constrained by all kinds of inhibition. Artistic activity namely may, by the untroubled surrender to momentary fancies or moods, and especially poetical activity by the facilitation of linguistic expression, experience a certain furtherance. (p. 17)

The connection between mood disorder and creativity is one that has been underscored in several studies. For example, Richards, Kinney, Lunde, and Benet (1988) observed that a genetic predisposition to manic-depressive illness accompanied a parallel predisposition to creativity. They found significantly higher scores on creativity measures among manic-depressives and cyclothymics, as well as their first-degree relatives, than in controls. Jamison (1989) similarly found that 38% of the outstanding British writers and artists she studied had been treated for affective illness. In 1993, she cited an impressive list—which includes the likes of Lord Byron, Robert Schumann, Herman Melville, Ernest Hemingway, Virginia Woolf, Alfred Tennyson, Vincent van Gogh, F. Scott Fitzgerald, and Robert Lowell—to make a convincing argument for the "compelling association, not to say actual overlap, between two temperaments—the artistic and the manic-depressive—and their relationships to the rhythms and cycles, or temperament, of the natural world" (p. 5). She refers to the episodic or cyclic nature observable in both creativity and bipolar illness.

In addition to demonstrating how the temperaments of artists and manic-depressives are equally characterized by sensitivity and imagination, Jamison explains how both manic and depressive aspects of the illness are capable of stimulating creativity. Perhaps the manic episode more obviously resembles creative processes in its frenzied excitement, visionary grandiosity, and generation of ideas and connections. The fluency, fluidity, and frequency of thoughts and associations, the intensity of emotional experience and expression, and the sharp focus and power of concentration are present in both hypomanic and creative states. In fact, one criterion for diagnosing mania involves original thinking, heightened sensitivity, and increased productivity. Neurologist Robert DeLong (1990) found that children who display early signs of bipolar illness show significantly more imagination than most children. Of course, shorter art forms, like poetry or painting, are more easily created in a hypomanic state than others (e.g., longer writing projects) that require sustained effort over a number of months (Andreason & Glick, 1988). Fitzgerald once apologized to his editor for his excessive drinking while writing *Tender is the Night*, explaining that "a short story can be written on a bottle, but for a novel you need the mental speed that enables you to keep the whole pattern in your head" (1994, p. 277).

Depression, too, encourages creativity in its sensitivity and compassion for the human condition as well as in its inward gazing and rumination. In their book *Saturn and Melancholy* (1964), Klibansky, Saxl, and Panovsky demonstrate how poetic melancholy is essentially an enhanced self-awareness. By cooling the ardor of mania, depression allows the slower pace necessary for the shaping and production of art, Kris's elaboration phase.

Not surprisingly, substance abuse plays a role in the intimate link between mood disorder and creativity. Andreason (1987) conducted a 15-year study of creative writers from the Iowa Writer's Workshop and compared them to a control group of nonwriters matched for age, sex, education, and intelligence. The group of writers were more often depressed (37%), more often manic (43%), and more often alcoholic (30%) compared with 7% in the comparison group of nonwriters. Overall, she found that 80% of the writer study sample met criteria for major affective disorder. Ludwig (1994) noted that Andreason's sample consisted primarily of male subjects and therefore tried to determine whether similar trends exist in a sample of women writers. He matched 59 women writers with a comparable sample of 59 nonwriters and found that 56% were depressed (vs. 14% controls), 19% manic (vs. 3% controls), and 17% drug addicts (vs. 5% controls).

A most useful way to comprehend the significant relationships that exist among alcoholism, drugs, mood disorder, and creative writing is to consider how writers (and other artists) may use and abuse alcohol (as well as additional substances) to regulate their feelings and sensibilities. Whereas Andreason's study observed that writers are at the very minimum 30% more inclined to have mood disorders and to be alcoholics than her nonwriter sample, it has also been found that at least 30% of addicts suffer from serious affective disorders (Krystal, 1995). Schildkraut et al. (1994), in their study of New York Abstract Expressionist artists, found that over 50% of the artists they studied had some form of psychopathology, predominantly mood disorders and preoccupation with death, often compounded by alcohol or drug abuse. Once again, 30% had substance-abuse histories.

Obviously, the studies mentioned above indicate a strong relationship between mood disorder and substance abuse but fail to clarify which comes first or how one contributes to the other. Krystal (1982, 1995) argues most convincingly that addicts employ substances to recognize and tolerate their emotional states. Here the condition is seen to precede the substance abuse. Khantzian (1995), too, proposes that addicts self-medicate and find a "drug of choice," or a combination of substances, to regulate difficult affect states. Therefore, what we observe is the transformative effect of drugs in their capacity to design a comfort zone for the artist who uses them. It is not merely about creating art; it is often about creating some ease in order to live. However, the very act of self-medication can eventually unleash the destructive and disruptive effects of addiction. Burroughs wrote that hashish "makes a bad situation worse. Depression becomes despair, anxiety panic" (2009, p. 224). Here we see that the relationship with a substance can be a sadomasochistic one.

The sensitivity attributed to the artistic temperament is regrettably the same sensitivity that may open doors to depression and to an intimacy with life's darker forces. Melancholia, or depression, involves a painful sensitivity, an unwavering vision that considers reality, morbidity, and death with less denial and sanitization than a "normal" frame of mind. Hanna Segal (1991) linked depression, with its accent on mourning, to the capacity for symbolization. Interestingly, the word *symbol* derives from the Greek *symbolen*, which means to reunite. Symbolization, then, can be thought of as the ability to ponder and realize what is absent. Through symbolization, we repair and reunite with whom and what has been lost to us. The depressive perspective, by definition, is one that embraces a particular and darker view of the human condition and does not shy away from experiencing guilt, loss, and the inevitability and finality of death. Such terror-driven experiences can act as a bittersweet muse to the creative process, yet they can also be felt as unbearable and lead to addiction. Baudelaire wrote: "One must always be intoxicated. That's the main thing; it's the only issue. In order to feel the horrible burden of Time which breaks your shoulders and bows you to earth, you must become intoxicated without respite" (1974, p. 5). Ultimately, one can say that it is the burden of mortality that is most deeply felt by one possessing the sensitivity of an artist.

FAME: THE DOUBLE-BIND

As a young child I wanted to be a writer because writers were rich and famous. They lounged around Singapore and Rangoon smoking opium in a yellow pongee silk suit. They sniffed cocaine in Mayfair and they penetrated forbidden swamps with a faithful native boy and lived in the native quarter of Tangier smoking hashish and languidly caressing a pet gazelle.

—William S. Burroughs

Ernest Hemingway, an alcoholic himself, believed that a large percentage of American writers became alcoholic due to ambivalent feelings toward their craft. On the one hand, they wish to be great writers who, on the basis of their work, stand proudly alone and apart from the hoi polloi and, on the other, they want to be rich and famous, admired and envied by others. Alfred Kazin, in support of Hemingway's theory, remarked on the strain on American writers that became noticeable in the 1920s, a time when big money and success became a real possibility for writers (Goodwin, 1988). Coincidentally, drinking writers emerged at the same time.

Desire for immortality and the hunger for fame is a two-sided coin. Freud (1908/1959b) was the first to connect creativity with fame when he wrote that writers find indirect routes, via their art, to gratify desires for fame, riches, honor, love, and power. Artistic production has long been considered a response to finitude because it serves as a special kind of immortality formula: The work of art outlives the artist/creator as if in defiance of physical mortality. Even though artists may feel like a vehicle for what they create as they form it, they also feel a sense of agency once it is done. And, in fact, others perceive artists as the creators of works rather than their instruments. Artists sign their work, an act that ties its creation to their identity.

The essential thrill of fame, then, is found primarily in the response of the audience, bestowing adulation and granting an elevated and even godlike status to the artist. The ambivalence about such bootlicking may be rooted in the fact that the feet of the artist-god, like all feet, are made of clay. Alas, as with all immortality formulas, art, too, is destined to fail. Both fool and genius must suffer the same fate. And so says an artist friend of mine: "Pass the bottle, please."

Many creative persons turn to substances only after they achieve fame, which suggests that limelight stress may trigger addiction. Since many creative individuals are loners, accustomed to honing their craft in isolation and, at times, against opposition, the sudden and unexpected attention and burden of fame is frequently experienced as overwhelming. When speaking of the pressures he and the three other Beatles endured at the height of their popularity, John Lennon complained of the expectation that they maintain a godlike demeanor and uphold the highest moral standards. Lennon may have been referring to superego dissociation. He wished to have a public persona and exploit fame, yet at the same time, he wanted to be able to act out his all-too-human foibles and fulfill his quotidian needs. Rolling Stones' Keith Richards, long addicted to heroin, explains, "I could face people easier on the stuff, but I could do that with booze too … I also felt I was doing it not to be a 'pop star.' There was something I really didn't like about that end of what I was doing … That was very difficult to handle, and I could handle it better on smack" (Kakutani, 2010, p. C6). Celebrity artists often endure constant scrutiny and have unreasonable demands and responsibilities placed on them. At the same time, drugs are easily available to them. All of these factors facilitate artists' surrender to the lure of chemical substances.

Drugs not only blunt the pressures of fame; they create a protective bubble, a safe buffer zone between the self and an impinging external and internal world. Rauch (2000) writes of the "protective layer around the individual's psyche" that drugs provide to shield the artist from environmental invasion. She even identifies the rush experienced by intravenous drug users as a clear marker that serves to delineate mental states and establishes a clear boundary between external and internal worlds. This "safe" zone, a physical and emotional drug-induced "holding environment," aims to set up the conditions under which the artist can continue to live a creative life while remaining unspoiled by fame.

Bobby, a man with a 30-year marijuana addiction, described the "room of one's own" created by the drug he craved: "Marijuana gives me a writer's room, a place for creativity that excludes much of the noise, demands, and impositions of the world. It allows a clear space that induces apartness and serenity." He added that the effect marijuana has on short-term memory actually helps him construct such a creative space: "The same thing that causes short-term memory loss also acts to effect a barrier between me and the world … to have interiority. I can worry about what's inside my head without worrying about the phone bill being due or the cockroach problem." Bobby claims to have been high on marijuana 90% of the time while writing his three novels. It is important to add that, for reasons connected to his prolonged drug use, this patient never published these works even though he has published his shorter writing.

THE COST OF ADDICTION

> There is a story about Dorothy Parker, who went with a friend to the funeral of a famous writer who had died suddenly. The friend sighed while gazing into the coffin, saying, "Doesn't he look just wonderful?" To which Parker replied, "Why shouldn't he? He hasn't had a drink in three days." (Goodwin, 1988, p. 6)

As we have seen, the benefits of drug-induced disinhibition are too often undercut by deficits in cognition and motivation. Aldous Huxley in *The Doors of Perception* wrote that "Though the intellect remains improved, the will suffers a profound change for the worse" (1956, p. 25). Clearly, unless both parts of the creative process—inspiration and elaboration—exist, creativity cannot be achieved. In a study of artists who create under the influence of mescaline, Hartmann (1974, p. 222) observed that much of art had an autosymbolic character. He adds that artists who continuously used drugs lost their capacity for judgment and reflectivity, resulting in their erroneous estimation of "artistic banalities as artistic breakthroughs," thus rendering their creations meaningless outside of the drug-induced state. "Opium enables, to give form to the unformed," wrote Jean Cocteau, "[but] it prevents, alas, the communication of this privilege to anyone else" (cited in 1957, p. 89). Although for some it seems that chemicals do promote some aspects of creativity (inspiration), they also endanger other aspects (elaboration), especially when addiction sets in.

In addiction, the drug becomes the point, and it frequently eclipses the artist and the work. Though drugs can set free one's creative reserves and sublime sensitivities, drugs can also toss users into a foul pit of desperation, leaving them feeling trapped and unsupported. Then Baudelaire's "artificial paradise" transforms into Artaud's "theater of cruelty," a cavity filled with pain and delirium. Baudelaire himself, who once lauded the saving grace of intoxication, eventually confessed "what hashish gives with one hand it takes away with the other" (1975, p. 122).

Thus, the artist who relies on intoxication to boost creativity faces a formidable double-bind. Prolonged usage eventually transforms the enhancement of reality into the avoidance of reality, which drains away both inspiration and motivation. Andy, the patient who as a child mourned the loss of egg yolk, came to my door as a chronic marijuana and alcohol user. "I use pot to lift me off and booze to help me land. The former loosens my heart while the latter numbs it," he said. Having published a minor but interesting first novel that showed great promise, he'd bogged down in writing the second, acknowledging that what once helped him to write now prevented him from doing so: "Because I spend so much time being fucked up, the drive to create has become diminished. I used to get excited when I smoked because a thousand lights would flash in my head at once, and the muses jammed the telephone lines trying to get in touch. Now my excitement involves getting high and hoping that happens again."

Indeed, with prolonged substance use, alert consciousness diminishes, and reality becomes increasingly frightening and undifferentiated. Timothy Leary's famous injunction from the 1960s to "Turn on, tune in, and drop out" describes the progressively antisocial process that dominates the long-term user. Even Dr. Jekyll in Stevenson's story can finally no longer keep his polar opposites apart and, one night, the transformation from Jekyll to Hyde takes place without the drug. The monstrous Hyde eventually replaces the good doctor. To clarify this type of development, Freud (1920/1955) moved "beyond the pleasure principle" to link the compulsive repetition of painful behavioral patterns to a death instinct attachment. Initially one who described the benefits of cocaine, Freud ultimately provided the first clues to understanding addictive behavior.

WHEN THE MUSIC STOPS

The case of David, a history teacher, illustrates how addiction can swallow creativity. From an early age, David was extremely sensitive and overwhelmed by everyday life. Remaining profoundly shy and insecure throughout high school and college, he experienced difficulties with women but wrote prolifically in his spare time. "It was my way of talking to myself because I felt no one really understood me. Seeing what I wrote made me feel worthy." He drank and got high, but women still eluded him. "I was like a blind man trying to touch smoke," he told me. David continued to experiment with various substances in a determined effort to chemically alter himself. "I felt I just couldn't do it on my own," he said.

Alas, when David stumbled upon the wondrous elixir Xanax, he likened it to meeting "a soul mate" after years of fruitless searching. Perhaps for the first time in many years Xanax made him feel "normal" by disconnecting him from neurotic thinking and freeing him to interact socially without debilitating anxiety. He felt powerful when on Xanax, able to face any situation—intelligent, well-spoken, secure in leading the classroom or coming on to a pretty girl at a club. Even his creative writing seemed to take off, and he furiously filled notebooks with fiction during his off periods and lunch breaks.

He penned a science-fiction novel in which every problem and feeling was controlled and regulated by medications. During this time, he consumed huge quantities of coffee to balance the sedative effect of Xanax. At night he guzzled beer so that he could sleep. Mornings found him totally exhausted and needing to start the cycle all over again. Similar to his protagonist, David lived a life dictated by his doctor's prescription pad.

The more Xanax helped David to construct an omnipotent inner self-state, the tighter the grip of its addiction became, and the more terrified David grew when he thought of being without the drug. Soon he began gobbling opiates to synergistically enhance the Xanax buzz. The small oases of euphoria became separated by ever growing stretches of deserts of misery and desperation. His life began to nose dive—school, writing, relationships, everything. One day David came to a session high.

[*David sat opposite me, silent, looking inward, eyes glazed.*]

DK: You look stoned today.
DAVID: Yeah. I ate a couple of footballs before I came. There you go.
DK: Xanax?
DAVID: My favorite.

DK: Do you think you wanted me to see you like this?

DAVID: Maybe. I don't know.

DK: Well, since you're stoned, and here, try to bring me into your experience.

DAVID: Nothing bothers me.

DK: Tell me more.

DAVID: I'm beyond needs, frustrations, desires. Nothing bothers me.

DK: I can see why that might be appealing to you.

DAVID: Hard to feel better than this.

DK: Continue.

DAVID: I don't care. I don't care that my mother never had time for me. I don't care that my father always criticized me. I don't care that my last girlfriend dumped me. I don't care if my students pass their tests. I've got that view from thirty thousand feet.

DK: Way up high. So nothing can hurt you now.

DAVID: Bingo.

DK: I'm wondering if you thought I might hurt you today?

DAVID: You? What do you mean?

DK: Well, last session, you told me about your first boss who made inappropriate passes at you and humiliated you. I think it was difficult for you to share that. How did you feel after you left here?

DAVID: I felt pissed off ... ashamed.

DK: So perhaps you didn't want to continue with that today.

DAVID: I guess not. Sometimes I get so tired of this talking shit. I'd just like it all to stop.

DK: What exactly would you like to stop?

DAVID: [*He looks at me wearily.*] I'm not sure. I guess what stops when I'm high. But that just doesn't stop the pain, it adds something too.

DK: What?

DAVID: Freedom. I can think more freely, make connections, get ideas. When I write, I can see my characters more vividly. A whole world comes alive inside my head. Time disappears. The weight of the day disappears. I feel free. Everything gets easier. [*He hesitates as if to say something, then falls silent.*]

DK: And yet?

DAVID: Well ... there's the addiction. The need for more. The drug. It's buying time on credit.

DK: What do you mean?

DAVID: I mean sooner or later it'll catch up with me. Sooner or later I'll pay back double what the drugs gave me. Every user knows that. I know that. But it's like, it won't be today. The drugs won't take me out today.

DK: So the drugs put you in stronger relationship to your ideas and your work. They allow you to relate more freely to women. But then they gradually put themselves in the place of these relationships?

DAVID: Yeah, the addiction. The growing hunger for the high. That's the problem.

DK: But it's not a problem today.

DAVID: No, it's not a problem today. Not yet. It's kind of like dying. I'm going to die eventually, but probably not today.

DK: No, today you're letting me in on the way you deal with your pain and limitations.

DAVID: Yeah, I guess so. I'm letting you in on my dirty little secret.

The dialogue neatly illustrates the difficulty in treating drug addiction. Why would anyone wish to stop doing something that alleviates pain while offering desired imaginative possibilities, the physical dependence notwithstanding? Usually the pain of the addiction has to reach a point where it overpowers the perceived benefit of the drug. The person must deeply desire and decide to stop taking the substance before he can actually do so. In this way drug use resembles perversion; that is, it provides a particular pleasure that is difficult to relinquish, and so it follows a predictable and scripted pattern.

In this session, David initially didn't want to dance with me because he wanted to be numb. But I tried to show him that even his wish to stay still and not have anything move him was his way of participating in the dance. His romance with benzodiazepines and opiates soon brought him to his knees. He involved himself with all sorts of sketchy individuals he knew very little about and put himself into risky situations several times a week. Only after being arrested for drug possession did he finally decide to end his relationship with drugs. Although it took him a couple of years to realize the truth, in hindsight, being arrested was the best thing that happened to him.

With regard to his addiction, David now says that he was "using drugs like a Band-Aid on the wounded part of my mind." He realized he had lived his youth in his head and now had to catch up with his age. At one point in the treatment, David discovered that I had a teenage-son. He asked many questions about the possibility of my son using drugs and what I would do if he did. I asked his advice on how he thought I might best handle such a dreaded scenario. Initially, he was very surprised by my request, but then he gladly offered his opinion. David told me to take careful note of my son's friends and their behavior, and to keep my eyes open for signs of drug use, withdrawal, anxiety, and depression. Although David was taken aback by my question, he seemed to appreciate being able to lead the dance between us.

As David's case shows, addicted artists face a "double descent" (Leonard, 1989)—the one of their addiction and the other of their creativity. Some creative artists, like Louis Armstrong and Ray Charles, descend with the help of drugs or alcohol and continue to create. Others, like Eugene O'Neill and John Cheever, find they must renounce their addiction in order to create because the addiction is destroying them as artists and people. Raymond Carver said that writing "under the influence" made his work inferior, adding that he considered giving up drinking to be one of his greatest achievements (Goodwin, 1988). Still others continue their addictions until it destroys their creativity and/or their lives. Truman Capote, Charlie Parker, Jack London, Rainer Werner Fassbinder, and Jackson Pollock are only a few who died young due to their addictions.

We all mourn the creative lives that are tragically cut short by addiction. We also rage at the decline or destruction of the artistic output of abusers. Due to his alcoholism, Truman Capote never finished *Answered Prayers* (1987), the novel he worked on for years. In *The Cup of Fury*, Upton Sinclair (1956) commented that through a miracle of physical stamina, Sinclair Lewis survived to the age of 66. More tragic than a life cut short, he believed, was Lewis's loss of productivity. What songs by Charlie Parker, Jimi Hendrix, and Elvis Presley, to name only a few, have we lost because they died so young of drug addiction? What paintings could we now view if it weren't for the alcoholism of Jackson Pollock or the narcotics addiction of Jean-Michel Basquiat?

Swiss art historian Michel Thevoz (1991) has lamented the fact that drugs yield more dollars than works of art. He encourages artists to discover and summon their own personal muses to create without risking the dangers that accompany actual drug usage. Although Thevoz means well, it is far easier to condemn artists who become addicts than to understand them. Here I want to illuminate the structure of the bond between creativity and substance (ab)use. As a result, I hope that the encounter with a creative addict who strives to break free of mediocrity and limitations will evoke empathy rather than quick, easy answers delivered in black-and-white terms.

Addiction is problematic, but so too is a human consciousness that loses its capacity to imagine and embrace new possibilities. In the end, both states can be said to have one important feature in common: they severely limit the expression of one's psychological idiom. They both result in a kind of dogma of self-destruction. Addiction narrows the world to the closed system of taking the drug over and over again. At first the drug appears to be the vehicle that liberates the user from the confines of social and personal limitation, yet "the senses grow skilled in their craving" and, eventually, one needs more and more to get less and less. On the other hand, a consciousness that cannot break out of its narrow confines, one that cannot question or find newness and joy, is equally immersed in lifeless repetition. Such a consciousness needs more and more (e.g., material possessions, status, normotic ritual) to "get high" and so narrows the world to a closed system of herd life and beliefs and values lived *in vacuo*, devoid of vision, inspiration, or delight. Again, "the senses grow skilled in their craving."

Studying the association between creativity and addiction highlights both the precious and the precarious states of being that artists inhabit and strive to sustain. The manifold reasons many artists turn to substances reveal the constant internal and external challenges encountered in creative lives. Some of these challenges concern receptiveness to regressive pulls and unconscious forces. Others result from artists' needs to fine-tune their exquisitely sensitive temperaments and affect states. Still others involve their attempts to come to terms with recognition and fame. Clearly, destruction of conventional reality is necessary for creativity, and substances are employed in the service of that destruction. Yet, the paradox of infatuation with drugs is that the tables eventually turn and the master becomes a slave, one left to succumb to the creativity-destroying and life-limiting processes of addiction.

Chapter 4

Creative Transformations of Trauma

Private Pain in the Public Domain and the Clinical Setting[1]

What is to give light must endure burning.

—Victor Frankl

One of the central ironies of the human condition is the consciousness of our mortality. On the one hand each of us knows we will die, and on the other hand we deny few things more vehemently than our death. Ernest Becker (1973) understood this denial as the basis of character construction and the very reason the human character is deeply flawed and conflicted. He saw the denial of death as the central driving force of human brutality as well as human magnificence. If we allow the irrefutable truth of death to enter too starkly into awareness, we can become paralyzed with terror. Life itself seems to require that we become forgetful of death, that in order to live effectively, we do not feel its presence too intensely. Freud (1915/1957c) alluded to this problem when he said, "Would it not be better to give death the place in reality and in our thoughts which is its due, and to give a little more prominence to the unconscious attitude towards death which we have hitherto so carefully suppressed?" (p. 299). That he framed his insight as a question is very telling. He himself was not certain of how much admission is too much. He also advised that just "a little more prominence" be given to the unconscious attitude toward death—not a lot, just a "little."

I have always believed that many artists walk with trauma and death, and even draw creative energy from that partnership. I agree with Robert J. Lifton (1987), who claims that artists who do not shy away from the subject of death or near-death offer us ways in which to recognize death, to touch it, to enter into it, and to expand the limits of our imagination and transcend our fear and clinging. In responding to the reality of death, which includes not only the fact of it, but the manner in which it occurs, the artist utilizes the limits of finitude in order to transcend them—more so, perhaps, if the artist has endured intense personal trauma, which is a kind

---

[1] An earlier version of this chapter appeared in Knafo, D. (2004). *Living with Terror, Working with Trauma: A Clinician's Handbook* (pp. 565–587). Lanham, MD: Jason Aronson.

of death before death. Mass death, senseless and violent death, state-sponsored death—these horrors that instill trauma in humanity and migrate across generations—can art address such atrocities? According to Becker, whether it is reckoning with individual or mass trauma, art is an immortality formula, and like all the other immortality formulas, art ultimately must fail in the face of finitude and annihilation. Yet art can put the artist (and audience) in a direct and authentic relationship with loss and death, and the horrors that attend them, and, therefore, also with life.

Nevertheless, a debate exists about whether mass atrocity and genocide can and should be artistically represented (van Alphen, 1997). Steiner (1967) argues that language has been demolished by the Holocaust and that "the world of Auschwitz lies outside speech as it lies outside reason" (p. 123). Adorno (1962/1992) proposes in his now-famous dictum that "after Auschwitz it is barbaric to continue writing poetry," a statement that created a tone of tremendous distrust of literary or artistic representation of the Holocaust. He and others concluded that although it is necessary to record and remember—that is, to be historians of the Holocaust—one must not exploit the pain of the victims by creating art that might allow others to derive aesthetic pleasure from it.[1] The controversy surrounding a 2002 exhibition at the Jewish Museum, *Mirroring Evil*, on Nazi aesthetics, confirms this point.

Despite the clamoring against an aesthetic response to genocidal trauma, equal claims exist that one *must* respond in order to master such trauma. Elie Wiesel, when writing about the Holocaust, describes the seemingly unresolvable paradox: "How is one to speak of it? How is one *not* to speak of it?" (as cited in Bohm-Duchen, 1995, p. 103). After author and Holocaust survivor Primo Levi complained of no longer being able to write, he continued to author seven books replete with powerful, desperate explorations of the essence of a human being in a world that stripped Jews of their humanity. Polish poet Czeslaw Milosz (1983) declared that, after horror, "people's attitude toward language ... changes. It recovers the simplest function and is again an instrument serving a purpose; no one doubts that the language must name reality, which exists objectively, massive, tangible, and terrifying in its concreteness" (p. 80). Indeed, art born of trauma is quite concrete and literal, as is the play of children who have been traumatized. When naming such realities one needs to color them with sorrow; one needs to acknowledge their terrible losses with mourning. How could such grotesque evil

---

[1] It is easy to understand and support Adorno's position when reading some artists' responses to the World Trade Center disaster. British artist Damien Hirst called the September 11 attacks "visually stunning" and even added that the perpetrators "need congratulating." New Zealand artist Gail Haffern said the attacks were "wonderful ... because it was a new idea." Experimental German composer Karlheinz Stockhausen called the destruction "the greatest work of art ever" (Freund, 2002).

and the devastation left in its wake be met with a mere historical or factual account? How could such text not be saturated with tears?

This chapter considers the ways in which some artists convert their private trauma into public works of art. It aims to show how these works provide meaning, connection, and continuity in times of social turmoil and rupture. The oeuvres of Charlotte Salomon, a German-born artist murdered in Auschwitz, and Michal Heiman, a contemporary Israeli artist, exemplify creative solutions to personal and political tragedy. A case illustration of Kasia, an artist and second-generation concentration camp survivor, is additionally presented to demonstrate the creative mastery of trauma in the analytic space.

Picasso once said, "Art is not Truth. Art is a lie to make us realize truth" (as cited in Chipp, 1968, p. 264). One can say something similar about psychoanalysis. Psychoanalysis is not life in the main, but through the illusions created by the transference and countertransference one learns to better appreciate life. Art and psychoanalysis help us to better realize truth and appreciate life, especially when both are instigated by trauma. I will attempt to show how both activities function in the service of making meaning and surviving in battle against despair, death anxiety, survivor guilt, and the psychic numbing associated with them.

CHARLOTTE SALOMON: *LIFE? OR THEATER?*

Charlotte Salomon (1917–1943) experienced childhood trauma (a family history of multiple suicides) that assumed a new form in the context of social tragedy (Nazi persecution). (See Plate 6.) Shortly before she was murdered in Auschwitz in 1943, 26 years old and 5 months pregnant, Salomon completed a barely veiled autobiographical picture-novel and musical theatre piece titled *Leben? oder Theater?* (*Life? or Theater?*)—a brave, life-affirming project that transcends the morbidity of its inspiration and content. Salomon crafted this amazing work of art because, in her words, "I have a feeling the whole world has to be put back together again" (Salomon, in Herzberg, 1981, 774).[1] Rather than follow in the footsteps of the women in her family—her mother, grandmother, and aunt—all of whom had committed suicide, Salomon chose instead to transform her private trauma into a work of art, a work that has become a noble testament to the power of spiritual preservation.

---

[1] The numbers in parentheses refer to numbered images or texts from Salomon's *Life? or Theater?* in Judith Herzberg's (1981) *Charlotte: Life or Theater: An Autobiographical Play by Charlotte Salomon.*

In *Life? or Theater?* (Salomon, 1981), more than 20 characters speak in soliloquies and dialogues in thousands of scenes from Salomon's external and internal life. Images are alternately presented as close-ups, long shots, flashbacks, and montages, winding from one person to another and from one angle to another in a serpentine composition. Sometimes the artist employs multiple angles to suggest the passage of time, placing the most recent events in the foreground and earlier incidents in receding planes. At other times she applies an aerial perspective; in one painting she dispenses with ceilings in order to peer into the rooms of a house (Herzberg, 19). In some, she sets the images floating about the page in no discernible order. And, finally, she sometimes breaks up scenes in a comic-book style. It is often difficult to know where one scene ends and the next begins.

Sometimes her use of multiple selves in one frame is dizzying. Many pages depict one or two characters, yet it is not uncommon for a page to be inhabited by dozens of characters, or for the same scene to be portrayed repeatedly in a whirlwind of text, color, and image that must have mirrored her confused and terrified state of mind. The work conveys her desperation to communicate, to render her vision before it is too late. It is as if she rushed to finish her work, pouring it on the page as image, text, and music while fleeing death. Finally, Salomon's oeuvre possesses a Joycean quality, as the repetition of scenes and sensibilities suggest the movement of consciousness and the way momentary events are seared into memory.

Similar to free association in psychoanalysis, the depiction of a stream of consciousness as opposed to a linear flow of events reflects Salomon's subjective reality. This stream shows how she needs to recollect and feel certain intense moments, especially the beautiful ones, as a way of building a potent inner life that could combat her family, its history, and the impending sense of doom that was the ambience of her time, an era of evil reaching mythic proportions. Pictures are not enough. There has to be description. There has to be music. She needs to turn her art into a theatre of what was most inwardly real. She is trying to capture her life, trying to make it mean something, and so she comes at us with everything she has.

"*C'est toute ma vie!*" ("It's my entire life!") Salomon exclaimed to Georges Moridis, a doctor and friend in the Resistance to whom she entrusted her *oeuvre* before being ushered to her death (Felstiner, 1994, p. 236).[1] This work, frantically produced between 1940 and 1942, while Salomon suffered exile from Germany, *was* her life and her art. In addition to being a poignant coming-of-age story set among increasing Nazi oppression, it was the way she found to stay alive, to manage ongoing trauma, to choose life over death, and to make an artistic bid for immortality.

---

[1] Biographical information on Salomon's life is taken from Felstiner's (1994) biography of the artist, unless otherwise indicated.

If we appreciate the deeper value of her statement to Moridis, then the bookends of this masterpiece are highly significant. Salomon chooses to open her musical theater with the suicide of her Aunt Charlotte, after whom she was named. Charlotte Grunwald (renamed Charlotte Knarre in the play) drowned herself at the age of 18 in Lake Schlachter outside Berlin in 1913. Salomon paints her aunt in an oval cocoon that resembles a womb, thus bridging (her aunt's) death and (her) birth. In the same image Salomon also joins together death and art. Born into a legacy of willful death, she would struggle throughout her life against her blood tie to self-extinction. Thus, despite the fact that her aunt's suicide took place four years before Salomon's birth, the artist considers this event an apt one to begin the story of *her* life.

The work concludes in France's Côte d'Azur, where she was sent to live in (temporary) safety with her maternal grandparents who had been there since 1934. While Salomon was in France, her grandmother, no longer able to bear life, made an unsuccessful suicide attempt by trying to hang herself. As if to speak both to her grandmother and herself, Salomon desperately draws attention to the sun, flowers, and mountains. She also sings Schiller's *Ode to Joy* from Beethoven's Ninth Symphony (Herzberg, 702-4) as she attempts to rescue her grandmother through music. Finally, she implores her grandmother to make a choice: to write or die. The grandmother jumps to her death from an opened window.

Not long afterward Salomon inevitably confronted the same choice: to take her life or to undertake something "wildly eccentric." She chose the latter; she chose the path of creativity. "I will create a story so as not to lose my mind" (Felstiner, 1994, p. 112), she proclaims in the stark and true assertion that creating art preserved her sanity. Ironically, this was her final communication to her father and stepmother before the Nazi invasion of Holland, where they had relocated. Between the bookends of death, Salomon created a space for mourning—mourning the many losses she had experienced, as well as the future she would never have, and offering up something beautiful, a gift launched into the void. Ultimately, Salomon's *Gesamtkunstwerk* [total work of art] can be considered a type of memorial, an artistic Kaddish, the Jewish prayer for the dead.

Salomon knew the essence of trauma—shock, helplessness, loss, disconnection, exclusion, and exile, a bleak future filled with ominous threat. She strove to make sense of the trail of family suicides under conditions in which she found herself increasingly isolated and endangered as a Jew. Unsurprisingly, then, her work came to reflect the familiar discontinuity, disruption, and fragmentation associated with traumatic experiencing. Although the entire oeuvre (1,325 gouaches, each measuring roughly 13″ × 10″; 784 were numbered into a final version by the author) was completed using only the three primary colors, indicating a strong life force, the content of the pictures reveals acute internal and external danger (Salomon, 1981). Both intimate and claustrophobic, it is a work of urgency that suggests impending doom.

The clustering of images also reflects the combination of memory and fantasy from which she drew the content of her stories. Some occurrences are fictional representations. For instance, her mother's death, which took place when she was a child of 8, was not an event Salomon actually witnessed or even knew about until she became an adult. She was originally told the lie that her mother had died of influenza. In fact, she was told of the history of family suicides only toward the end of her own young life, soon after her grandmother tried to hang herself in Nice. Her grandfather, apparently upset by Salomon's rejection of his sexual advances, the encroaching war, and his wife's suicide attempt, cruelly and callously confronted the artist with the family tragedy (four women and two men had committed suicide), even prodding her to take her own life.

It is not difficult to understand why her grandmother's attempt and eventual suicide and her grandfather's malignant communication served as catalysts for Salomon's creative endeavor. She wrote of her survivor guilt in an unsent letter:

> My life commenced when my grandmother wanted to take her life, when I found out that my mother had taken hers, as had her entire family—when I found out that I was the only survivor and when deep within me I felt the same inclination, the urge towards despair and towards dying. (Herzberg, 1981, p. vii)

Salomon depicts the suicides of her mother and grandmother similarly, one witnessed and one imagined, condensing the important women in her life and thus uniting adult pain with childhood longing. The bodies of both women lie on the ground in a pool of blood, a single, naked, raised leg the only sign remaining in defiance of the downward thrust (Herzberg, 32, 748; see Plate 7).

The impetus to create her life's work began at the moment Salomon realized that her life up until that point had been built on a lie. *Life? or Theater?* represents her attempt to re-imagine her life in order to make it bearable and to right the wrong of it being based on misinformation. Salomon realized that she had been mired in deception meant to protect the familial relationships that had become toxic. Hidden alliances and splits regulated the closeness and distance in family relationships she could no longer trust. Her entire internal reality had been eviscerated, for nothing was as it seemed. Even many of her memories no longer meant what they once did. From such terrible pain she began her creation.

Salomon's strong need to imagine how the event of her mother's suicide took place made her depict the episode from many perspectives. In one frame, we look directly into the mother's face, which is attached to profiles

of her husband and daughter. Immediately afterward, we see mother gazing dreamily out of the window. As the coloring becomes darker and
more ominous, we observe her from behind. Finally, all that remains is
a stark, empty window frame. The next frame is a close-up of her dead
face (Herzberg, 137–141). Before the death, we witness a child who is very
attached to her mother and who empathically yet naively observes her
mother become increasingly depressed and disinterested in life. Intimate
conversations take place in a shared bed where mother tells daughter how
beautiful it is in heaven and that she would like to go there and become an
angel (see Plate 8). She promises to write from heaven and, after her death,
Charlotte repeatedly checks the mail for letters that never arrive.

Although Salomon's work is primarily visual, it is accompanied by text
and is sometimes called a *singespiel* (operetta); scenes are paired with sug-
gestions for musical accompaniment culled from opera as well as popular sources. Both Paula Lindberg (her stepmother, renamed Paulinka in
her play) and Alfred Wolfsohn (her stepmother's voice therapist, renamed
Amadeus Daberlohn) possessed strong ties to music. Salomon observes that
from the time Paulinka is introduced into Charlotte's life, her "feelings are
expressed in songs" (Herzberg, 58). Daberlohn, too, believes that "singing
is more closely bound up with life than anything else" (Herzberg, 251).
Thus, music connected Salomon to the important people in her life at a
time when she was forced to be apart from them. In fact, Salomon hummed
as she drew (Salomon, 2006), thereby fashioning a type of "holding environment," a safe space in which to create.

In the first part of her work, Salomon adds text onto tracing paper, which
is superimposed onto the painted pages. It is possible that these overlays
provide the author with the necessary distance from the tragic events she
portrays. The overlays also can be understood as representing what Freud
(1900/1953b) called "secondary revision," the ego's organizing, interpreting, and narrating function for the dream's somewhat puzzling visual imagery. Thus, she recounts her entire life from the viewpoint of revising her
memory. The alter ego lives the life she would have lived if she, Salomon,
had known the truth. Salomon's seemingly disconnected fragments are
allotted meaning and coherence in the textual narration and commentary
provided in the overlays.

Salomon dispenses with the tracing paper and prints the text directly on
the painted pages upon the arrival of the play's pivotal character, Amadeus
Daberlohn, who soon becomes Charlotte's mentor and lover. Obviously
he comes to represent the breaking down of barriers and the removal of
defenses.[1] Furthermore, since he was probably her first sexual partner,

---

[1] Wolfsohn (Daberlohn) noticed Salomon's strong defenses and her withdrawn nature.
He stated, "Certain reasons induced me to undertake an attack on those fortifications"
(Herzberg, 1981, p. xi).

the overlay could be likened to the female hymen, a virginal interposition between picture and text, penetrated by his presence. It is he who awakened her sexuality, and he who helped her break through her limitations to become more innovative in her artistic project and in her life. Thus, Daberlohn represents the connection between image and speech, a connection that ultimately became Charlotte's song.[1]

Daberlohn was a voice coach, called in to help Salomon's stepmother, singer Paulinka Bimbam. Charlotte idolizes Paulinka and receives much love, warmth, and attention from this positive figure, who replaces her own mother and who, coincidentally, had been an orphan herself. Adolescent idealization swings back and forth between her stepmother and her Svengali-like mentor, Daberlohn, both objects of serious crushes, which creates palpable and shifting Oedipal tension. One painting pictorially illustrates Charlotte's own primal scene tableau: she is in the lower right corner facing the viewer while, in the background, Daberlohn and Paulinka crowd the piano and literally make beautiful music together (Herzberg, 236). Charlotte is inspired by her exclusion; she wants in (see Plate 9).

Charlotte meets with Daberlohn, often in secret, and absorbs many of his ideas, which are evident in the play. Daberlohn's theories, clearly influenced by psychoanalysis, are allotted a great deal of space. His axiom: "You must first go into yourself—into your childhood—to be able to get out of yourself" is quoted numerous times, echoing early psychoanalytic views, which stress the importance of childhood in depth psychology. Daberlohn believes that geniuses are made, not born, and that one becomes an artist only by getting in touch with one's inner self. He also preaches that creativity is born of trauma and suffering. "The emotional life of the singer," he says, "must suffer a great upheaval to enable that singer to achieve exceptional results" (Herzberg, 379). When reading these words, it is impossible not to think of the exceptional results achieved by Salomon in her artistic tour de force.

Salomon's epic, although heavily influenced by the political conditions under which she lived, gives surprisingly little space to the actual depiction of these events. She does, however, present us with the flavor of European prewar anti-Semitism. Interestingly, in nearly all cases, she does so with a healthy dose of humor, perhaps to render these noxious experiences more aesthetic and palatable both for her readers and herself. To give but one example, during a visit to Italy with her grandparents, Pope Pius XI inquires, with arms open to those before him, "Tiens, tiens, tiens. What are those little Jews doing here" (Herzberg, 176).

---

[1] Wolfsohn was no stranger to trauma. He suffered shell shock in World War I as a result of having been buried alive for several days beneath a pile of dead soldiers. He lost his voice after hearing dying soldiers cry for help. He then developed a theory connecting voice and soul, and dedicated his life to healing others and himself through song.

Salomon also depicts with brutal clarity a scene of marching, mechanized Nazis who are melded into one mass; they are nondescript in personal features but clear in the uniforms that create a grotesque brown tapestry broken only by red and black flags bearing the swastika. Salomon purposely paints the Nazi symbol in reverse at all times both to mock it and to diminish its power (Herzberg, 152).

Salomon illustrates, too, how her stepmother's celebrated singing career is brought to an abrupt end with the depiction of her final concert during which a crowd shouts her off the stage. Likewise, her father's university professorship is withdrawn. A scene shows him performing surgery with a large red X over it; now he is allowed to work only in a Jewish hospital. Both parents were ousted from their professional milieus with the harsh commands, "*Aus—Raus* (Get out—out—get out)" (Herzberg, 154, 156). Salomon chronicles the Nazi attacks on the Jews that accelerated in 1938 and culminated in Kristallnacht, November 9, 1938. Her father was arrested and sent to Sachsenhausen, a labor camp. Nine thousand Jews passed through the camp ruled by Rudolf Höss. In one painting, a guard stands over the bowed shadow figure of her imprisoned father. The guard's words—"You have to work here, there'll be no loafing. You've done enough loafing in your lives" (Herzberg, 644, 645)—literally and figuratively weigh down on the father's hunched body. Interestingly this is the first time Salomon employs a muddy palette. Paulinka, using her considerable charms, obtains false papers, granting Albert's release from the camp; he was nonetheless forced to walk 15 miles home in his weakened state. The man who walked with him perished. Albert survived but was bedridden for 4 weeks (Felstiner, 1994).

No image of Gurs, the French Transit camp in the Pyrenees where she and her grandfather were inmates during the summer of 1940, exists in her work, but it is known that art supplies were delivered to the camp by the Red Cross and that a large amount of art was produced there, so it is possible that Salomon reconnected to her art and to Wolfsohn's spirit while an inmate at Gurs. The transit camp served as a transition between life and death and between art and death.

Toward the end of Salomon's play, text progressively crowds out image until it completely takes over. This is partly due to the fact that Salomon shifts her focus from actual memories to psychological complexities. For example, in one image of her grandfather after his wife's suicide, he makes sexual advances to Charlotte, and in response she covers his body with text to diminish the power of his words. It is clear that Salomon was feverishly trying to complete her work as she sensed that time was running out. At one point, she paints herself with brown-lettered words, "I can't take this life any more, I can't take these times any more" (Herzberg, 636).

Irregularly sized letters and disembodied words become bolder and demand more room, often with barely a space between them. The last words in *Life? or Theater?* are: "And with dream-awakened eyes she saw all the beauty around her, saw the sea, felt the sun, and knew: she had to vanish for a while from the human plane in order to create her world anew out of the depths. And from that came *Life? or Theater?*" (Herzberg, 782–783). Her final image is one of herself seated at the beach in her bathing suit, paintbrush in hand. Interestingly, her pad is transparent in her last painting, indicating that in the end her art and her life became completely joined through a clear window of vision existing between both domains. She looks out to sea and contemplates her death, a death she willingly embraces but, notably, a death not caused by suicide. In large letters printed across her back are the words "LEBEN ODER THEATER" (see Plate 10). The question marks are gone, revealing that in the end Salomon chose both life and theater. Salomon chose life, with its chaos and broken promises, its cruel surprises and assaults on meaning, its precious beauty that still shines through its seeming indifference. Salomon also chose to transform all this, every bit of it, both bitter and sweet, into theater, into show and song and, most of all, into a meaningful and beautiful story forged from her own bleeding depths.

In September 1943, Charlotte Salomon was taken from Nice, along with her husband, Alexander Nagler, to Drancy, a camp a few miles from Paris where more than 70,000 Jews passed through on their way to German camps. It is assumed that she was murdered upon arrival in Auschwitz on October 10, 1943. Although her work did not succeed in saving her life, it seems to have saved her spiritually, in that it recontextualized her existence in a form and meaning that transcended its tragic personal and social context. It allowed her to visit (and recreate with truth) her past, no matter how painful, in the context of a terrifying present and future. It brought to life her youthful passion and creative spirit. It connected her, in her isolated, exiled state, to those most dear to her and breathed life back into the dead, in blatant refusal to accept their disappearance from her life. It helped her battle the numbing death forces, by allowing her to face the truth about her family and the world. It helped her to find herself. She wrote: "The war raged on and I sat by the sea and saw deep into the heart of humankind. I was my mother my grandmother indeed I was all the characters in the play. I learned to walk all paths and became myself" (Felstiner, 1994, p. 141).

MICHAL HEIMAN: MAKING ART BETWEEN BOMBARDMENTS

Michal Heiman glances into the rearview mirror of her car as she films herself.[1] She wants to see her face. She needs to see her face (see Plate 11).

---

[1] Information about Michal Heiman's life and career comes from many personal interviews and conversations with the author over several years.

She seeks the mirroring validation of the many fear reactions she experiences as she drives in a car on her way to Jerusalem from Tel-Aviv to teach at Bezalel Academy of Art. Rather than focus on visions of external damage and ruin, she conveys what life under terror is like from the inside, using a fish bowl perspective. When she began to make this art in 2001, Heiman's car wound through streets that, over a period of 3 years, had become perilous sites inviting numerous attacks by suicide bombers. Heiman wanted to document her fear as well as create a womblike protective cell against external menace. She wished to block out the danger by replacing her rearview mirror with one that mirrors herself, her emotions, and her reactions. Ironically, in her attempt to protect herself, she endangers herself, because while thus preoccupied, she might crash or fail to see a road sign designed to preserve her life.

Heiman, born in 1954, is a prominent contemporary Israeli artist who transforms her private pain in the public domain. She is also a curator, theoretician, and creator of the *M.H.T. (Michal Heiman Tests)*. For several decades, she has been creating a space between art and psychoanalysis, photography and diagnosis. Having been an analysand for over a decade herself, Heiman incorporates into her art her interest in projective techniques for personality assessment as well as her awe of psychoanalysis. She screens the *Michal Heiman Test (M.H.T.) No. 3: What's on Your Mind?* in a theatre space containing six couches. Six people have to come up with one story; they have to agree. Is it possible for her films to elicit only one story? Is it possible for different minds to come to a complete agreement about the meaning of a given reality—reality as a set of facts and an objective condition? The projective quality of Heiman's work, as well as the fact that no one "story" exists about the land of Israel, a land whose borders and character are forever changing, renders such a task daunting, surely even impossible. Heiman's forcing one story is so interesting because traumatized individuals try to find a definitive answer—a single, correct, objective story—to convey what they have experienced; they try to find one truth that will make sense of the senseless. Yet Heiman knows on some level that it is not the story per se that saves the traumatized, but the work with others to communicate one's pain and to create meaning from it.

Heiman does not merely create from the present-day trauma and turmoil she experiences and witnesses. As a young adolescent, she entered a closet she shared with her brother only to find her uncle who had hanged himself among her clothes. Because the family's public account of the uncle's sudden death involved his having suffered a heart attack, Heiman had to keep the trauma to herself, and to this day vows that a mirror in the closet saved her life. Rather than remain trapped and suffocating in a restricted space with the dangling body of her uncle, she instead saw her own image reflected in the optically expanded room behind her. Trauma has the power to rupture one's sense of identity, and Heiman claims that her timely reflection in the mirror offset more serious repercussions because it assured her of her existence. She wasn't simply there with her dead uncle, suffering a psychological assault of potentially lethal proportions. Because of the mirror she bore witness to herself under that assault; in this way she was a level removed from it, a level above it.

The significance of Heiman's car mirror recalls the mirror that "saved" her in the confined closet of her youth. In both situations, she succeeds in overcoming the threat of death and self-annihilation by literally expanding the space beyond that of death's imprint and by reasserting her sense of self. Unsurprisingly, then, the mirror—whether real or figurative—has become an essential component of her art. Heiman looks into the rearview mirror as she drives to Jerusalem. When viewing her art, we look at her while she looks at herself, mirroring her existence as well as her (and our) death anxiety.

Artists like Heiman respond directly to the political tension and violence they are forced to live with. Making art in an age of terror, as she does, requires a curious amalgamation of the traumatic and the life affirming: a claustrophobic reality is transformed into a realm involving multiple possibilities. Yet, as in life, the artist does not allow for all possibilities, once elicited, to be actualized. Forcing her respondents to overcome the impossibility of interpretive closure places them in situations not unlike that of political leaders in the Middle East, who seek one answer to an endlessly complex question. It also puts respondents in the place of a traumatized victim, needing to have some kind of monolithic answer. For Heiman, the personal is political and the political personal. Both the personal and the political are subject to analysis. And, in the end, it all becomes fodder for her art. Ultimately, the art seeks to transcend the trauma by simultaneously absorbing and expressing it. If nothing else, it can be given meaning through art.

When she was 30, and already a well-known artist, Heiman had encountered difficult times. She sought assistance and was administered projective tests to aid in her diagnosis. She was so fascinated by the tests, and especially by the shared viewing of images, that she later used those very tests as raw material for her creative endeavors. Heiman transposed the private encounter between diagnostician and subject to a public site, giving her own artistic spin to psychology's use of visual imagery and reversing the power dynamic she had taken part in. Heiman created her own projective test, the *Michal Heiman Test* (*M.H.T.*) *No. 1*, whose box and procedure were first exhibited as *Documenta X* in Kassel, Germany (curated by Catherine David) in 1997. The *M.H.T. No. 1* is modeled after the Thematic Apperception Test (TAT), a psychological test composed of black and white drawings about which the subject makes up stories (see Plate 12).[1] By replacing the drawings with photographs and adding several plates in color, Heiman plainly states that the Israeli external reality—replete with its imagery of war, soldiers, and occupation—is so compelling and oppressively omnipresent that Israelis cannot avoid its influence on their unconscious lives. Thus, her photographs consist primarily of people posing in front of "sites where battles were fought and memorial monuments were erected to the fallen, places of national heritage, of grief where blood was spilled" (Agassi, 1997, p. 10).

Heiman's version of the TAT is clearly more personal and deliberately political than the original. It also takes the ambiguous, abstract, impersonal images and makes them all too real. These are not projections of inner wishes and psychic reality. These are real events impinging from without. By having art spectators sit and volunteer to be "tested" in the space of a gallery or museum, she brings her projective technique into a collective cultural space. How can one, Heiman asks implicitly through her art, ever truly separate the private from the public, the personal from the collective, the projective from the objective, and the past from the present? How can art not reflect, reconfigure, and re-imagine reality? Heiman's use of real images in an artistic context evokes powerful reactions that are quite different from those given to typical TAT cards: a young girl in a 1930 classroom in Tripoli, Libya, pointing to the ever-changing map of Israel; two hands holding the mangled face of a corpse; an Israeli soldier with a rifle and a club staring at the back of a Palestinian man standing with his face to the wall in a refugee camp; a group of Egyptian prisoners with their arms in the air; a group of young Israelis posing atop an enemy tank; a family posing in front of the Tel Hai monument; a stone pedestal whose inscription reads: "It is good to die for our country" (see Plate 13). Incidentally, this plate comes from a photograph of Heiman's own family taken in 1962, and it is she who stands on the right posing and smiling as a child in front of the monument.

Heiman's test is clearly one that fills in for most psychological tests' cultural blind spots. It is a test that highlights the ways in which Israeli identity is composed of violent encounters, sacred places, tourist sites, evasive borders, heroic myths, defensiveness, guilt, denial, states of annihilation anxiety, emergency, and terror (Katz-Freiman, 1996, p. 10). Through her art, Heiman also creatively plays with the dual struggle of surmounting the trauma of being terrorized and the trauma of being forced into the role of occupier and aggressor.

---

[1] In 1998, Heiman created a second "test" modeled after the TAT. Her *M.H.T No. 2: My Mother-in-Law, Test for Women*, includes 66 plates with photographs of Keila, Heiman's mother-in-law at the time, and five other women, and one blank plate.

Heiman created art in response to the Second Intifada (Palestinian uprising, begun in 2000). Continuing her interest in projective techniques, she produced a series of works reminiscent of the Rorschach inkblot test that she calls *Blood Test* (see Plate 14). Heiman replaces ink with images of bloody scenes taken from newspaper clippings, blood being the unifying element of this work and what it represents—blood from victims of terrorist attacks; the blood of former prime minister Yitzhak Rabin after his assassination; and blood from Arabs, Jews, and foreign workers as well as blood from the attackers.

In all these works, Heiman addresses the issue of repeated exposure to sensationalist images of atrocity. In our time, and especially in Israel over the years, daily newspapers assail their readers with endless images of violence, blood, carnage, and destruction. Viewing these images on a daily basis eventually inhibits their inherent shock value and diminishes one's interest in and compassion for the personal suffering of those depicted. One suicide bomber's portrait begins to resemble another's, and one victim's body becomes indistinguishable from the next. Heiman's aesthetic recycling of these horrific images compels viewers to undo their numbing defense so that they no longer remain indifferent (Sontag, 2003). They are forced to notice, contemplate, learn, and study the reasons for mass affliction. Heiman's focus on enlarged and close-up images of bloody hands and wounds divorced from personal signifiers additionally has spectators personalize these politically motivated acts. The crimson blood that pours from us all when brutally injured or killed eliminates all differences between Arab and Jew. Thus, we all become would-be victims, and we all have blood on our hands.

Heiman was inspired by another visually based diagnostic tool, the Szondi Test, in the creation of her most recent artistic test, the *Michal Heiman Test No. 4: Experimental Diagnostics of Affinities* (2010). The now defunct Szondi Test is a psychological test created by Hungarian psychiatrist Leopold Szondi in the 1930s and published in 1947. Szondi's test had subjects respond to a group of 48 photographs of mental patients and criminals by choosing those they found most and least appealing. The *M.H.T. No. 4* aims to explore visual attraction and repulsion, instinctual reactions, and even "incestuous" receptiveness of subjects who choose from 60 cutout photographs culled from a variety of sources, including those of herself, members of her family, artists, theoreticians, and her art works.

The shifting boundary between private and public permeates Heiman's art, whose subject matter always emphasizes the powerful stimulus value of pictures. She has collected photographs of homes, buses, and vehicles that have been blown up and ripped apart. Photographers do not knock on doors in order to request permission to photograph. What was once a private enclosed space, privy to a select few, is transformed into public ruin for anyone to observe and even walk through. Photographers invade these spaces, just as the Palestinian bombers or the Israeli military already have. Her horror at the intrusiveness of photography in these cases has led Heiman to title an exhibition *Photo Rape* (2003), a title that raises ethical questions regarding the rights and privacy denied the subjects whose interior homes and private selves lie ravaged and exposed. Heiman transforms these images into works of art that juxtapose emotion and history, public and private, outside and inside.

The photographs are mounted onto enormous canvases, and their realistic yet strangely lit atmospheres create a Vermeer-like impression that succeeds in offsetting the grim subject matter. The tension between the erotic pleasure of color and the scenes of destruction results in an uncanny attractiveness. Placing the photographs on walls as backdrops for her spectators, Heiman poses the ultimate psychoanalytic question, "WHAT'S ON YOUR MIND?" next to them. She thus forces her audience to concede a personal connection to what it sees. They, too, are indicted for blood lust. They too must at some level acknowledge human madness.

But Heiman's maneuver cannot be contained in any simple reduction. It also elevates the effect of witnessing brutal, raw images that are potentially traumatizing when left alone by inviting symbolic, verbalized accounts. By having her spectators/patients associate to what is seen, or attempt to provide meaningful formulations for their reactions, Heiman becomes the artist/analyst who provides the structure in which to reexperience trauma in order to help work through its consequences.

Yet unlike Winnicott's (1951/1975) soothing and reassuring transitional space between me and not-me, these images provide no comfort or safety; instead they graphically depict how easily life is shattered and how utterly fragile and ephemeral are the connections among people, places, and objects. Children, like victims of bombings, are helpless and unable to survive on their own. Indeed, Heiman is acutely sensitive to such juxtapositions. In one series of photographs, baby carriages and children's wagons are heartbreakingly strewn alongside dead bodies and ruins from bombsites. There is no safe haven, no third space; here you cannot even be comfortably inside your own skin, nor can you seek refuge from without. Everything is blowing up. Everything is ablaze. Childhood illusions are withered to ash. Mothers cannot guarantee safety, and neither can museums or therapy.

One might begin to think of the artistic rendering of trauma as repetitive, life negating, preoccupied, or self-defeating. Yet all is not hopeless in Heiman's world, because her transformations of trauma into artistic expression reflect her desire and ability to transcend what would otherwise be an overwhelming and unbearable situation. She is taking the trauma that surrounds her and the trauma she embodies and working through it the only way she can. Surviving trauma, according to Robert J. Lifton (1987), involves being able to continuously imagine the encounter with death "in order to create past it, stay in it, and use it, yet move beyond it" (p. 258). A space beyond trauma and death can be opened by repeated acts of creative imagination.[1]

Heiman, like other artists (think of Picasso's *Guernica*, Goya's *Disasters of War* prints, or works by Otto Dix, George Grosz, and Käthe Kollwitz) who create in an age of war and terror, engages herself and her audience in a conversation with violent death. Dialoging with Goya's painting, *The Third of May* (1808, completed in 1814), in which French soldiers are about to execute a Spanish citizen at point-blank range, she juxtaposes it with an image from the Israeli newspaper *Haaretz*, which shows a Palestinian man facing an Israeli military vehicle with his pants down, because he is probably suspected of being a terrorist who might be wearing a belt with explosives (see Plate 15). She transposes the yellow pants onto the Palestinian man, causing the bright color and thus the figure of the man to stand out from these violent scenes. Both images show men wearing dazzling yellow trousers with their hands raised in supplication and surrender. Heiman's artistry here is multileveled: she covers the Palestinian man with the yellow trousers to make his image less humiliated and humiliating; she connects both men across a great span of time and distance in their posture of helplessness and terror in the face of hate-driven brutality; and in so doing she suggests a universal image of the terrorized individual, hands raised, pleading with mouth agape and eyes agog as he faces annihilation.

The traumatic reaction to disastrous events damages social connections and erodes the healthy illusions that are needed to make a more tolerable fabric of life (Benyakar & Knafo, 2004). The art object attempts to restore these broken connections and impose form onto the destruction if only by representing it within a new structure: the structure of art. The art object, by inviting dialogue with its spectators, also acts to restore threatened social connections (Rose, 1995).

An excellent example of this is Heiman's 2002 series, *Holding*. She purposely adopts Winnicott's term, which denotes the mother's and therapist's creation of a protected physical and emotional space in which the child and patient may safely regress and grow. Modeled after the famous movie poster for *Gone with the Wind*, of Clark Gable holding Vivienne Leigh in his strong, manly arms, Heiman juxtaposes endless images of bombing victims being carried in the arms of their saviors (see Plate 16). Mirroring the exact pose of the cinema's romantic couple, Heiman's acerbic humor has us witness the passing (*gone* with the wind) of romantic fantasies of love and Eros, only to be replaced by desperate couples—both Palestinians

---

[1] Indeed, art is and always has been the primal therapy, the first activity (along with sacred celebration) that comprised a naked bid for transcendence. Even the earliest prehistoric works were rooted in an existential need to transform a hunting scene or an animal into something more permanent—to depict the ephemeral and, by doing so, transform it and go beyond it.

and Israelis—scrambling for cover or medical assistance in a life or death situation. Heiman's art, with its fluid and interchangeable roles, points to the unsettling awareness that aggressors and victims, saviors and attackers, can be the same people or even the same person. This is the new pairing, she seems to be saying. *This is today's most dramatic form of human contact.*

The images of terrorized couples are horrific, not only because they are bloody but, more important, because they show the terror, confusion, and desperation in the eyes of the people who run for their lives. Yet, as she documents the state of emergency and alarm, Heiman masterfully creates a literal "holding environment" in her work. The gesture of having one's fears and wounds physically and symbolically held reflects the artist's ability to contain her audience's most primal emotions and provide a safe space in which to express them.

Other *Holding* scenes appear in her *Do-Mino* (2008) series that depicts tragic Middle Eastern scenes adjacent to canonical Western art masterpieces, thus forcing a connection between high art and political violence. In Hebrew, *do-mino* means bisexual. Heiman's variation of the word refers to the fluidity of roles and also to the cascading—domino—emotional effect the scenes in these images have on us. In one, the dead Christ in Raphael's *Deposition* (1507) is presented next to a scene portraying the aftereffects of an incident that took place in Bidu in the West Bank (see Plate 17). Both images show compassionate people carrying the dead, their bodies creating a pyramidal form inviting the viewer's eyes to move back and forth between the dead body and those holding it. In *Deposition* emotions appear sorrowful, while in the newspaper photo they seem desperate. Both deal with the tragic dimension of life. Both reveal trauma that has taken place in the Middle East. And both show that trauma can and must be embraced with care. In fact, the two images are reminiscent of Michelangelo's *Pieta* (1498–1499) in which Christ is held by his mother Mary after the Crucifixion. All three images denote a sentient as well as spiritual view of human suffering. The similar features in all three works equate the suffering of Israelis and Palestinians. Indeed, Heiman has found a way to bring Palestinian suffering to her viewers' consciousness. If it is art, then no one can tell her it is unacceptable. One message that comes through loud and clear from her work is that suffering does not privilege one people. Suffering is human and universal.

In her 2008 solo exhibition at the Tel-Aviv Museum, Heiman adopted the term, "attacks on linking" from Wilfred Bion (1959/1984), an analyst who was marked by war trauma himself. She presents her viewers with disruptive and disastrous scenes, only to question them with the words, "What did you see?" and "What didn't you see?" in a series of movies and lectures titled *Attacks on Linking*. Heiman shows catastrophes while acknowledging our need to become absent and evade, to turn away, dissociate, and even go blind temporarily. It is as if she is reminding us of

T. S. Eliot's (1963) observation in his poem "Burnt Norton" that "Human kind cannot bear very much reality" (p. 190). She is well aware of the fact that she assaults our empathic sensibilities with images that have the potential to traumatize us, to attack our links to reality and to our own thoughts. Yet she does so within the context of art and art, like psychoanalysis, has a healing potential.

Thus, rather than simply experience, or re-experience, the trauma, Heiman has us reflect on it—"What's On Your Mind?"—ask questions and make connections, name and contain the destructive elements. In this way, her art helps detoxify and contextualize horrific experiences, helps us recover our sense of self and the symbolic and reflective function. If we can construct a trauma narrative, then we can avoid the extremes of feeling either overwhelmed or deadened by a mind and self that have collapsed under pressure (Boulanger, 2007).

The films, lectures, and photographs that make up Heiman's *Attacks on Linking* series all unite to create links as well as destroy them. In *Clinging 1* (2004), she juxtaposes a painting of the Madonna and baby Jesus by Raphael (1505) alongside a newspaper photograph of a Palestinian mother with child (see Plate 18). Both women have beatific expressions on their faces; both women's eyes look downward rather than meet their child's gaze; both women are wrapped in green and red cloth. Both children raise a hand to meet the mother's body. Yet, next to the vision of the Holy Virgin is that of the wife of a suicide bomber who blew himself up the day before. Despite this knowledge, we are still moved by the maternal holding. It seems that no matter how gruesome the world becomes, no matter how many links are broken, one link persists: compassionate holding. As long as there is holding, hope remains. The Palestinian woman, I am told, was 5 months pregnant at the time she was photographed. With a new life comes new links.

PSYCHOANALYSIS IN CHAINS

Clinicians can learn from artists who are adept at finding ways to combine reality with fantasy and rationality with imagination in a seriously playful engagement with their pasts and with death, all the while creating a transformational object of art, an object that synthesizes loss and attempts to repair it at one and the same time (Knafo, 2002; Segal, 1991). Though analysts do not necessarily create an object of art, they can be instrumental in the facilitation of their patients' and their own creativity within the analytic space. One of the important objectives in the treatment of individuals who have experienced trauma, then, is the provision of creative, rather than destructive, outlets for the expression of aggression.

I already mentioned authors like Adorno and Milosz who referred to the nearly impossible task of putting traumatic experience into words, a difficulty also recognized by researchers who find that severe trauma is apparently not processed symbolically (e.g., van der Kolk, 1997). Clinicians who treat severe trauma are therefore well aware that verbalization, the very tool of psychoanalytic therapy, is difficult to access. Along with the challenge of employing language to surface an event that is not processed linguistically is the challenge of working within a human relationship after circumstances have proven that human beings cannot be relied on. This is why clinicians need not be too disheartened by the profound difficulty of treating personal trauma, because nothing we say can erase the memories or bring back lost loved ones, and nothing we do can make the world a safe place or guarantee that horrific events will never again be repeated.

Still there is much we can offer. We can be there with our patients, share their pain, contain it, and bear witness to the events that caused it. We can help them reflect and symbolize their experiences, express their feelings so they don't choke on them, and give words to their thoughts so they are not mute (or vocal solely through the body). We can allow our patients to use us as needed, staying with them and working through the most awful experiences, however rough the going gets. In this way we may return to them the possibility of trust. Most of all, we can assist our patients in finding meaning in their suffering, the only thing that ultimately helps them bear it. I sometimes find it useful to recall Becker's (1973) view on the essence of transference as "a taming of terror" (p. 145). In the analysis of one who has suffered trauma, one tries to find a way of helping the traumatized person go from being or perceiving herself as a victim, with its concomitant helplessness, passivity, and dependence, to being a survivor, a person capable of taking action to control her destiny.

Analysts can help their patients achieve this state by providing a creatively flexible analytic space, a space that at times may even come to resemble a torture chamber. The analyst might also assume the roles of victim, tormentor, and helpless bystander, as needed. Transference in these cases often entails a destruction of the therapist's preferred role as caregiver. I am reminded of a patient who consciously identified with Palestinian suicide bombers as she perceived herself as destroying the treatment, herself, and me in one massive wave of aggressive acting out (Knafo, 1999). In such cases, one faces the challenge of transforming immense rage and the need for revenge into self-assertiveness, play, humor, and, occasionally, a creative product. Creativity and humor should not be considered mere peripheral or defensive activities because they allow us to appreciate the ridiculous, absurd, and tragic dimension of life.

Kasia sought psychoanalysis to overcome a paralyzing speaking phobia. Her difficulty as a political activist, whose work demanded public speaking, drove her to my door. A woman in her 30s, Kasia was the product of forced immigration from post–World War II Eastern Europe. She was born in a displaced-persons camp, the stark land of the lost and the dispossessed, and introduced to the world's cruelty at a young and tender age. Her father, who was blinded in a concentration camp "experiment" during the Holocaust, was responsible for Kasia's most prominent childhood memories of suffering and abuse. Family members excused his erratic, violent, and sometimes insane behavior, rationalizing that he couldn't help it because "his nerves were shot."

Despite his multidimensional traumatic handicaps and the fact that he worked at a menial job, Kasia's father stood out as a powerful and influential man in the immigrant Eastern European community to which his family belonged. Kasia's mother, a career woman, remained away from home much of the time, leaving Kasia with her father for long hours, a situation that reinforced their inordinate attachment to each other. Kasia contained her father's pain and became his seeing-eye dog as well as his voice in the outside world. He took her with him everywhere he went, and she described what she saw to him and translated his words to others. A powerful mutual dependency developed between the two.

In the privacy of their home, Kasia's father, a strict and psychologically tortured man carrying profound and unresolved trauma from his sojourn through hell, never hesitated to use corporal punishment on Kasia, and theirs became a relationship expressed by sadomasochistic enactments. Kasia often described how, as a child, she provoked her father to administer harsher beatings by hiding from him, compelling him to aimlessly flail and thrash about the house until he found her. This battle of wills evolved into a game of mutual torture in which each party alternatively took turns playing the roles of victim and victimizer, but always ended with the father confusing past with present by "ripping into" Kasia and beating her ruthlessly as if his life depended on it.

Predictably, Kasia's choice of vocation was rife with ambivalence and conflict. Whereas she viewed herself as a photographer, she associated that art with luxury, selfishness, and neglect of her Eastern European/father tie. The irony of her taking pictures while having a blind father to whom she remained inordinately close did not escape her. Additionally, she knew that through photography she expressed herself, but had difficulty exhibiting her emotional contours in a context devoid of abuse and mutual violence. Not surprisingly, Kasia photographed people in hiding. Hidden faces and covered bodies tease the viewer by dropping visual clues but withholding answers. Hiding identifying features additionally conveys that the people depicted in her photographs are devoid of identity, as were the inmates in the concentration camps. Playing this visual hide-and-seek game with her viewer, as she had done with her father, demonstrates the ways her art both expressed and worked through her unconscious issues. Furthermore, perfectly expressing her conflict, ambivalence, and creative inhibition, Kasia hung her photographs with the picture side facing the wall. Whereas she had become her father's eyes and captured the visual world for him, she simultaneously symbolically blinded herself (and her viewers), by depriving herself (and them) of the ability to view and portray the world from which he was excluded. As a result, she reduced her visual voice to that of "speaking to the walls."

Kasia soon strongly associated psychoanalysis with photography and self-expression, in her mind, self-indulgent activities that triggered conflicted anger and aggression. Not surprisingly, then, she imported her powerful emotional issues around her father, her ethnic identity, and her art into treatment. Consciously, she appreciated the difference in our backgrounds and expressed relief at the fantasy that I was in a position to regard her objectively because I did not belong to her community. Unconsciously, she was hoping to steer clear of the sadomasochism associated with her world by being in treatment with someone whom she viewed as outside of it. Alas, her embodied sadomasochistic rage proved unavoidable as it entered the treatment and at times even co-opted it.

Kasia's self-perception as a victim had been so deeply ingrained that it formed an integral part of her character. Life to her was a prison; trauma and pain were even idealized in her worldview. She saw herself as a martyr, and her language became especially vivid when communicating profound feelings of persecution. She shouted at the top of her lungs for the duration of most sessions as she related her experiences of being metaphorically "spit on," "beat over the head," and "pinned against the wall" by her boss, her friends, and her family.

Initially she could see herself only as the slave in relationships, a helpless prey of torture and cruelty. Nevertheless, in the transference, Kasia acted out primarily as victimizer, missing sessions or coming late and delaying the payment of her bills. She did not call to cancel her sessions and thus recreated the hide-and-seek game she had once played with her father. Like her blind father, I could not see her, did not know where she was, and felt angry at being treated so disrespectfully. And as with her father, Kasia confessed her expectation/wish that I beat her and, ultimately, throw her out of treatment. "I want you to hit me, kick me, throw me out of here!" she shouted in response to my questioning her absences.

Her intense aggression and angry tirade upset both of us. Four times a week she screamed so hard that she left her sessions red-faced, sweating, and shaking. Aside from the commotion she created, her language was packed with curses to express the primal nature and boundlessness of her emotions. I sometimes didn't even hear her words, just the vibrations of her voice that shattered my composure and strained my ability to sustain emotional attunement. I wanted to cover my eyes, block my ears, look the other way. But Kasia didn't allow me to remain on the outside, a mere spectator to her fear and fury. She screamed until I took notice. She got under my skin, and I embodied her world of torture and violence. Because

I held up an empathic mirror to her behavior while containing her boiling rage and intense pain, it soon became impossible for her to avoid recognizing the pervasiveness of her sadomasochistic view of life and her disavowal of the part she played in it. We analyzed her relationships outside of the treatment and then connected them to the transference along with its extreme enactments. The patterns she imported into treatment became obvious to her, and she began to actually feel how they continued doing damage to her and her relationships. Indeed, she needed to bring those psychosocial scripts into our sessions in order to change them. In fact she temporarily transformed the analytic space into a kind of "concentration camp" with either she or I cast in the role of prisoner and held in bondage. Kasia's comparison of analysis to a concentration camp was a very somber matter; yet by casting me in whatever role she wished and watching me survive her repeated attacks, the echo of this world and her father's horrific past ultimately began to fade and threaten her less. When she was not making me feel like a sadist by forcing her to look inward and take responsibility and do things she wished to avoid, I felt shackled by her screams and the intensity of her pain. Our relationship became the transparent vehicle and literal crucible in which transformation took place. I contained her pain the way she had contained her father's.

The fact that I am a woman also played a significant role in Kasia's treatment. Her mother had been absent during much of her childhood and, when she was present, Kasia developed a disrespect for her that generalized to all matters feminine. Her overattachment to and overidentification with her father prevented her from incorporating softer, more nurturing, elements into her personality. Instead, she viewed reality as an arena in which she needed to fight for her life. And fight she did. Fighting with me and against me in the analytic space without being attacked in return gradually led Kasia to allow herself to be "held" by me, which, in turn, allowed for a degree of internalization of my mothering behaviors toward her. As she became gentler toward herself, the world became a kinder and less persecutory place in which to live. One outcome of this change was that she married her longtime boyfriend with whom she established a home.

It was at times difficult to reconcile Kasia's world of misery and torture with her artistic world. Much of her emotional life seemed unsublimated, raw, powerful, and angry. Photography was psychologically loaded and guilt-inducing due to its connection to her father's blindness, which resulted in Kasia's experiencing acute bouts of creative inhibition. At these times, I directed her to experiment in a medium other than photography, and she chose clay. Because making art with clay involved tactile sensations more than visual ones and could easily be performed by a blind person, Kasia's guilt was alleviated and her creative impulses liberated. Clay also represented Kasia's being molded by her father; her creations were of diminutive persons huddled into fetus-like shapes. Expressing her trauma and pain in clay helped free Kasia's creativity enough that she was able to return to photography, her artistic medium of choice.

It is important to note that during the entire time that the analytic space took the form of a torture chamber, this milieu simultaneously became an artist's studio, a place where Kasia imaginatively created embodied images that would ultimately set her free. It was in this third space (Ogden, 1994a, 1994b; Winnicott, 1951/1975), a space that bridged the past with the present and external and internal worlds, that Kasia was able to finally sculpt a new self, a self whose anger became one of agency rather than destructiveness. Accepting this change was inevitably fraught with conflict for Kasia, because it represented Americanization and the possibility of getting her needs met and of being treated with dignity and respect.

As Kasia gradually relaxed her masochistic stance, she began to take on more assertive roles in her life. Although photography did not entirely disappear, it receded into the background. In its place, Kasia's political activity, initially employed in defensive identification with her father, became an area to which she brought her creativity and in which she took charge and legitimately sublimated and expressed her angry feelings. Her activism required multiple national and international public-speaking engagements in which she came to excel, which is significant, since she began treatment with a phobia of public speaking. She did find her voice after all.

Considering both the intensity and extent of Kasia's identification with her immigrant parents, their experiences during the Holocaust, and their visions of the past, there were limits to the extent of Kasia's separation. Whereas she had initially used her culture to avoid separation, Kasia now employed it to achieve independence. Perhaps not so ironically, the focus of Kasia's political activities centered on the struggles of her parents' native land to separate and attain complete autonomy from the Soviet Union. As she was able to achieve greater independence from her father and her past, Kasia became increasingly instrumental in helping their native country achieve independence for the future.

CREATIVE REPAIR: THE ART OF TRAUMA

The art discussed in this chapter is an art created at the intersection of personal, aesthetic, social, and political experience. It is art made in the service of survival and meaning making. The creation of art when addressing trauma or facing death, whether real or imagined, involves the aesthetic response to human emergency. It represents an attempt to shift the power relations by handing power to those most in need of safety and support. It is a warning system as well as a form of resistance against destructive forces (Stiles, 1992). Kristine Stiles has given the label "destruction art" to works that "situate the body in the center of the question of destruction and survival" (p. 75). Paradoxically, although the content of this art is destruction, its purpose is to prevent and relieve trauma, thus preserving the survivor's power to live, to be spontaneous, to fantasize and to dream. This type of art is in the service of mastery over destruction, loss, numbing, and mourning. Laub and Podell (1995) provocatively assert that survival itself can be viewed as an art of trauma (e.g., Plates 4 and 5).

Freud realized the relevance of mastery in such phenomena when he wrote *Beyond the Pleasure Principle* (1920/1955). He observed that nightmares of shell-shocked soldiers challenged his theory positing that all dreams are representations of the fulfillment of ungratified wishes. Freud came to regard such dreams as constituting a violent and frustrated attempt to master and overcome trauma. Children's games (e.g., *fort da*), played in the shadow of loss, were understood as serving a similar function. In their play, children repeat events that have made strong impressions on them in real life, and through abreaction they decrease the strength of the impressions and attempt to make themselves masters of the situation (Freud, 1920/1955, pp. 16–17). Freud extended this argument to artists, especially as it concerned creativity related to trauma. Not surprisingly, the works of both Salomon and Heiman involve repetitive attempts to master a situation veering out of control. Their aesthetic repetitions assault viewers and induce in them sensations felt by the artists themselves, and thereby have viewers share the psychological burden as well as the ethical responsibility of containing the trauma.

Although it is possible for us to feel traumatized by witnessing repeated scenes of bombings or suicides, the aesthetic response to such art is far from simple. Despite the difficult content of the artworks discussed here, there also exists a clear attempt to discover, create, and communicate truth— truth about humankind and truth about one's inner world. This attempt is not unlike the task facing psychoanalysis. We too embark on a joint journey with our patients that takes us to the depths of the human condition. Sometimes we do not like what we see or recoil from the intensity of emotion and experience. Nonetheless, we know that it is truth that ultimately sets people free from their pain and symptoms. Although Salomon and Heiman have clearly struggled to deal with their experience of personal and collective trauma, their art compels us to acknowledge, if only through unconscious identification, that we are all survivors of devastation from wars, holocausts, and natural and man-made disasters, and we all live with the imprint of death and the guilt that surrounds that fact. Artists possess the gift of using aesthetic forms to present us with these unpalatable truths in order to help us digest them. They can wrest beauty from horror and transform the trauma in themselves and around them into a larger world, one that is more than a sequential collection of facts to which is attached a monolithic (and sometimes necessary) interpretation. They assume an active role in revisioning their lives, and they show us that our greatest power lies in the creative use of our imagination. We can create our lives, not simply live them. Thus, acts of imagination reveal that a life has an infinite number of profiles, each of which shares the facts freely with alternate interpretations and combinations of ideas. In this way one's personal life becomes every life.

In addition to their heightened sense of inner and outer reality (Greenacre, 1957/1971a), artists also have a strong need to repair the bleak and damaged world they see before them. According to Melanie Klein's theory (1946/1984), creativity is born of the depressive position. It is the infant's wish to repair the destroyed harmony with the mother that propels it toward a creative solution: the restoration and recreation of a lost world. "True reparation," writes Segal (1991), "must include an acknowledgement of aggression and its effect" (p. 92). Art, therefore, involves the balancing of destructive and reparative elements because it takes into account the reality of separateness and loss.

In certain ways, Klein's theory reminds me of the response found in the Jewish mystical tradition of the Kabbalah to people who question why there is evil in the world or how a benevolent God can allow evil to exist. The Kabbalah teaches that because God made humans his partner, Creation remains unfinished. It is only through Tikkun Olam, acts of healing and repair, that Creation is completed and the world restored. Indeed, artists possess the singular ability to restore life from the most broken and damaged pieces. Thus, Charlotte Salomon adds color and humor to the tune of suicide and mass annihilation in her epic tale, and Michal Heiman takes a world shattered by human bombs and uses blood and embraces to glue the shards back together again.

The artist, like the mother in Bion's theory (1967), becomes the container of malignant projections from the environment and gives them back to spectators in a form they can handle. This does not mean that art born of terror is easy to look at. It simply means that such art may render our reality easier to look at and our lives easier to bear.

Psychoanalytic treatment of trauma offers the patient similar avenues of repair. Although Kasia captured the world in her photography, she was initially unable to look at that world or have others look at it. Only after transforming the analytic space into a cruel and sadomasochistic play arena was Kasia able to confront her darker side, the side that was passed onto her by family tragedy. The psychoanalytic space, with its continuity and freedom from judgment, created a structured and accepting setting in which to play with and play out the most horrific experiences. Psychoanalysis, then, offers its traumatized patients the ultimate creative experience: the possibility of creating a survivor who is strengthened rather than destroyed by trauma. If analysts succeed in achieving this, then they too participate in the creative process, a process that ultimately embraces life while unflinchingly looking loss and death in the eye.

Chapter 5

Alone Together

Solitude and the Creative Encounter in Art and Psychoanalysis[1]

Ideas are like goddesses who appear only to the solitary mortal.

—Marcel Proust

The answer is that when a man has been there and undergone the baptism of solitude he can't help himself. Once he has been under the spell of the vast, luminous, silent country, no other place is quite strong enough for him, no other surroundings can provide the supremely satisfying sensation of existing in the midst of something that is absolute. He will go back, whatever the cost in comfort or money, for the absolute has no price.

—Paul Bowles

The Diving Bell and the Butterfly (1997), a heroic and poignant memoir by French journalist and *Elle* magazine editor Jean-Dominique Bauby, describes Bauby's horrific condition after suffering a massive stroke that left him with a rare and horrific disease called locked-in syndrome. Bauby remained conscious, yet unable to speak or move, except for one eyelid which he learned to use to communicate. One would be hard-pressed to find a more solitary condition—a completely functional and active mind cut off from all forms of discourse and incarcerated in an immobile and nearly useless body. Understandably, Bauby felt intensely suicidal until he discovered the two gifts his stroke had not eradicated—memory and imagination. Little by little, one eye blink at a time—translated by Claude Mendibil into one letter at a time—Bauby wrote his brief memoir. The diving bell refers to his deadened body sunk in the gloomy depths of immobility, while the butterfly is a metaphor for the flight of his imagination, delicate and ephemeral, rising above the wreckage of his despair.

Artistic creation is a solitary vocation, usually not forced upon the artist, as in the case of Bauby, but chosen and even cultivated. In his *Letters*

---

[1] An earlier version of this chapter appeared in *Psychoanalytic Dialogues*, 22(1), 2012.

to a Young Poet (1992), Rilke advised Franz Kapus to foster solitude first and foremost: "What is necessary, after all, is only this: solitude, vast inner solitude" (p. 54). Indeed, the artist eschews social intercourse to engage the world anew through acts of imagination. Of course, this is true not only for artists, but for anyone undertaking an intricate, creative task. Scientists, scholars, and all manner of thinkers and planners may retreat from others to bring their ideas into being. However, it is especially true for the serious artist who might spend the greater majority of his adult life in the solitary pursuit of creation. Furthermore, the work of most thinkers necessarily brings them into relationship with others for the purpose of verification, validation, and collaboration as they work out their creations. Though artists occasionally collaborate, more often they prefer to fly solo until their work is complete and ready for judgment. Perhaps only the lone mystic spends more time alone than does the dedicated artist.

Expressionist painter Agnes Martin said, "I paint with my back to the world" (Smith & Kuwayama, 1997). Françoise Gilot (2001), painter and one-time wife of Pablo Picasso, when asked by her students how one would know if she were an original artist replied, "I can tell you that it's very simple. How many hours can you remain alone during a day, a week, a month, a year, a lifetime? If you can remain alone almost all of the time you can be a painter" (p. 164).

Nearly anyone who consciously retreats from the many to commune with the one, whether that one is oneself, nature, art, or a divine presence, is practicing a disengagement that can have many benefits. What all these "loners" have in common is that they are in passionate pursuit of some private project. For many of them the most significant relationship, the very *causa sui* of their lives, is *the project*. Otto Rank, in his book *Art and Artist* (1932), concluded that one must choose to dedicate one's creativity either to art or to one's personal relationships.

This chapter examines some of the creative and transformative aspects of solitude, especially as they pertain to artists and their objects, and shows how both solitude and relationship are interrelated and layered states existing in dynamic interaction. It also considers the relational needs that art objects serve for their creators, and specifically addresses the uniqueness of women's solitude. Finally, a clinical vignette illustrates the interplay between solitude and relatedness in analytic treatment.

PERMUTATIONS OF SOLITUDE

Solitude is the physical and psychological withdrawal from others, a condition of being alone with oneself, either by choice or by virtue of an undesired circumstance. Radical or primary solitude, the condition of being alone in one's experience, is the basic state of human existence. Whether alone or with another, each human being maintains an existential aloneness throughout the course of life. Winnicott (1988) claims that prior to the "capacity to be alone" we exist in "a primary state of being," a "pre-primitive stage of development" that predates relationship (p. 133). Making a similar observation, Bollas (1989) states that "shadowing all object-relating is a fundamental and primary aloneness which is inevitable and unmovable. And this aloneness is the background of our being; solitude is the container of the self" (p. 20). Eigen (2009) calls this "boundless aloneness brought to us, in part, by who we are, an inherent ingredient of our basic nature" (p. 14). I cannot feel your toothache. You cannot taste my orange. I cannot live your life and you cannot die my death. You cannot love my love and I cannot hate your hate. You can never fully know what it is to be me nor I to be you. At best, we can develop empathy for one another and imagine what it is like to be the other.

At the heart of human experience, solitude is that burden of indescribable and seemingly impenetrable aloneness. It drives us to reach through the bars of our solipsistic cage of subjectivity and connect with others, whether through art or love or rage or the necessary goals of community. This movement itself is already an act of creativity, for each individual must find a way to deal with his own solitude. Creativity, then, is not an option; it is a natural response to being radically alone, and needing contact and encounter to realize and enlarge oneself.

Layered upon this core aloneness are two derivative states of solitude. Enforced solitude is a state of incarceration imposed either by oneself or another. This state of aloneness causes one to hunger for the company of others. The second kind is voluntary solitude, the intentional and happy retreat from others for some private purpose. Either of these two types of solitude may be beneficial or detrimental. Voluntary or enforced solitude may be *generative* and provide personal growth through special exercises or creative pursuits.[1] Either kind may become *defensive* when used to avoid relationships one finds painful and overwhelming. For example, one may feel authentic and safe only when alone. Either type of solitude may eventually become *degenerative*, which is indicated by the loss of the ability to connect with others, a sense of exile and despair in relationships, extreme loneliness, and negative health consequences and degradation of self-care (Cacioppo & Patrick, 2008). To be sure, voluntary solitude, enforced solitude, and defensive solitude can be generative, though the latter two are more likely to deteriorate into degenerative solitude that hastens the movement toward death. Artists (and others) have of course been subject to the dangers of solitude, especially when they feel they have failed to achieve a

---

[1] Many prisoners, whether incarcerated by the state or by the self, have enjoyed creative production. Cervantes's *Don Quixote*, Malory's *La Morte d'Arthur*, Wilde's *De Profundis*, Genet's *Our Lady of Flowers*, among others, were all penned in prison.

worthy and laudable product or have abused substances to enhance their creativity (see Chapter 3). Kurt Gödel, one of the greatest mathematicians of the twentieth century, literally starved to death in the last years of his life, overwhelmed by paranoid terror (Dawson, 1997). Yet we know that relationships can also become degenerative and destructive.

Though I have defined solitude simply as being apart from others and by oneself, that idea can be challenged, along with the somewhat static categories outlined earlier. Also subject to interpretation is what exactly solitude consists of. How much solitude constitutes a defensive position is clearly an open question, one sometimes examined in therapy. Secondary questions that can help address the larger issue are: What is the individual doing when alone? Is the solitary activity constructive? Is the activity enough of an "other" to constitute continued interest and absorption? Is there some kind of personal development taking place? Is the solitary activity a replacement for actual relationships with others? Such questions do not have clearly objective answers, nor can they be effectively addressed without inclusion of the person under examination. So long as there is no clear idea of what constitutes the "good life" in a "free" society, the answers to such questions necessarily involve a mutually creative examination on the part of the questioner and the one being questioned.

Terms like *solitude, relationship, intimacy,* and *connectedness* are dynamic, mutually permeable, and even simultaneous states in constant dialogue. Solitude and relationship cannot be seen as dichotomies, but rather as the background–foreground of human experience. Thoreau famously said, "I have a great deal of company in my house; especially in the morning, when nobody calls" (2009, p. 101). Indeed, we can feel alone with someone who does not understand us or is narcissistically self-involved. We can feel close to someone during her absence. Our attention drifts during a dialogue and we can leave the other feeling momentarily abandoned. We connect, disconnect, leave, come back, move in, move out; boundaries are drawn and erased as a relationship expresses the flux of its function and meaning.

Like relationship, solitude is a layered state. One artist asked rhetorically, "How can I give to anyone after I have just gone through labor?" She explained that following the solitary state of her creativity, she needed "a break to be even more alone."[1] One can detest solitude or covet it or, of course, use it defensively. It may be synonymous with loneliness and fear, or freedom and even ecstasy, all in the same day or even in the same hour. It can be connected with renewal and creation. It can be the harbinger of destruction and death. Just as there are dimensions within relationships,

---

[1] I asked 20 artists to write me a page or two on their thoughts regarding the relationship between creativity and solitude. When unnamed artists are mentioned or quoted in this chapter, they are either taken from this pool or from artist patients whom I've treated in psychoanalysis or psychotherapy.

even within a single one, there are dimensions within solitude: levels of creativity, self-discovery, flight, return, fear, longing, fantasy, introspection, communion, and silence. One patient, a stained-glass artist, once told me, "I can live and die in the same hour—bow down in gratitude when I am gifted with a new vision of glass or have the urge to break a plate into shards and cut my throat in despair when nothing will come."

What distinguishes artists from nonartists is their particular personal, historical, and psychological response to experience. Artists are so affected by experience (see Chapter 3 and its section on the artist's sensitivity) that they actually seek solitude to create something that stands apart from experience while conversing with it, and which reveals the multiple profiles and the possibilities embedded in its reality. The personal reasons artists create may be linked with awe, pain, loss, trauma, or even some idiosyncratic aspect of character. Nevertheless the end effect is the same; they withdraw from the general course of life, returning to aloneness for the purpose of creating a product that speaks in a new way to others about existence. Small wonder solitude is a site of terror and delight, of harrowing self-diminishment and ecstatic self-expansion where human creation takes place, sometimes at the highest levels.

WHAT IS THE ARTIST DOING ALONE?

Few psychoanalytic writers have addressed the question of solitude. In particular, the abundant attention recently directed toward relational and attachment needs has eclipsed the need for and benefit of aloneness. Of course, Winnicott (1958/1968) is an exception, and his groundbreaking paper on "the capacity to be alone" stands nearly alone in its argument that solitude can be regarded as a developmental milestone that is "nearly synonymous with emotional maturity" (p. 31). Winnicott's understanding of this capacity, however, assumes that safe and secure mothering establishes the ability for the child to feel comfortable being alone. For Winnicott, being alone paradoxically implies that someone else—a good and reliable object—has been introjected and is therefore present. A graphic artist alluded to this state when she exclaimed, "Ah, the sweetness of walking into my silent studio space after being with people. It smells of me and my work. I almost call out, 'I'm home, Mom!'" On a similar note, Modell (1993) claims that the muse, an internally constructed, mainly female and maternal presence, exemplifies the artist's continued connection to the mother despite apparent solitude.

Winnicott's assumption that only one who has had "good enough mothering" can attain such a capacity for aloneness is illuminating, yet I question its generalizability, because it is known that many highly creative artists have experienced poor parenting or early trauma and loss (Eisenstadt,

Haynal, Rentchnick, & De Senarclens, 1989). Indeed, the graphic artist quoted earlier grew up in a home with an absent mother and a bipolar father. Keen on this aspect of solitude, Michael Balint (1968) wrote about the space of creation as one in which there is "no external object present, no object relationship and no transference." Although I disagree with this statement in ways I will make clear shortly, Balint deserves credit for bringing attention to artists' creative regression from "harsh and frustrating" object relationships in order to "create something better, kinder, more understandable, beautiful, and above all, more consistent and more harmonious than the real objects proved to be" (p. 68). Along this line, Storr (1988) argues that artists' primary source of self-esteem and personal fulfillment often derive from their artistic output rather than from their interpersonal relationships. Likewise, artists often regard their own maturation in terms of the development of their art rather than according to changes in their relational world. Thus, self-understanding and self-regulation often take place in the privacy of the creative space. One patient recounted that when he was a young child, his mother kept him locked in a room for days at a time. "I had nowhere to go but inside," he said. It was during that time he developed a complex, imaginative world. Although he was "incarcerated for the crime of being a small boy," he cultivated a fertile, dynamic inner life that he later accessed for his writing. This is an example of how forced solitude can also lead to generativity.

So far we have two seminal ideas about solitude and creativity. For Winnicott solitude is an ability gained from being in the presence of a positive, nurturing mother, what Bowlby (1969) would call a secure attachment. For Balint solitude is a space of safety, predictability, and creativity to which one runs away from a frustrating or abusive environment. I would argue that both of these views are correct, and to them I add a third. Sometimes artists seek solitude to engage the bad object of their childhoods—Fairbairn's (1943/1952) unpredictable yet exciting objects—with whom they have unfinished business. Thus, there is a continued wrestling with one's objects even in the state of solitude, a need to seek resolution with the object world through the product of creativity. Austrian Expressionist artist Egon Schiele (see Chapter 7) harbored enormous resentment toward his mother for neglecting him as a child. As an adult he repeatedly killed her in a series of *Dead Mother* portraits (see Plate 23). Serving a dual purpose, these portraits expressed his anger toward his mother by killing her as well as the inner deadness he experienced from her. Interestingly, most of these portraits include a baby—himself—inside the womb in an ultimate state of fusion (Knafo, 1993). During the time he created these eerie and compelling works, he lived alone and eschewed contact with others, except to spend time sketching mothers and babies, both alive and dead, at his friend Dr. Graff's gynecological clinic. Later self-portraits would depict him as a lone monk, hermit, and saint (see Plate 24).

Thus, even in their generative solitude, artists are engaged in important and influential relational processes. Eagle (1981) writes of interests as a critical feature in the development of object relations, and I (Knafo, 2002) have written about how artworks function as a type of object relationship that can provide a site for transformation and change. Artist and psychoanalyst Julia Schwartz says, "With the first marks on the canvas, there begins a dialogue" (personal communication, January 16, 2010). Such a dialogue can carry profound unconscious communication. For example, one married patient spent over a year writing a novel about a woman whose husband commits adultery. After finishing the novel, this writer was ready to "discover" the obvious signs that her husband had been unfaithful for quite some time. In her life she had been unaware of what was happening, and yet in her writing she struggled with characters coping with infidelity.

Indeed, creative activity, though usually requiring solitude, produces a locale wherein the artist seeks objects, engages with them, and sometimes even reenacts reunion with them. Many artists identify with their original objects in the creative process and thus embody maternal generativity, which exemplifies, in part, Winnicott's theory of the capacity to be alone (Knafo, 2002). For example, following a terrible accident at age 18, Mexican artist Frida Kahlo was forced to spend much time alone, in hospitals, in bed, away from friends and family. She offered self-portraits to her friends so they would not forget her. She also painted their portraits and surrounded herself with them to keep them with her (Herrera, 1983).

Kahlo's emphasis on self-portraiture had earlier origins. Her mother was unavailable to her as an infant and, consequently, her early mirroring experience was derailed (Knafo, 2009b). The dozens of self-portraits she painted throughout her life represent the means by which she was able to perform a maternal function by acting as a mirror to herself, reflecting her need for self-definition while simultaneously attempting to achieve it (see Plate 3). Next to several small self-portrait drawings, Kahlo wrote, "The one who gave birth to herself" (Knafo, 2009b, p. 78). These stunning little portraits clearly indicate her identification with the mother. (See Chapter 7 for more on psychological mirroring.)

The work of art additionally can incorporate containing properties (Bion, 1959/1984). The poet patient mentioned earlier who was locked in a room by his mother clearly had a childhood filled with enforced isolation, trauma, and abuse. He responded to my suggestion that he try to write about his mother by writing a poem filled with profound longing, rage, and despair, evident from even these few lines:

> Then came the door, the door that would not
> open even when I had to piss, Mom, how could
> you, and the keyhole clogged with toilet paper
> so I could not see and the sheet stuffed beneath the

door so I could not hear, while the man with the
hatchet face became my next father as he hammered
you into the mattress all summer and the heat baked me
into a cinder … Even when I got out
I didn't. The room locked itself inside me and inside it
I still am, still enclosed now as an old man … All the
rooms I lived in after that, Mom, they were lifeboats,
intensive-care units, barrels thrashing over the falls …

After he wrote the poem, he rekindled what had been a very strained relationship with his mother. The poem, rooted in her solitary confinement of him, now contained all the toxicity of their connection, and could transform the trauma into images and connections he created and controlled. This new expressive relationship with his "created" mother helped free him to lessen his anger toward his actual mother. He told me:

As a kid I was terrified of being alone. She'd leave to go to the store, and I thought she'd never come back. She'd sleep and I was afraid she'd die. I hated my room. I hated being locked in. I hated being alone. Now I embrace my aloneness. It renews me. From it I draw out from myself that which is both beautiful and ugly. It is my aloneness in which I fully experience the terror of being a man with the wonder of being a man. If I couldn't be alone and create, I'd find it very hard to live.

Some artworks possess self-object properties (Kohut, 1971) and function in mirroring or idealizing capacities. American assemblage artist Joseph Cornell was a well-known recluse who worked in his basement from dusk to dawn creating his exquisite art boxes. He made boxes for women he admired from afar, like Lauren Bacall, Lois Smith, and many ballerinas. He was extremely shy and did not have the nerve to approach these women, so he sent his boxes in his stead. The boxes he created clearly functioned for him as self-objects, both representing the women he longed for and interacting with them in ways he could not (Salomon, 1997).

Thus, even though they are usually alone, artists are constantly talking to and creating for others, including, of course, a reader, a viewer, an audience. One writer described the interaction and overlap of solitude and relationality that takes place in creativity like this: "I am never alone (or lonely) when I write. When the going is good and the writing is white-hot, I am surrounded by my characters. They're huddled over my shoulders and around me, talking to me. That's one of the reasons I like to be alone: so I can hear them." The poet who was locked in a room explained:

Paradoxically, my inner life demands both the presence and the absence of others. Without them my experience is barren and stark. I need them to live, to love, and to feel. But I also need to retreat from them as well, to turn away and turn inward so that I may understand what I did and what happened to me when I was with them. They necessarily return me to myself, and my solitude necessarily returns me to them. I need to be with them and to not be with them, knowing that I am still alone when I am with them and still with them when I am alone.

Because solitude is often connected with isolation, abandonment, and death, most people, including artists, fear entering solitary spaces, experiencing painful emotions, or confronting difficult truths. Yet they do so because they hope that the risks will pay off. One poet described the fear that accompanies her transition into solitude:

> Going into solitude can be like snorkeling, which I always begin by reminding myself that I must now switch from nose breathing to mouth breathing, and that this will not make me drown. There is a moment of hesitation and discomfort, almost fear, as I make the change, before I can descend into the joy of being alone underwater with the magical contents to be found there.

Being "underwater" means being immersed in another world, leaving behind a familiar one; it also implies the risk of drowning. Adam Phillips (1993) claims that "the risk of establishing one's solitude is the risk of one's potential freedom" (p. 39), and we know that freedom is something most want to escape from (Fromm, 1941) but something many artists seek. Indeed, in order to gain access to such freedom, artists rarely create in the presence of others. Franz Kafka's fiancée once asked him if she could sit with him while he wrote, to which he replied:

> Listen, in that case I could not write at all. For writing means revealing oneself to excess; the utmost of self-revelation and surrender, in which a human being, when involved with others, would feel he was losing himself, and from which, therefore, he will always shrink as long as he is in his right mind ... That is why one can never be alone enough when one writes, why even night is not night enough. (Kafka, 1973, pp. 155–156)

Interestingly, Kafka's response not only speaks about the utter solitude needed to create what he did, the existential nakedness that gave rise to works like *The Castle* and *Metamorphosis*, but it also beautifully illustrates the regression needed for creativity.

The interplay of aloneness and relatedness brings to mind Ogden's (1994a, 1994b) conceptualization of a "third analytic space," created from projections and identifications of both the analyst and the analysand. As mentioned in Chapter 1, Ogden is referring to the co-creation of an inter-subjective space that transcends each individual and even the analytic pair. This third space, like Winnicott's potential space, is the space of creativity, the space where we discover and experience something new, where we transcend our own limits and knowledge. At the very least a third space can be constructed through the relationship with an assumed presence as an embodied act of imagination. The other is imagined as already being in relationship with the artist. From the interplay between the mind and the figure of fantasy emerge new thoughts and feelings, ideas and images, situations and fabrications. In the movie *Cast Away*, Chuck Noland, played by Tom Hanks, imaginatively transforms a soccer ball smeared with his bloody handprint into "Wilson," a friend whose presence comforts him and even saves him from utter madness from his enforced solitude. So real is this relationship, and the space for dialogue that it creates, that Chuck nearly drowns trying to "save" Wilson when "he" comes loose from the raft and falls into the sea.

In his book *The Invention of Solitude* (1982), Paul Auster beautifully portrays the intersubjective interaction taking place in the third space that exists between writer and reader:

> Every book is an image of solitude, the outcome of a great deal of time spent alone in a room. Literature is at once the product of an author's solitude and a means by which a reader reaches through his own and the author's solitude. In reading, an isolated individual becomes absorbed in something beyond his own preoccupations and communes with another mind ... It is possible to be alone and not alone at the same time. Reading literature creates a kind of companionship that preserves the solitariness of reading and writing. (p. 136)

Auster and the other artists I have quoted demonstrate that creative solitude is not necessarily an escape from the world but, rather, a different kind of participation in it.

BY HERSELF: WOMAN, SOLITUDE, AND CREATIVITY

> I am a writer who came from a sheltered life. A sheltered life can be a daring life as well. For all serious daring starts from within.
>
> —Eudora Welty

Solitude for women is different than it is for men. Evolution and biology have shaped culture to place the female primarily in the caretaking role, and she is expected to be the more social, communicative, and nurturing gender. Even feminist psychologist Carol Gilligan (1982) writes about the female's self-definition in terms of her relationships as opposed to the male's who finds his in independence and achievement. French feminist psychoanalyst Luce Irigaray (1985) has gone so far as to locate woman's relationality in her labial anatomy—lips speaking to one another!

It is true that solitude cannot be isolated from gendered, cultural, and historico-political contexts (Miller, 1992/1993). Its luxury has traditionally been linked to the wealthy and the upper classes whose resources of money and time lent access to books, education, and other forms of self-engagement. Solitude is also usually associated with men because of the independence and self-reliance implied by it—the privilege of the male, a rite of passage, a search for adventure and knowledge. The monastic tradition of leading a contemplative life while withdrawing from the mundane world has historically also been primarily a male prerogative.

Women in retreat, on the other hand, have been regarded with suspicion, perceived as dangerous or evil, a menace to society (recall the witch hunts), selfish, indulgent, irresponsible, neglectful of their duties as nurturers and caretakers, even miserable and pathetic (think of the spinsters, the old maids). Additionally, solitary women have been considered insane. Mr. Rochester's mad bride from *Jane Eyre*—hidden and locked in an attic—though nameless, has come to stand for the countless solitary women deemed mad by those around them (Gilbert & Gubar, 1979). Finally, the lone woman in old age is often presented as an ugly hag, horrifying and predatory. Emily Dickinson, who was a notorious recluse, is at times remembered more as an abandoned woman and invalid of love than as the great poet she was.

Are these dominant cultural images of female solitude reflective of a more profound problem in women? Anthony Storr's popular book *Solitude* (1988) never once mentions gender differences, and nearly all of his examples are taken from men. Philip Koch, author of *Solitude: A Philosophical Encounter* (1994), devotes a chapter to women and solitude, and concludes that two major obstacles block the path to female retreat: social norms and violence against lone women. Nancy Burke (1997) examines the psychological dimension of female solitude by applying the feminist psychoanalytic theories of Nancy Chodorow and Jessica Benjamin to explain why women may have greater difficulty developing the capacity to be alone. Burke argues that the mother's differential treatment of her daughters and sons results in greater difficulties for girls in the negotiation of separation and individuation. Accordingly, the bond between mother and daughter inhibits the development of strong self–other boundaries in the daughters, which makes it more uncomfortable for them to be alone. This discomfort is reinforced by cultural expectations that women be more social than men. Burke mentions borderline personality disorders and eating disorders as primarily female maladies, and ties them to the difficulty women have in being alone.

Yet women can break free of the group and find themselves by themselves. When they do, they subvert social stereotypes and cultural expectations, and challenge the idea of women as chiefly familial and relational beings. Women artists have even invented new words to describe female solitude, a state that involves nurturing of the self and of one's creativity. Alice Koller, author of *The Stations of Solitude* (1990), isolated herself in Nantucket for 3 months and created the words "loning," "singling," and "instasis" for "standing inside oneself, in full and rapturous control begotten in doing one's work" (p. 56).

Tillie Olsen wrote in her book *Silences* (1965) that most women writers have been unmarried and childless. Although this situation has changed since Olsen wrote her book, many women artists who are married with children, like author Ruth Setton, still have to steal moments from a hectic life to write, always in anticipation of interruptions, because "in a minute the door will burst open and a voice will cry, 'Mom, I'm home!' And I will wrench myself from [the writing world] while I return to the other world—the family world—where I am Mom and I have children and they need to eat and we're out of milk and I have to do laundry." Unsurprisingly, Setton adds, "Solitude is an aphrodisiac to someone who is rarely alone" (personal communication, March 18, 2009).

Women artists are solitary in another sense, too, because they lack lineage, a tradition of well-known and well-respected women artists who have made their mark in the art world (Miller, 1992/1993). Significantly, women artists have had to fight for the space and time in which to create, for education and recognition. In her famous article, "Why Have There Been No Great Women Artists," art historian Linda Nochlin (1971/1988) answers her own question by explaining that for centuries women were denied access to art education. When they were finally admitted to select institutions, women were forbidden to attend anatomy classes. When I interviewed feminist performance artist Carolee Schneemann, she told me about the isolation she felt upon encountering the exclusion of women artists in her art history studies:

> In my college years I was outraged by the linguistic masculinization of all texts: "Man and His Images," "The Artist and His Materials," "Every student will remove *his* car from in front of the art building." I was automatically a girl gender criminal, because I didn't think that "He must empty his locker" really meant me. At the same time my creative essence was also denied its erotic core: there was no female genital sexuality ... women's explicit sexuality belonged either to medical issues or to pornography. My lived experience was taboo, occluded. (Knafo, 2009b, p. 90)

Schneemann is best known for the instrumental role she played in launching nude female performance art in the 1960s and in advocating the validity of female sensual pleasure. She led the way for generations of women to literally put their bodies in their work.

Recent progress notwithstanding, women artists continue to struggle to be taken as seriously as male artists and to have their works exhibited in major museums and galleries. Many women seeking creative lives, like Virginia Woolf, feel the need to open a literal or metaphorical "room of one's own," a place of refuge and renewal, a crucible of interiority for delight, surprise, and transformation. Yet such a space, when not chosen freely, can be a prison, as in the case of French novelist, Colette, who was locked in a room by her husband and only allowed out when she had written the required number of pages. Her *Claudine* series, written under these conditions, was highly popular, but the author's name was her elderly husband's (Willy), not her own. Colette's case is another example of involuntary yet generative solitude.

Whether a room of one's own becomes a prison or a sanctuary naturally depends upon the circumstances, and we have seen that both have the potential to be generative. Virginia Woolf's "room" connotes a "stage for a single actor; a house of soliloquy; a studio of rich, internal echoes; a closet of expression; a safe cell for the incubation of ideas" (Malin & Boynton, 2003, p. 144). Author May Sarton wrote in her *Journal of a Solitude* (1973):

> I am here alone for the first time in weeks, to take up my "real" life again at last. That is what is strange—That friends, even passionate love, are not my real life unless there is time alone to explore and to discover what is happening or has happened. Without the interruptions, nourishing and maddening, this life would become arid. Yet I taste it fully only when I am alone here and "the house and I resume old conversation." (p. 11)

Sarton's house is her significant other, whom she names "Nelson," and refers to it as her bridegroom and host. Indeed, sometimes a woman's "love affair" with her home provides an alternative to a real person. Carolyn Heilbrun, famed author of the Amanda Cross mystery series, wrote in *The Last Gift of Time* (1997), "Solitude late in life, is the temptation of the happily paired; to be alone if one has not been doomed to aloneness is a temptation so beguiling that it carries with it the guilt of adultery, and the promise of consummation" (p. 11).

Heilbrun's observation points to changes that take place with age in woman's relationship to her solitude. Artist Erika Harrasch confessed that after her brother died when she was 10, she instantly became an only child and despised being alone. Many years later, when she became an artist, she began to enjoy her solitude. Harrasch calls her painting practice a

"Labrynthic Solipsism," a space that is alternately "peaceful, meditative, exciting, and energetic" (personal communication, December 18, 2009).

Storr (1988) writes of the increasing solitude that takes place in the "third period" of life and claims that as one ages, emotional dependency declines and one becomes preoccupied with internal concerns. The self-portraits of German artist Käthe Kollwitz represent a major psychological and formalistic shift as she grows old. In her own words, she went from being a "revolutionary to being an evolutionary" (Knafo, 2009b, p. 33). Whereas early self-depictions are of an ideological fighter, albeit one who is often forced to surrender to powerful external forces, later works focus on acceptance rooted in inner strength and faith. Storr explains the transformation that takes place with aging in terms of the individual entering a phase that allows the freedom to break free from attachments in preparation for loss and death. It is no surprise that as Winnicott (1988) aged, his attention to solitude increased and that the final essays of both Frieda Fromm-Reichmann (1959) and Melanie Klein (1963/1975) were on the subject of loneliness.

Koch (1994) claims that women's art possesses unique qualities because women require different strategies of disengagement than men. Indeed, there is a gendered connotation to spaces, a spatial particularity to women's imagination. Erikson (1968/1974) observed that the play of girls, unlike that of boys, is concerned with the creation of inner spaces, an interior well of resonance and being. Thus, women are not really strangers to solitude, for their bodies come with an inner space—the womb—the biological foundation for creation. The womb has its correlate in female experience as having space within for birth, both literal and figurative, a kinesthetic connection with a pulsing interiority rich with creative possibility.

Some thinkers remark on the highly personal quality in women's art especially obvious in self-representational art (Knafo, 2009b) and journal writing, a common form of female literary art (Buchholz, 1997). Between the covers of a journal is a set amount of pages, blank leafs that one fills with meaning, a textual offspring enclosed in white space. Anaïs Nin, famous for her journals, wrote: "Playing so many roles, dutiful daughter, devoted sister, mistress, protector, my father's newfound illusion, Henry's [Miller] needed, all-purpose friend, I had to find one place of truth, one dialogue without falsity. This is the role of the diary" (Moffat & Paynter, 1974, p. 14).

Writing in a diary represents permission for solitude and allows a private work for a private voice. Journal writing not only results in generative solitude; it also conveys the aesthetic aspects of women's daily lives. I would like to mention only a few of the better known works belonging to this genre. Most popular is May Sarton's *Journal of a Solitude* (1973), which offers an account of a feminist, lesbian, single child, writer, and poet. Sarton writes: "The fact that a middle aged single woman, without any vestige of family left, lives in this house in a silent village and is responsible only to her own soul means something" (p. 40). Annie Dillard's *Pilgrim at Tinker*

Creek (1974) brings us to the Blue Ridge Mountains of Virginia; Doris Grumbach's *Fifty Days of Solitude* (1995) takes us to Maine; and Sister Karen Karper's *Where God Begins to Be: A Woman's Journey into Solitude* (1994) describes six years in the West Virginia backwoods. (Karper and her husband later founded a newsletter for hermits called *Raven's Bread*.) Stephanie Mills' *Epicurean Simplicity* (2002) reflects upon a life of solitude and simplicity, and Jane Dobisz's *The Wisdom of Solitude* (2004) describes her 100-day experiment of solitude as enlightenment. All of these women, and many others whom I cannot name here, offer the kind of attention to detail and introspection particular to a female sensibility conversant with solitude. "By making my focus smaller and smaller," writes Dobisz, "everything is getting bigger and bigger" (p. 120).

SOLITUDE AND THE ANALYTIC SITUATION

Before turning to a brief case illustration where issues of solitude and journal writing were central, I want to say a few words about analytic solitude. The analytic encounter exemplifies the coexistence of solitude and relatedness. People often seek therapy because they feel painfully alone, anxious, and depressed, and because they cannot connect with others. In general, pain— both physical and emotional—tends to separate one from others and to foster the feeling of unwanted isolation. Furthermore, the patient who lies on the couch, though speaking to the analyst, is placed in a solitary state. In fact, this condition is meant to achieve some of what the artist's solitude does: a removal from the influences and demands of social interaction and a refocusing on the interior world. But the expressive component of analysis moves it from a purely private to a shared analytic space.

Analysts, too, confront solitude as they listen to endless stories that leave them questioning the meaning of their patients' lives, their lives, and life in general. The analyst is Sullivan's "participant-observer," the juxtaposition that comprises a paradox: engagement and disengagement, relatedness and solitude. The analyst simultaneously participates in the transference and countertransference while attempting to stand outside as an observer of the patient's and her own psychodynamics and defenses. In some cases, the analyst sits behind the couch, out of view, a solitary figure set in a singular personal space, attentive to the patient yet open to private reveries, so as to engage the patient on conscious and unconscious levels.

Warren Poland (2000) rightly observes that silently witnessing the patient's self-inquiry is a major part of the analytic process, and Charles Hanly (1990) states that genuine analytic work involves respect for the solitude of each person as he relates to himself. The analyst often feels alone and adrift in a sea of confessions; though the analytic relationship is deep and intimate, cracking open the patient's most private and personal inner landscape, it by necessity must exclude the analyst as a fully expressive individual.[1] Additionally, the analyst is forbidden to speak of these intense encounters due to confidentiality concerns. Indeed, it can be lonely work. At the day's end, the analyst may carry in her heart and to her home worlds of sorrow and loss, the angst of human existence along with its innumerable forms of pain. She will need time to reorient and return to herself and the world.

ECHOES OF SOLITUDE: A CASE STUDY

Liz is an attractive, assertive, intelligent, middle-aged woman who sought therapy because she found herself at a crossroads in life. Both she and her husband retired early from demanding professions in which they earned a lot of money and could, as a result, settle in New York City. Enthralled by the cultural possibilities offered by the city, Liz frequented the theater, museums, concerts, and continuing education classes. Her husband, on the other hand, preferred the adventure of being alone, holed up in his room with a hobby that he turned into a second profession. His reticence about journeying forth infuriated and frustrated Liz and became a site of intense conflict between them. She disliked being alone and wanted her husband to go out with her more. Additionally, she resented being his sole connection to the outside world. She became anxious when she did not have plans to do something with someone. Unsurprisingly, at the outset of treatment Liz expressed some discomfort with the unstructured nature of psychodynamic therapy because she tended to avoid solitary ruminations.

Liz challenged me from the start when she asked me about my background. She came from a family of Holocaust survivors and wished to know if I did too. I gently responded, asking her if she wondered whether I could understand her. Yes, she agreed, how could I understand her if I had no direct experience with the darkness and pain often associated with that situation? Later I realized how important it was for her to assess how alike we were. One day she expressed her delight at seeing us both dressed in the same color. Interestingly, Liz had a fraternal twin, Julia, from whom she felt painfully alienated despite their common background.

Liz was able to recognize some of her reasons for feeling anxious with me, and she efficiently and quickly got on with the business at hand. Why was she uncomfortable being alone? Why couldn't her husband be more

---

[1] Although it does seem that contemporary—especially relational and interpersonal—analysts are more apt to disclose personal feelings or experiences in sessions than was done previously, this does not, however, indicate that these analysts are less solitary in their work. We can be genuinely authentic as people and disclose when we feel it is helpful, but most of us do not open ourselves up in a way that we would with someone who is not a patient. Genuine communication does not preclude solitude.

like her? After all, isn't that what marriage was all about, sharing activities with one's partner? Why did he find it more desirable to steer clear of social gatherings in favor of his solitary pursuits? Was she avoiding something by keeping busy with friends and cultural activities all the time? If so, what was it? Was the thing she might be avoiding the very thing that wouldn't let her think about anything else when she was alone except how to get out of being alone? And, most important, why did she feel sad and have trouble getting out of bed of late?

To Liz's credit, she quickly relinquished her strong façade and willingly began to disclose her vulnerabilities. At times, her friends used her and even called her mean. Her mother and sister thought she was selfish for setting boundaries. Yet, she held fast to those boundaries because she felt both of them had exploited her, expecting help she wasn't always able or willing to give. Could they be correct? When she spoke of her childhood, Liz told me that both her parents had survived the Holocaust and experienced unbearable trauma. She quickly added, almost automatically, as if she'd said it many times before, "My parents never had a normal life or childhood. They didn't know how to raise a family or rehabilitate themselves." As the sessions progressed she repeated these thoughts, always immediately following them with "It wasn't their fault," or "I forgive them." Rather than find solace in her twin sister, Liz bore resentment toward Julia while refusing to acknowledge anger toward her parents.

I found most poignant the revelation that as a child Liz stole away from agonizing family fights and hid in the laundry room, a small white cubicle that became her safe haven. The laundry room, clearly a transitional space for Liz, became that space she both discovered and created (Winnicott, 1951/1975) to appease and nurture herself when her family could not. It was also a place associated with profound pain and sadness.

One level of Liz's fear of aloneness began to come into view. To be alone, for her, was equivalent to being huddled in the laundry room, tortured by tumultuous and painful memories—the shrill and bitter voices of her parents and sister—and yet struggling to find a way to care for and soothe herself. Ironically, the laundry room, a place of cleansing, became her only hope for renewal of spirit.

I began to conceive of the goal of treatment as one in which the laundry room, filled with its painful memories, would be replaced by the therapy room, a new space that could serve as a container for her sorrowful memories and provide her with novel ways to deal with them. Therapy could offer Liz a healthy possibility to know herself by herself. The treatment setting would become a model for a relationship in which we could each be present to the other while also able to maintain a comfortable sense of being alone.

I found it very interesting that Liz and I were thrown together by the fates. We are the same age and, under different circumstances, we would have become good friends. Like her, I love culture and have an immigrant background, and although I am not a twin, I was born on the same day as my sister. Yet unlike Liz, I am far from retiring and, although I enjoy my work very much, I experienced some envy at her ability to retire at such a young age. The most marked difference between us is that I have always found great comfort in being alone and value my solitude to the point of considering it a sacred space. We were two sides of a coin, a new type of twinship; perhaps we could enlighten each other. Only later did I realize that on a deeper level, the transference and countertransference contained mother–daughter dimensions.

In time Liz's trust grew, and she brought her first dream. Describing a dance, it was a metaphor for the intersubjective tango we were beginning to do together. She danced with her husband, a man who does not like to dance, after which she changed partners and danced with someone who was a perfect match. Liz felt in the dream, and in therapy, that she had found a fitting partner. She was opening up to her unconscious, to her past, and was in a budding collaboration with me and her treatment.

A few months later, Liz came in one day and announced that she was going to write her memoirs. "It will give me something to do when I am alone," she added. Knowing that she would now need to confront her past and her defensive stance—her "well-known tactic of walking away" from conflict and emotional pain—she also claimed, "I am ready." The following week, she shared with me some of the entries she had written. I always loved being read to, and so I sat and listened with pleasure as she read to me. I enjoyed learning more about her life and was impressed with her surprising facility with language, especially since English was not her mother tongue. Some of her writing depicted her early memories of growing up with limited resources and the shame that accompanied it. Other pieces had to do with her relationship with her mother. She shared a visit the two of them took to Auschwitz together and her mother's advice, "Enjoy life because you never know." It became clear that Liz felt pressured to live a life that her mother and father could not.

Liz described her mother as cold and detached. When she tried to approach her mother after the Auschwitz visit, to reach and soothe her with empathy and concern, the mother pulled away. Her father never spoke about the war (he lost his entire family), and when he was angry he'd stop talking to his family for weeks to express his rage. Unlike her father, Liz's mother spoke to her about her wartime experiences and even wrote a memoir about them that Liz shared with me. Liz reacted most strongly to the pain her mother expressed at being alone, the anguish of being separated from her own fraternal twin sister at age 14. I imagined how lonely Liz must have felt as a child in the face of her mother's coldness and her father's silence. I commented on how terrible both words and silence, imbued with trauma and destruction, might make being alone unbearable.

In one session, Liz read me what she wrote about her sister Julia. It turns out that Julia was born six minutes before she was, and that the two girls had experienced a close relationship until high school, when Julia's grades began to slip and she was held back a year. From that time on, Julia became the little sister who resented Liz for being more academically successful than she. The parents deepened this split because they compared Julia to Liz, constantly reminding her that she was not as smart, strong, social, or successful as Liz. Indeed, Julia was a troubled adolescent and adult. She lived with a chip on her shoulder and blamed Liz for all her shortcomings. Julia became Liz's albatross, a weight around her neck serving as a constant reminder of what she feared most: failure, conflict, and disconnection. As her twin Liz was Julia's perfect and awful mirror. In her writing, Liz explored her feelings toward Julia and, as she wrote, her understanding grew and so did her empathy.

Unlike Liz, her mother had enjoyed a mutually supportive relationship with her twin sister. Yet the girls were separated during the war, each hidden in different places to prevent discovery. As Liz recounted the story of her family, I began to question how much of her aversion to solitude might also have been passed down to her intergenerationally, unconsciously, and without words. Her parents were hidden children who needed to hide who they were, children for whom solitude meant separation from family and danger at being discovered. To be hidden, couched in darkness—and her mother was sometimes required to hide under a floorboard in a tiny dark space shared only with mice—to be separated from everyone and everything you loved, to tremble in exile, meant exclusion; it meant being a Jew; it meant trauma; it meant the constant threat of annihilation. Yet, solitude also meant one might survive!

I wondered what additional chain of events unfolding between Liz's parents and their children had repeated a drama of separation between Liz and her sister. It was fascinating how Liz and her twin became estranged at the same age that her mother and her twin had been separated. My making this connection brought to light the intergenerational transmission of trauma that had become imbedded in Liz's fear of being alone. Certainly Liz knew early on about what had happened to her family but, more important, the terror of the pursuit and potential annihilation of innocent family members formed the very parental context of Liz's young life; such was the atmosphere of her embodiment, absorbed by mood, identification, suggestion, and direction. She fled to the laundry room; this she knew, but she learned that she also fled that condition of senseless annihilation and loss.

Since her family and childhood friends lived in a distant land, Liz's search for constant company and friends "who replace my family" was one way she not only showed she was different from her parents; it was also her attempt to fill in the blanks of her silenced history, to inhabit the empty spaces left by all of those who had been murdered by the Nazis. "I like people around me," she was fond of saying, "It's like a security blanket." Yet, ironically, no matter how many friends she surrounded herself with or how many activities she took part in, Liz always felt like an outsider. She eventually wrote about her experiences of being an outsider, which began with attending a private, elite high school and studying abroad in Europe, and ending in her living and working in the American South. Being an immigrant myself, it was easy for me to relate to Liz's experiences of being an outsider. Immigration enforces a type of solitude on the transplant because the true sense of "home" is something one never quite recaptures (if one had it in the first place). Of course, immigrants, exiles, or those who experience social discrimination are often the most creative due to their unique perspective derived from detached observation. In *An Autobiographical Study*, Freud (1925/1959a) observed that the anti-Semitism he experienced while at the university was to prove important for him because it placed him "in the opposition ... of the 'compact majority,'" thus laying the foundations for "a certain degree of independence of judgment" (p. 9).

Each of Liz's parents dealt with solitude in a unique way. Liz's mother went out a lot, loved to dance and socialize. Like Liz, she complained about her husband who preferred to stay home. Liz described her father as a man who lived his life within the four walls of one small room, with his chair, books, and television. She spoke of his solitude with disdain, probably imitating her mother's contempt. Yet, when I questioned her about her father's inner world, she lit up and told me how he, unlike her mother, was able to discuss any topic under the sun. He loved politics and kept abreast of world events by reading three newspapers a day. Liz began to understand and accept the true scope of his experience in his physically circumscribed world.

Most enlightening was Liz's realization that her marriage in many ways replicated that of her parents. This frightened her and fueled her anger toward her husband whom she had married because she thought "he's different from my father." In fact, Liz's husband is a solitary type just like her father. He is also a constant reminder of what she must face: herself at last with no external buffers.

Liz's parents were unable to help her address the problem she inherited, that of senseless murder, unbelievable loss, and the specific forms of horror that shaped their lives. This dark world could be avoided but it could not be dismissed. It resided in Liz's very flesh; therefore, it needed to be made coherent, and its devastation somehow had to be mourned. What once seemed impossible has begun to be possible. This has been accomplished through Liz's writing, most notably in two moving entries she wrote on the ways her life has been influenced by each of her parents. Coming to terms with the past was also facilitated through her maternal transference to me. When she wrote in her journal, assembling her past, surely I was with her in a ghostly but potent form, standing behind her, reading as she wrote.

And when she brought her work to our sessions, I was again involved in a birthing process that helped her develop a richer and deeper subjectivity capable of incorporating her personal and historical reality.

As she has come to appreciate her connections to her family, Liz's solitude has gradually become more tolerable. It is no longer synonymous with irrevocable isolation and the imminent threat of annihilation. At the beginning of treatment, she filled her world with people and activities to fill a deep void in her. Now she has begun to realize the ways she has avoided dealing with loss—her own and that of her parents—and this has helped her to courageously let go of some others to whom she clung just for the sake of not being alone or feeling abandoned. She recently returned from a trip and told me that her best times were the daily two-hour walks she took alone on the beach. We still have work to do, but Liz is clearly on her way. Putting her life into words, both in therapy and in journal writing, has helped transform an anxiously filled emptiness into a generative creativity.

This chapter began by evoking the terrible, irreversible solitude suffered by Jean-Dominique Bauby, which he powerfully rendered in *The Diving Bell and the Butterfly*. Though most of us will never have to suffer the extremes experienced by Bauby, each of us incarnates those two sides of existence, the diving bell of solitude and the butterfly of imagination. And those experiences can be deeply expressed though artistic creation. Liz has begun a foray into the depths with her memoir writing, which uses the same powers that saved Bauby: memory and imagination. What she has shared with me has caused me to consider the layered complexity and reciprocal engagement of relationship and solitude.

Lacan (in Evans, 1996) believed that the end of an analysis should aim not for happiness, but for a patient's coming to terms with his or her utter solitude. Similarly, Quinodoz (1996) states that the developed capacity for solitude is often a criterion for termination. To this I would add that even when going alone we take all those we have known with us. When Liz and I part company, we will each go our own way, carrying the other inside.

Plate 1 Martha Posner, *Dancers for Boscobel* (2011). Honeysuckle vine, bamboo, and jute. Photo: George Paichas.

Plate 2 Pablo Picasso, *Bust of a Woman in a Hat* (1970). Musee des Beaux-Arts, Rennes, France. Scala/White Images/Art Resource, New York.

Plate 3 Frida Kahlo, *My Nurse and I* (*Mi Nana y yo*) (1937). Fundacion Dolores Olmedo, Mexico City, D.F., Mexico. Schalkwijk/Art Resource, New York. © 2011 Banco de México Diego Rivera Frida Kahlo Museums Trust, Mexico, D.F./Artists Rights Society (ARS), New York.

Plate 4 Bracha L. Ettinger, *Autistwork, n. 1* (1993). Courtesy of the artist.

Plate 5 Bracha L. Ettinger, *Untitled* (1988–1989). Sketch. Courtesy of the artist.

Plate 6 Charlotte Salomon, *Self-Portrait* (1940). Jewish Historical Museum Collection, Amsterdam. © Charlotte Salomon Foundation.

Plate 7 Charlotte Salomon, from *Life? or Theater?* (1940–1942). Gouache, 13 × 10 in.
Jewish Historical Museum Collection, Amsterdam. © Charlotte Salomon Foundation.

Plate 8 Charlotte Salomon, from *Life? or Theater?* (1940–1942). Gouache, 13 × 10 in. Jewish Historical Museum Collection, Amsterdam. © Charlotte Salomon Foundation.

Plate 9 Charlotte Salomon, from *Life? or Theater?* (1940–1942). Gouache, 13 × 10 in. Jewish Historical Museum Collection, Amsterdam. © Charlotte Salomon Foundation.

Plate 10 Charlotte Salomon, from *Life? or Theater?* (1940–1942). Gouache, 13 × 10 in. Jewish Historical Museum Collection, Amsterdam. © Charlotte Salomon Foundation.

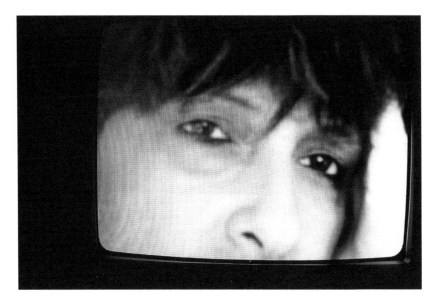

Plate 11 Michal Heiman, *Mirror Test* (2001). Courtesy of the artist.

Plate 12 Michal Heiman, *Michal Heiman Test (M.H.T.)* (1997), with Plate 15S (4). Courtesy of the artist.

Plate 13 Michal Heiman, *Michal Heiman Test (M.H.T.)* (1997), Plate 7. Courtesy of the artist.

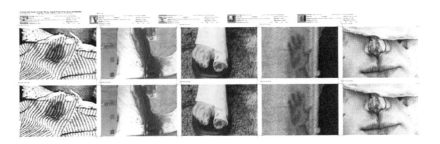

Plate 14 Michal Heiman, Blood Test, No. 4 (series A) (2002). Courtesy of the artist.

Plate 15 Michal Heiman, *3 May 1814–6 December 2001* (2002). Courtesy of the artist.

Plate 16 Michal Heiman, *Holding, no. 15* (2002). Courtesy of the artist.

Plate 17 Michal Heiman, *Holding, no. 13* (2002). Courtesy of the artist.

Plate 18 Michal Heiman, *Do-Mino (Clinging I)* (2004). Courtesy of the artist.

Plate 19 Egon Schiele, *Two Reclining Nudes* (1911). Watercolor and pencil on paper, 56.5×36.8cm. Bequest of Scofield Thayer, 1982 (1984.433.309). The Metropolitan Museum of Art, New York. © The Metropolitan Museum of Art/Art Resource, New York.

Plate 20 Egon Schiele, *Self-Portrait (Head)* (1910). Gouache, watercolor, and charcoal, 42.5 × 29.5 cm. Private Collection. Erich Lessing/Art Resource, New York.

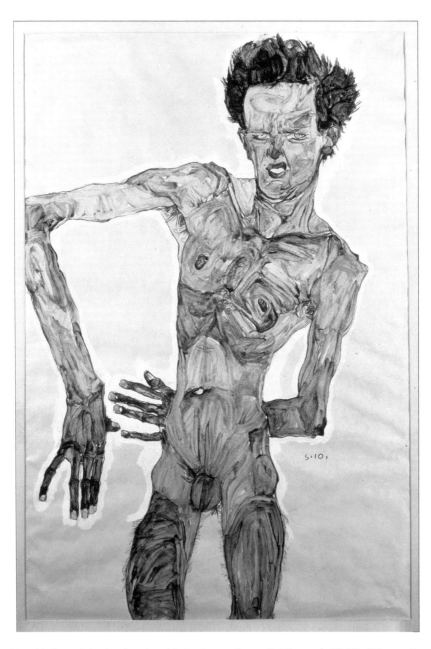

Plate 21 Egon Schiele, *Standing Nude, Facing Front (Self-Portrait)* (1910). Watercolor. Graphische Sammlung Albertina, Vienna. Art Resource, New York.

Plate 22 Egon Schiele, *Death and Man* (*Tod und Mann* or *Selbstseher II*) (1911). Oil on canvas, 80.5 × 80 cm. Museum Leopold, Vienna. Erich Lessing/Art Resource, New York.

Plate 23 Egon Schiele, *Dead Mother (Tote Mutter I)* (1910). Oil on wood, 32 × 25.7 cm. Museum Leopold, Vienna. Erich Lessing/Art Resource, New York.

Plate 24 Egon Schiele, *The Hermits* (*Eremiten*) (1912). Oil on canvas, 181 × 181 cm. Museum Leopold, Vienna. Erich Lessing/Art Resource, New York.

Plate 25 Egon Schiele, *Death and the Maiden (Man and Girl)* (1915). Oil on canvas, 150 × 180 cm. Österreichische Galerie im Belvedere, Vienna. Erich Lessing/ Art Resource, New York.

Plate 26 Egon Schiele, *Seated Couple (Egon and Edith Schiele)* (1915). Gouache and pencil, 52.5×41.2cm. Graphische Sammlung Albertina, Vienna. Erich Lessing/Art Resource, New York.

Plate 27 Egon Schiele, *Embrace (Lovers II)* (1917). Oil on canvas, 100 × 170.2 cm. Österreichische Galerie im Belvedere, Vienna. Erich Lessing/Art Resource, New York.

Plate 28 Ana Mendieta, *Tree of Life* (1976). Color photograph, 20 × 13¼ in. The Estate of Ana Mendieta Collection. Courtesy of Galerie Lelong, New York.

Plate 29 Ana Mendieta, *Untitled (Fetish Series)* (1977). Color photograph, 20 × 13¼ in. The Estate of Ana Mendieta Collection. Courtesy of Galerie Lelong, New York.

Plate 30 Ana Mendieta, *Untitled* (from *Silueta* works in Mexico) (1973/1991). Color photograph, 20 × 16 in. The Estate of Ana Mendieta Collection. Courtesy of Galerie Lelong, New York.

Plate 31 Ana Mendieta, *Untitled* (from *Silueta* series in Iowa) (1976/1991). Color photograph, 16 × 20 in. The Estate of Ana Mendieta Collection. Courtesy of Galerie Lelong, New York.

Plate 32 Ana Mendieta, *Untitled* (from *Silueta* works in Mexico) (1973/1991). Color photograph, 20 × 16 in. The Estate of Ana Mendieta Collection. Courtesy of Galerie Lelong, New York.

Plate 33 Ana Mendieta, *Untitled* (from *Silueta* series in Iowa) (1977), Ana Mendieta. Color photograph, 13¼ × 20 in. The Estate of Ana Mendieta Collection. Courtesy of Galerie Lelong, New York.

Plate 34 Ana Mendieta, *Untitled* (1980). Black-and-white photograph, 40 × 55 in. The Estate of Ana Mendieta Collection. Courtesy of Galerie Lelong, New York.

Plate 35 Ana Mendieta, detail of *Rastros Corporales (Body Tracks)* (1982). Blood on tempura paint and paper, 38 × 50 in. The Estate of Ana Mendieta Collection. Courtesy of Galerie Lelong, New York.

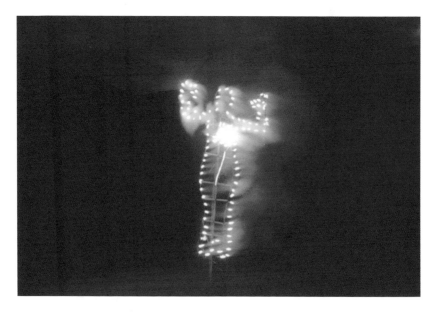

Plate 36 Ana Mendieta, *Ánima, Silueta de Cohotes (Soul, Silhouette of Fireworks)* (1976). Color photograph, 13¼ × 20 in. The Estate of Ana Mendieta Collection. Courtesy of Galerie Lelong, New York.

Plate 37 Bruno Schulz, *Jacob Flying* (c. 1935). Courtesy of Marek W. Podstolski, Köln.

Plate 38 Bruno Schulz, *The Pilgrims* (from *The Book of Idolatry*) (1920–1922). Courtesy of Muzeum Literatury im Adama Mickiewicza, Warsaw.

Plate 39 Bruno Schulz, *The Beasts* (from *Book of Idolatry*) (1920–1922). Courtesy of Muzeum Literatury im Adama Mickiewicza, Warsaw.

Plate 40 Bruno Schulz, *Two Naked Women and a Man (Self-Portrait)* (no date). Courtesy of Muzeum Literatury im Adama Mickiewicza, Warsaw.

The Psychoanalysis of Art

Chapter 6

Dreams of Genius

Sigmund Freud and C. G. Jung[1]

> Whenever I began to have doubts of the correctness of my wavering conclusions, the successful transformation of a senseless and muddled dream into a logical and intelligible mental process in the dreamer would renew my confidence of being on the right track.
>
> —Sigmund Freud

> The dream is a little hidden door in the innermost and most secret recesses of the soul, opening into that cosmic night which was psyche long before there was any ego consciousness, and which will remain psyche no matter how far our ego-consciousness extends.
>
> —Carl Gustav Jung

In the ancient world, genius was linked to divinity (Hirsch, 1931), and thinkers as late as Emerson considered genius to be an expression of the God within (Bloom, 2002). Indeed, genius invokes the extraordinary and the inspirational, the highest possibilities of mind and actuality, the root and bloodline of visionary expression. Whether in the realm of number, letter, or image—in the rarified atmosphere of the abstract or the iron firmness of the immanent—the elevated mind is capable of producing ideas that transform human life.

Both Sigmund Freud and Carl Gustav Jung were men of genius, trailblazers whose powers of imagination and reason allowed them to see what others did not. Freud, the father of psychology and psychoanalysis, created a completely innovative theory of the mind, which cited and analyzed unconscious processes underlying thought, memory, sexuality, and behavior. Freud's theory revolutionized our view of human nature and its application became a therapeutic technique for alleviating suffering. Psychoanalysis

---

[1] An earlier version of this chapter appeared in *International Review of Psychoanalysis*, 19(3), 1992, pp. 351–358.

uses the concepts of repression and transference and the techniques of free association and dream analysis to understand and address the unconscious. When one considers the edifice of Freudian thought, the comprehensive body of work produced by a single man, one stands in awe of his achievement. Jung was greatly influenced by Freud, though he eventually broke with him to elaborate an analytical psychology of his own with a focus on the self and its individuation. Jung believed in a collective unconscious that contains universal archetypes found in art, religion, myth, and dreams. He was the first to pay attention to changes that take place in midlife and, open to both Eastern and Western influences, he focused on the spiritual elements of life.

Among other things, genius is known for its capacity to extrapolate universals from particulars. Myers's (1907) theory of genius refers to the power of appropriating unconscious contents to serve conscious thought. Research clearly shows that unconscious mental processes help solve problems that require creative insight (Simonton, 1999). As mentioned in the introduction, all conscious thought depends on unconscious processes— parallel operations of the brain that form the basis of cognition, memory, intuition, and imagination. Freud and Jung realized that one of the key expressions of the unconscious mind occurs in dreams. Both also understood that it is primarily in dreams where the unconscious appears to speak of the deeper and often denied dimensions of thought and experience.

In dreams we find representations and elaborations in a symbolic code that expresses unconscious wishes, desires, and knowledge made available for conscious consideration and elaboration. We simultaneously dream our lives as well as live them consciously. Radically speaking, the two realms are equally important, two halves of the same whole, inseparable dimensions of mind and life. The mind of a great thinker is like any other mind, in that it must dream—but in the case of a genius like Freud or Jung, great thoughts will be disguised in unconscious representation.

This chapter will demonstrate how these two psychoanalytic geniuses dreamed their visions and, in fact, used those very dreams to shape their respective theories of mind. Normally, when two systems of thought are compared, one examines content, logical connections, historical context, influences, and so forth. In other words, they are compared rationally, logically, and consciously. Here I take a different approach by comparing these two systems of thought based on the dreams of their originators. As such these dreams express the particular idiom of each man's psyche as well as each man's system of thought. Such an approach allows us to think about their systems from the perspective of their dreams and how they themselves analyzed their dreams. The genius of their dreams is reflected in the genius of their thought and especially in how they themselves turned their thought to their own dreams and their dreams to their thought. Thus, we will also be paying attention to the irrational underlying the rational: symbolic order, hidden desire, and the errant and denied impulse. The interpretation of the dreams of Freud and Jung reveals the unconscious aspects of their genius.

DREAMS AND CREATIVITY

Dreams and their interpretation play a central role in the theories of Freud and Jung. For Freud the dream was the "royal road to the knowledge of the unconscious activities of the mind" (1900/1953b, p. 608). He insisted that dreams are not chance waste products of mental life but, rather, intelligible, even intellectual, human operations that have meaning and are capable of being interpreted. Freud believed dreams provide a persuasive challenge to the traditional supposition that psychic acts are primarily conscious. He understood dreams as the symbolic representation of the fulfillment of unconscious wishes, usually sexual and infantile in origin. He was interested in the dream's latent, unconscious content more than its manifest covering (1923/1961d), believing dreams to be disguised and therefore requiring decoding akin to cryptography (1911/1958a). Later (1920/1955), he added that some dreams express the unconscious attempt to master traumatic experiences. In all, Freud regarded dreams as involving a regression from motor to sensory channels of perception and to earlier (primary process) forms of thinking. In treatment, he believed dreams provide a perfect means to interest patients in the unconscious, to undo repressions, and to express transference aspects that are otherwise unverbalized (1900/1953b, 1923/1961d).

Like Freud, Jung considered the dream as a major avenue to gaining knowledge of the unconscious mind. Yet, unlike Freud, Jung did not believe dreams were deceptive but, rather, expressive and revealing. In his words, dreams are "impartial, spontaneous products of the unconscious psyche...[that] show us the unvarnished, natural truth, and are therefore fitted, as nothing else is, to give us back an attitude that accords with our basic human nature" (1933/1964, p. 149). Jung thought dreams serve a compensatory function, regulating the self by bringing to the surface repressed, neglected, and unknown elements. He saw the dream as helping to access archetypal symbolism from the collective unconscious. Whereas Freud believed dreams inform us about our past, Jung believed dream symbols possess the value of a parable by teaching and anticipating future directions.

The theories of both Freud and Jung reveal the unconscious mind, as represented in the dream state, to be active and imaginative in organizing conscious experience. Furthermore, both men used their own dreams to aid them in their respective self-analyses. It is significant that both Freud and Jung considered the works that contained analyses of their own dreams to hold their major creative discoveries. In *The Interpretation of Dreams* (1900/1953b),

Freud uses his dreams to both illustrate and give birth to his discoveries about the unconscious workings of the mind. Looking back at his accomplishments toward the end of his life, he claimed that his "dream book" was his most important work: "It contains, even according to my present-day judgment, the most valuable of all discoveries it has been my good fortune to make. Insight such as this falls to one's lot but once in a lifetime" (p. xxxii).

Jung also went through a period, between 1914 and 1930 (see *The Red Book*, 2009), during which he wrote about and drew images from his dreams, which led to his discovery of archetypes belonging to the collective unconscious. Toward the end of his life, he wrote:

> The years ... when I pursued the inner images, were the most important time of my life. Everything else is to be derived from this. It began at that time, and the later details hardly matter anymore. My entire life consisted in elaborating what had burst forth from the unconscious and flooded me like an enigmatic stream and threatened to break me. That was the stuff and material for more than only one life. Everything later was merely the outer classification, the scientific elaboration, and the integration into life. But the numinous beginning, which contained everything, was then. (p. vii)

Two dreams—one of Freud's and one of Jung's—demonstrate how the manifest content, with its use of imagery from the lives of these men, conceals a deeper, latent content derived from their unconscious minds and their childhood experiences. Both dreams are significant not only for revealing the way these men dealt with their childhood—including their Oedipal feelings—but also for indicating how resolutions to their own childhood conflicts found expression in their respective theories.

Incidentally, the dreams of geniuses sometimes directly lead the way to theoretical discoveries. German organic chemist Friederick Kekulé woke from a dream state in which he had a vision of a snake biting its own tail to discern the chemical structure of benzene. Niels Bohr conceived his model of the atom in a dream. The extraordinary mathematical genius Srinivasa Ramanujan claimed that a family goddess appeared to him in his dreams to give him whole formulas, which, upon waking, he would verify. Einstein, too, said that his theory of relativity could be traced to a dream he had in adolescence of riding a sled down a hill. When the sled accelerated until it approached the speed of light, stars became distorted and colors resplendent. He later said that his entire scientific career could be an extended contemplation of that early dream (Taylor, 1983).

No record exists that would present a similarly stark or obvious unconscious revelation in the dreams of Freud and Jung. Nevertheless, we will see how the theories of these two men are reflected in their dreams and how self-work with dreams shaped their theories. Fortunately, each man wrote associations to his dream, and these associations (Freud, 1900/1953b; Jung, 1961), along with other information known about them, will be applied in my own analysis of the dreams. Following are the two dreams under examination.

FREUD'S DREAM OF THE THREE FATES

> I went into a kitchen in search of some pudding. Three women were standing in it; one of them was the hostess of the inn and was twisting something about in her hand, as though she was making *Knödel* [dumplings]. She answered that I must wait till she was ready. (These were not definite spoken words.) I felt impatient and went off with a sense of injury. I put on an overcoat. But the first I tried on was too long for me. I took it off rather surprised to find it was trimmed with fur. A second one that I put on had a long strip with a Turkish design let into it. A stranger with a long face and a short pointed beard came up and tried to prevent my putting it on, saying it was his. I showed him then that it was embroidered all over with a Turkish pattern. He asked: "What have the Turkish (designs, stripes …) to do with you?" But we then became quite friendly with each other. (1900/1953b, p. 204)

Freud included this dream in a chapter of his opus on dream interpretation to help demonstrate how "long-forgotten experiences in childhood" become sources of a dream (1900/1953b, p. 204). He had this dream between September and October of 1898, following his summer holiday. Freud wrote that he went to bed "hungry and tired." He was most probably sexually excited as well (he and his wife had been separated for a time during his journey) because all of his "major vital needs" are present in his dream. Freud's dream has two parts. In the first, he enters a kitchen feeling hungry and wishing to eat. Three women are present, but one informs him he will have to wait to have his needs met. Narcissistically, and by implication physically, injured (castrated) by his exclusion and the necessity for delayed gratification, he sulks and leaves disappointed as in the typical Oedipal situation.

Freud offers many associations to this dream, popularly known as the dream of The Three Fates. The first association is to a novel he read at age 13. Although Freud cannot remember the title of the novel, Grinstein (1980) correctly designates it as *Hypatia*, a popular historical romance by the Reverend Charles Kingsley. In it a young monk is attracted to two women: Hypatia, an older, clever Greek teacher of philosophy who represents the good mother, and Pelagia, her beautiful erotic sister who belongs to someone else. A third woman in the monk's life is Miriam, the Jewish, sinister, bad mother figure. It is interesting to note in this context that Freud often mentioned that he had two mothers, his true mother Amalia, and his nursemaid, Teresa, who cared for him during the first three years of his life. This awareness even informed his analysis of Leonardo DaVinci's two mothers in his paper on the artist (Freud, 1910/1957a). Freud later called his dream a "hunger dream" and not coincidentally associated that "love and hunger meet" at a woman's breast. He even quotes a man who had been fed by a beautiful wet nurse as a child and later regrets not having taken full advantage of it. Freud's relationship to his five sisters is unknown; however, they, along with his younger brother and parents, lived in three cramped and, perhaps we can assume, not too private bedrooms. Since the incest taboo includes both mother and sister, Freud's dream, along with his associations, seems to relate to the significant and sexually arousing women of his childhood.

Philammon, the hero of *Hypatia*, does not go mad as Freud recalls (Anzieu, 1986, p. 364). His memory is meaningful nevertheless since it probably alludes to Freud's own notion of one of the outcomes that may befall a man who covets the forbidden women in his life. Another no less ominous outcome emerges from Freud's further associations to the three fates from Greek mythology: Clotho, who spins the thread of life for each mortal; Lachesis, who determines its length; and Atropos, who cuts it off. In his paper "The Theme of the Three Caskets" (1913/1958d), Freud viewed the fates as "the three forms taken by the figure of the mother in the course of a man's life": one woman bears man, another is his mate, and a third (death) destroys him. Associating to the present dream, Freud cites Shakespeare's lines from *Henry IV*, "Thou owest God a Death" which he misquotes as "Thou owest Nature a Death." Once more, Freud's mistaken recollection is noteworthy for he affirms, through it, that the covenant with woman—as Mother Nature—is a covenant with death.

Aside from his associations to the significance of the three women in his life, Freud's emphasis on the number three further indicates a meaningful allusion to the triangular Oedipal situation, a situation in which, according to his own theory, the incest taboo renders infantile sexual desires forbidden and punishable. Thus, although this scene takes place in the kitchen and supposedly deals with hunger (pudding, a milk-based food, is associated with the breast and female nourishment), there are many clues that suggest it is also concerned with sex. In particular, Freud's association to his childhood memory from the age of 6 of his mother rubbing her palms together can be understood as a screen memory for the primal scene, another central concept in Freud's theory: the child's observation of the parents during sex. His "astonishment at the ocular demonstration" which "knew no bounds" (1900/1953b, p. 205) suggests the shock of the young child who first perceives his parents having sex— the rubbing together of two bodies.

His mother, he says, taught him his first lesson—"that we are all made of earth and must therefore return to earth"—a lesson referring to humility and the ephemeral nature of human life, but also to the sexual knowledge he attained in the witnessing of the primal scene with its rubbing. The rubbing, as sex, is associated with the blackish scales of the epidermis, or dirt and anality. As Freud noted in his "Three Essays on the Theory of Sexuality" (1905/1953c), the child's first theory of where babies come from usually references the anus as the origin. Thus, the mother's rubbing produces not only dirt, but *Knödel*, or dumplings (i.e., babies). The rubbing can, of course, also refer to masturbation, which, in Freud's young mind, equally deserved punishment. Thus, as in the making of dumplings, the penis, when rubbed, grows erect.

Whereas the first part of the dream relates to women—who represent Freud's mother and sisters—the second part of the dream relates to men, and in particular, Freud's father. Having been rejected and disappointed by women, Freud turns to a world that promises to be more rewarding: the world of men.

Freud associates to Ernst Brücke, the German physiologist who, in Freud's words, was "the greatest authority that worked upon me" (Gay, 1988, p. 33). Brücke is the bridge between the two parts of Freud's dream, especially since the word *brücke* means "bridge" in German. Freud worked in Brücke's laboratory from 1876 to 1882, where he worked on the puzzles of the nervous system, first using fish and then humans. Brücke, who was 40 years older than Freud (nearly his father's age), was clearly a paternal figure and mentor to Freud. After Brücke died in 1892, Freud named his fourth child, Ernst, after him.

In Freud's mind, however, Brücke represented more than a kindly mentor. In his *non vixit* dream, for example, he recalls Brücke's unforgettable "piercing look." He says, "No one who can remember the great man's eyes, which retained their striking beauty even in his old age, and who has ever seen him in anger, will find it difficult to picture the young sinner's emotions" (Freud, 1900/1953b, p. 422). The "young sinner" in this dream is Freud, and Brücke, as father, is a powerfully admonishing man who becomes converted into Freud's own conscience.

The male "stranger" in the second part of the dream is, therefore, most probably a reversal for a man with whom Freud was actually quite close: his own bearded father. The overcoats that Freud wishes to wear consequently possess multiple meanings. To begin with, the first overcoat is too large and the second has a long strip (penis) like the long face of the stranger; by implication both belong to the father, for whom they would be a more suitable fit. Second, the father (recall Brücke's look), the rightful owner, prohibits Freud from wearing them. Third, the first overcoat may represent the mother's "fur-trimmed" vagina that is also too large for the young boy's genitals. Finally, the overcoat, with Freud's fish bladder (*fischblase*) association, of course, also could refer to the male contraceptive sheath or condom, used when having sex with forbidden women.

Several men's names come to Freud's mind and continue the theme of food and nourishment: *fleischl* means "flesh or meat," and *knödel* means "dumplings." Reminded of his teachers at the Institute of Physiology where he spent his "happiest hours," Freud's oral and sexual needs for his mother become displaced and sublimated into higher learning in the company of men. Fleischl was a colleague whom Freud introduced to cocaine to treat his morphine addiction. Freud considered cocaine a miracle drug because it "removes hunger." Fleischl injected the drug and suffered from terrible hallucinations and seizures, which Freud witnessed and was traumatized by, partly because he felt guilty for the part he played in Fleischl's suffering and eventual demise. In his associations to an earlier dream, he wrote: "I had been the first to recommend the use of cocaine, in 1885, and this recommendation had brought serious reproaches down on me. The misuse of that drug had hastened the death of a dear friend of mine" (Freud, 1900/1953b, p. 111). It is not surprising, therefore, that it is here Freud stops his associations, stating "I must desist at this point because the personal sacrifice would be too great" (p. 206).

Freud continues associating along other lines, however, and makes much of the use of common names that appear in his dream. He states, "My own name had been the victim of feeble witticisms ... on countless occasions" (Freud, 1900/1953b, p. 207). Indeed, Freud, which means "joy" in German, seemed to mark him out for the pleasures of the flesh. We learn from Freud that Goethe claims one wears one's name like a skin, and Freud's skin, by implication, is pleasure, which many might believe fits him like a glove. *Freudenhaus* or *freudenmädchen* ("house of joy" and "girl of joy") means whorehouse and whore, and further suggest that the scene in the kitchen could very well be one that takes place in a brothel. In his dream associations, he recalls a joke Herder played on Goethe's name: "Thou who art the offspring of gods or of the Goths or of dung." Both references to Goethe refer to the lesson Freud's mother gave him and echo her demonstration of our origin from the earth, dirt, and even dung. Freud paraphrases Goethe's Iphigenia from *Iphigenia auf Tauris*: "So you too, divine figures, have turned to dust!" (1900/1953b, p. 207, n. 3). Indeed, upon witnessing the primal scene, with its anal connotations, Freud's disillusionment with his godlike parents began, and his own identification with his "filthy" origins became inescapable. Like the skin (skin = epidermis), his name, and the condom, Freud's sexual desires are born, and the relationship between sex and death is established. So too is the hidden admonishment not to take himself—despite his godlike abilities—too seriously, for he too will die as all humans do.

Freud recalls his wife making a purchase in Spalato, which reminds him of another that took place in Cattaro, both towns on the Dalmatian coast. He remarks that he had been "too cautious" in Cattaro, again echoing the theme of wasted opportunity. Freud's sexual thoughts are forbidden, and acting upon them with women—his mother, sister, even prostitutes— results in punishment or *catarrh*, inflammation of the mucous membrane. He makes a great deal of catarrh in the case of Dora (Freud, 1905/1953a), where he interprets it as her identification with her syphilitic father (p. 82).

In "The Psychical Mechanism of Forgetfulness," which Freud wrote in 1898, the year of his dream, he mentions an incident that seems to be the one he alludes to in the present context. Traveling with a man after separating from Martha, who because of gastric disturbances had gone to recuperate in Merano, Freud enters into a scintillating discussion about Turks. With some bewilderment he notes that Turks make sex a top priority in their lives and, once again, he connects sex with death by recalling a man who killed himself upon learning that he was suffering from an incurable sexual disease. Freud associates to Turks in the present dream by recalling the first purchase his wife made in Spalato: she bought "Turkish stuffs." The name Popović comes to his mind too as a word that contains papa and refers to backside—*popo*—in childish German language. The Turks mentioned in the dream are also associated with their anal sexual positions. Thus, the father, the Turks, and the catarrh all represent potential punishment for sexual misbehavior.

Freud's dream, then, reveals his internal conflicts regarding sex and his sexual life in particular. While, on the one hand, the dream warns of punishment for his "childhood naughtiness" (Freud, 1900/1953b, p. 207), on the other hand, his further association revels in the hedonistic slogan, *carpe diem*, which Freud is sure to mention includes a sexual meaning. As he states, "One should never neglect an opportunity, but always take what one can even when it involves doing a small wrong. One should never neglect an opportunity, since life is short and death inevitable" (1900/1953b, p. 207). Thus, it appears that consciously, Freud was in favor of taking advantage of a sexual opportunity because life is short and death inevitable. Unconsciously, however, he was afraid that doing so might be punishable by death.

One of Freud's associations refers to plagiarism, the appropriation of something that belongs to someone else. This association also links the two parts of the dream. Wanting something (drive gratification) from his mother in the first part, he turns to take something belonging to his father (the coats) in the second. As plagiarist, Freud desires his mother whom he knows belongs to his father. Another meaning of plagiarism relevant at the time of Freud's dream concerns his troubled relationship with Wilhelm Fliess. Freud may have been feeling guilty for "borrowing" Fliess's theory on the universality of human bisexuality (Grinstein, 1980, p. 164). Indeed, the dream, with its first part illustrating a heterosexual theme and its second part a homosexual one, is itself an example of the bisexual theory in its wishes—both active and passive—for both sexes. Indeed, there are two overcoats, the first trimmed with feminine fur and the second with a long, phallic strip, again perhaps illustrating Freud's bisexual leanings as well as his and Fleiss's theory.

This is an exemplary dream that demonstrates Freud's desire for an adequate and complete resolution to his Oedipal conflict. In it we observe the Oedipal conflict symbolized. We also see its repressed desires encoded in its imagery. Following an expression of sexual longing for the mother related to having witnessed the primal scene, threats of exclusion, postponement, and punishment flood Freud's chain of associations. It is the father, as "stranger" and true possessor of the overcoats, who enters in the second part of the dream as the source of the threat to the boy. (He challengingly questions: "What have the Turkish (designs, stripes ...) to do with you?") Rather than engage in a conflict with the father/rival, in his dream Freud makes peace with the man. Thus, the dream ends with the words: "But we then became quite friendly with each other." The "but" here is significant. As in his theory of the Oedipal conflict, Freud realizes that he cannot take his place with his mother and submits to his father. He thus renounces his claims on the incestuous object of his desires and, instead, identifies with his father, with whom he leaves in peace and friendship. He ends his associations with the solution of "restraining thoughts of every kind and even threats of the most revolting sexual punishments" (1900/1953b, p. 208). Freud's psychic solution is to repress his desires and sublimate them into intellectual pursuits. His final words reveal nostalgic longing for a time when such diversion from his needs was easier, "a time when the dreamer was content with *spiritual* food" (p. 208).

JUNG'S DREAM OF THE HOLY GRAIL

I had dreams which presaged the forthcoming break with Freud. One of the most significant had its scene in a mountainous region on the Swiss-Austrian border. It was towards evening, and I saw an elderly man in the uniform of an Imperial Austrian customs official. He walked past, somewhat stooped, without paying any attention to me. His expression was peevish, rather melancholic and vexed. There were other persons present, and someone informed me that the old man was not really there, but was the ghost of a customs official who had died years ago. "He is one of those who still couldn't die properly." That was the first part of the dream ...

The dream had not reached its end with the episode of the customs official; after a hiatus came a second and far more remarkable part.

I was in an Italian city, and it was around noon, between twelve and one o'clock. A fierce sun was beating down upon the narrow streets. The city was built on hills and reminded me of a particular part of Basel, the Kohlenberg. The little streets which lead down into the valley, the Birsigtal, that runs through the city, are partly flights of steps. In the dream, one such stairway descended to the *Barfüsserplatz*. The city was Basel, and yet it was also an Italian city, something like Bergamo. It was summer-time; the blazing sun stood at the zenith, and everything was bathed in an intense light. A crowd came streaming towards me, and I knew that the shops were closing and people were on their way home to dinner. In the midst of this stream of people walked a knight in full armor. He mounted the steps towards me. He wore a helmet of the kind that is called a basinet, with eye slits, and chain armor. Over this was a white tunic into which was woven, front and back, a large red cross.

One can easily imagine how I felt: suddenly to see in a modern city, during the noonday rush hour, a crusader coming towards me. What struck me as particularly odd was that none of the many persons walking about seemed to notice him. It was as though he were completely invisible to everyone but me. I asked myself what this apparition meant, and then it was as if someone answered me—but there was no one there to speak: "Yes, this is a regular apparition. The knight always passes by here between twelve and one o'clock, and has been doing so for a very long time (for centuries, I gathered) and everyone knows about it." (Jung, 1961, pp. 163–165)

Jung had this dream in 1910, while working on his book *Wandlungen und Symbole der Libido (Symbols of Transformation)*. He describes it as one of several dreams he had which "presaged the forthcoming break with Freud." The first part of Jung's dream takes place on the Swiss-Austrian border, a "mountainous region" signifying the conflicted nature of the relationship between the Austrian Freud and the Swiss Jung. Freud is depicted as an old, weakened, stooped-over customs official who "couldn't die properly." Much as he would like to get rid of Freud, and much as he weakens him in his dream, Freud's power remains great and does not cease to haunt Jung.

Jung had a very ambivalent relationship with his father, a poor country parson, who is frequently described by Jung in his autobiography in pathetic terms—like those referring to the Freud dream figure. On one occasion, Jung wrote that he had the most "vehement pity" for his father in whom he saw "the tragedy of his profession and his life" (1961, p. 55). He explains how much of his youth was spent questioning his father's religious beliefs, a process that ended in his losing respect for his father. On the other hand, Jung reveals a strong early attachment to his father; the two even shared the same bedroom (p. 18). Jung began the account of his life by noting that for him, "Father ... meant reliability," but he adds "and—powerlessness" (p. 8).

Interestingly, Jung describes the break in his relationship with his father: "An abyss had opened between him and me, and I saw no possibility of ever bridging it, for it was infinite in extent" (1961, p. 55). Following his father's death, Jung wrote that he "took his place inside the family" (p. 96). Revealing his guilt over this Oedipal triumph, Jung suffered from repeated dreams of his father coming back to haunt him as Freud does in the present dream. He wrote then, "I reproached myself because I thought he was dead. Later I kept asking myself: 'What does it mean that my father returns in dreams and that he seems so real?'" (pp. 96–97). Could Jung be denying his death wish for his father as he tries to deny his death wish toward Freud when he defensively claimed: "I could find no part of myself that normally might have had such a wish" (p. 164).

Freud, as customs official, suggests the role Freud played in examining Jung's (unconscious) baggage, revealing potential contraband, items made illicit and uncontrolled once they illegally cross borders. Jung not only kills off Freud, as father figure in the dream, but he also alludes to trying to illegally appropriate things from him, things he should not possess, hence the customs check. Certainly these might be some of Freud's key ideas as well as the homoerotic feelings Jung may have harbored for Freud.

Like Freud the "plagiarist" who borrowed from Fliess, Jung borrowed heavily from Freud's theories and made them his own—most significantly the universality of the unconscious, a subject on which he was writing a book at the time. Interestingly, these two men, known for their originality and creativity, feared being found out as frauds. Indeed, creativity and even genius never takes place in a vacuum, and, therefore, the "anxiety of influence" (Bloom, 2002) often exists in the adoption and reworking of others' ideas. In this case, Jung states that in the border examination, "unconscious assumptions are discovered" (1961, p. 163). In his book, as in his dream, Jung tries to transcend Freud's theory of the individual unconscious by expanding its contents to include mythological material. Perhaps part of Jung's anxiety refers to his dreaded anticipation of Freud's reaction to his amendment. He writes, "I alone logically pursued the two problems which most interested Freud: the problem of 'archaic vestiges,' and that of sexuality." He argues that sexuality did indeed play an important part in his theory but that he wishes to "investigate ... its spiritual aspect and its numinous meaning, and thus to explain what Freud was so fascinated by but was unable to grasp" (p. 168).

The second part of the dream, therefore, can be read literally as revealing the contents of Jung's unconscious baggage, most notably his unacceptable wishes concerning Freud, and on a more latent level, his father. Jung is justified in describing the latter part of the dream as "the more remarkable part," since it deals with deeply repressed fantasies and wishes. The essence of Jung's wish is his desire to overshoot the dying/dead Freud/father by becoming a knight in shining armor, perhaps like Sir Galahad, who surpassed his father, Lancelot, in the quest for the Holy Grail and, in doing so, discovered a special power to heal. The kinesthetic dynamic in this dream is significant. The knight is ascending the steps while Jung is descending them. He and the figure are coming toward each other as they move in opposite directions. Here we have the collision of the personal with the mythical, the absorption and salvation of the individual by the universal, and the ascension of life as a result.

Jung associates the second part of his dream to his interests in the Crusades of the 12th century. When he was 12 years old, he was traumatized in a cathedral square, apparently the same one in Basel described in the dream. He was shoved by a boy, fell, and hit his head and subsequently developed fainting spells for which he was excused from school for some time afterward (Jung, 1961, p. 30). During this period, he spent his time drawing battle pictures and war scenes. As in his imaginary childhood games, Jung reverses the painful reality in his dream. He is now protected and ready for battle. Years later in Basel, where Jung attended his father's university and joined his father's fraternity, intense feelings of competition arose: "In Basel I was stamped for all time as the son of Reverend Paul Jung and the grandson of Professor Carl Gustav Jung ... I could not and would not let myself be classified ... the pressure of tradition was too much for me" (p. 111).

Thus, Basel is the city that for Jung evokes feelings of battle and competition. Jung's father, who attended the University of Basel before him, was in Jung's opinion, "a Ph.D. but *merely* a philologist and linguist" (1961, p. 76, emphasis added). Jung juxtaposes his special powers and brilliance with the dying father whose "days of glory are ended" (p. 91), and with the Jewish founder of psychoanalysis whom he positions at death's door as well.

Jung did not deny the fact that he had a father complex. In *Civilization in Transition* (1964), he wrote, "I also admit my so-called 'father complex'; I do not want to knuckle under to any 'fathers' and never shall" (p. 540). Indeed, Jung rejected the traditional religious dogma of his father only to replace it with a new belief system (yet one that also contained mystical elements). It is interesting that Jung eventually rejected Freud's atheism as he had previously rejected his father's religion, seeking instead to become the "father" of a theory involving archetypes.

In the first part of the dream someone tells Jung the custom official is a ghost. In the second part, it is only a "voice" that tells him about the eternal purpose of the knight. It is possible that Jung is here referring to the voice of God. Transferring his father complex onto his psychoanalytic mentor, Jung once told Freud, "You are dangerous competition, if one wants to speak of competition" (Gay, 1988, p. 227). Both Jung's son and wife recognized Jung's father complex with regard to Freud. His son Franz keenly observed,

"Father was very disappointed in his own father, and ... he became very critical of everything Freud said as he had not believed in his own father. He had a negative father complex, and he brought it to his relationship to Freud" (Donn, 1988, p, 98). Jung's wife, Emma, similarly commented in a letter to Freud, "Carl was waiting for your opinion ... with some trepidation. Of course this was only a residue of the Father Complex" (Donn, 1988, p. 138).

Jung's associations to the second part of his dream reveal a self-perception as a crusader on a difficult and perilous quest. He identifies with Christ (who was resurrected from the dead), perhaps even with his ability to see beyond—the insight of genius. Jung is reborn between 12 and 1 o'clock as the knight in shining armor who emanates light. Unlike the primal scene association to the visual in Freud's dream, for Jung, the visual "apparition" is emphasized to demonstrate that only he has the power to see what others do not. Seeing and being seen are condensed, and he is the revealer of the "great secret" (Jung, 1961, p. 165). Thus, from the legend of the Holy Grail emerges Jung's appreciation for universal investigations: "My whole being was seeking for something still unknown which might confer meaning upon the banality of life" (p. 165). His lesson is given him by an unseen someone (God) in the words: "Yes, this is a regular apparition ... for a very long time ... everyone knows about it."

In Jung's dream, both the customs agent and the knight are apparitions. As a child, Jung was known to have had visions. In fact, he had one when he was 12 that may well be the source of this dream. While he was crossing the Münsterplatz in Basel he was struck by the sun's brilliance on the cathedral's rooftop. He pushed away a sinful thought that caused him anguish for days to follow. Finally, he concluded that God wished him to have a vision of God defecating on the cathedral and smashing it. Jung then experienced a sense of bliss and was convinced he had come in touch with the "direct living God, who stands omnipotent and free above the Bible and Church" (Jung, 2009, p. 194). Jung distinguished this direct and immediate experience of a living God from his father's God. For Jung, his father's religion and church had become a place of death.

Jung's associations to religion and Christianity abound. First, he identifies with the Crusades, whose aim was to aggressively spread Christianity. Indeed, Jung is dressed for combat in his Oedipal confrontation. He does not wear a Turkish embroidered coat like Freud. Instead, he is dressed in full armor to defend himself and protect himself from potential attacks. The red cross he bears represents the organization, founded in Switzerland, aimed at relieving human suffering. The red cross on a white background is also the reversal of the Swiss flag, a white cross on a red background. Clearly Jung's Oedipal conflict is viewed by him as a battlefield and he, representing Switzerland, Christianity, and newly discovered healing powers, is prepared to fight it out with Freud, who stands for Austria, Judaism, atheism, and classical psychoanalysis (and, of course, his father). Like Galahad who breaks up the knights of the Round Table, Jung, Freud's favored son, perceives himself as breaking up Freud's "disciples" and finding his own path; he would not be a mere follower. Importantly, Jung attributes a great significance to the motif of hero in the book he was working on at the time that he had this dream. In this work he writes, "The hero represents man's unconscious self. This appears empirically as the sum total and the quintessence of all archetypes, and thus, it also includes the type of the 'father,' that is, the wise old man. In this sense the hero is his own father, and begets himself" (Wehr, 1988, p. 36). Eliminating the real father in both theory and dream, Jung as hero became responsible for his own creation.

Thus, Jung's dream is also an Oedipal dream that includes elements of both past and present. The first part refers to the real friction that existed between Freud and Jung at the time of the dream. The second part reveals his unconscious wishes and motivations that are discovered, as it were, by the border police. What we find are grandiose wishes on Jung's part to kill the father, take his place, and outshine him. Jung's wish acknowledges the need for confrontation, and, therefore, he is dressed to kill and protected from anticipated attack. The father figures are weakened, yet they do not cease to haunt him; his moment of glory is thus far limited to one hour a day. But that hour is also the hour of the day's greatest power. It symbolizes the hour of the hero, even the hour of God, a drama played out again and again, and one that must fall to the night/knight. This is a drama known to all, recognized by all people (future ghosts), yet enacted only by few of them.

DREAMING THE REAL

There are many similarities and differences in the dreams of Freud and Jung. Both have two distinct parts that are clearly differentiated from one another. Both deal with the psychic interplay of three stages of life: adulthood, puberty, and childhood. Both demonstrate how infantile—here, Oedipal—material reverberates throughout one's life and becomes reactivated in one's dreams and, in this case, in the dreamer's theories.

For Freud, current preoccupation involved his rivalry with Fliess. Pubertal interests were demonstrated in the book he remembered with its incestuous theme. Childhood concerns led back to his maternal longings and the observation of the primal scene. The witnessing of the primal scene evoked strong desires in Freud that he repressed due to paternal prohibitions and guilt. Freud's Oedipal conflict found resolution in his dream—as it did in his theory—with the boy renouncing his sexual longings for his mother and submitting to, and identifying with, his father.

For Jung, the current preoccupation involved his rivalry with Freud. This rivalry echoed his earlier feelings toward his father. Pubertal interests were evidenced in his visions of God as well as his fascination with legends of the Crusades and the quest for the Holy Grail. Childhood concerns similarly involved Jung's witnessing of the primal scene as an "apparition." At age six he went to a museum in Basel with his aunt wanting "to look at everything carefully." He found himself standing before naked statues, marveling at their beauty. His aunt pulled him away, saying, "disgusting boy, shut your eyes!" (Jung, 1961, p. 16). This memory could be a screen memory for primal scene exposure, which initiated Jung into the world of sexuality.

As with Freud, Jung's dream, on all three levels, deals with his attitude to the Oedipal conflict. Unlike Freud, Jung perceives the Oedipal situation as a battleground where he refuses to submit and, instead, oversteps the father and even emerges as hero. Whereas Freud wears a jacket too large for him, Jung wears a suit of armor. Each man carries the defense of childhood into adulthood and into his theory. While Freud and his theory remain steeped in immanence—in the body, in biology, in the earth, in history—Jung takes to the skies, seeking transcendence in the form of archetypes, synchronicity, and integration. Freud dreams of dumplings and disguised parents and overcoats that are too big for him. Jung dreams of a ghost official who cannot die properly and a knight, brilliant with noon light, ascending a staircase. Freud's dream reflects the conflict between pleasure and death. His resolution involves the curbing and prohibition of instinctual drives, the renunciation of the pleasure principle, and sublimation as a consequence of the acceptance of the reality principle, as represented by the father. When he writes about the artist Leonardo da Vinci he might be writing about himself:

> He had merely converted his passion into a *thirst* for knowledge; he then applied himself to investigation with the persistence, constancy and *penetration* which is derived from passion, and at the *climax* of intellectual labor, when knowledge had been won, he allowed the long restrained affect to *break loose and to flow* away freely, as a stream of water drawn from a river is allowed to flow away when its work is done. When, at the *climax* of a discovery, he could survey a large portion of the whole nexus, he was overcome by emotion, and in *ecstatic* language praised the splendor of the part of creation that he had studied, or—in religious phraseology—the greatness of his Creator. (Freud, 1910/1957a, pp. 74–75, emphasis added)

Of interest is Freud's use of sexual metaphors when describing da Vinci's creativity, indicating Freud's perspective on the genius's sublimation of sexual needs.

Jung, on the other hand, asserts that behind the real father stands the archetype of the father and that "the predominating influence of the father's character in the family often lasts for centuries" (1909/1985, p. 230). Thus,

Jung's dream symbols include those from religion and history, which he strongly believed possess the power to transform him into a mythic hero, albeit one for whom the Oedipal conflict is kept alive until his father, as shadow, is conquered. When Jung describes the creative process, one can easily discern his own:

> The creative process, so far as we are able to follow it at all, consists in the unconscious activation of an archetypal image, and in elaborating and shaping this image into the finished work. By giving it shape, the artist translates it into the language of the present, and so makes it possible for us to find our way back to our deepest springs of life. (1922/1971, p. 321)

The personal factors that paralleled and gave rise to elements in Freud's and Jung's theories might tempt one to discredit the universality of the theories. Certainly, with time, each theory has been shown to be limited in its generalizability. Yet, this is true of all philosophical and psychological theories. The theorist makes the great leap of thought and leaves it to his or her followers to iron out the details, and to elaborate and modify its contributions. Indeed, creativity can never be divorced from its creator, since it consists in the ability to make something universal from something personal.

Chapter 7

Egon Schiele

A Self in Creation[1]

I want to tear into myself, so that I may create again a new thing which I, in spite of myself, have perceived.

—Egon Schiele

So many young girls! Nymphets—naked, undressing or fetishistically flaunting their stockings and shoes, masturbate when alone and embrace when together (see Plate 19). Though childlike in their simplicity, they deftly strike erotic poses reminiscent of adult pornography. Some express hesitancy or shy embarrassment by hiding their eyes. Others face forward, daring one to voyeuristically behold their private pleasures. Still others gently close their eyes to reveal the sleepy aftermath of sexual fulfillment. Genitals are exposed. Labia are exaggerated and drawn in obsessive detail. Color is sometimes added to accentuate sexual desire. Engorged nipples and lips shine in bright red hues. White auras produce an electric effect. An arm grows redder as it approaches swollen, spread fingers burning for touch. Patches of color blend into one another, signaling excitement as they travel across the body.

By 1912, such visions of childhood sexuality proliferated in the ouevre of Austrian Expressionist artist Egon Schiele (1890–1918). In these drawings, Schiele repeatedly demonstrates that innocence and lasciviousness exist side by side. At the turn of the century, Freud shocked the scientific community with his theories of infantile sexuality. For years afterward, he was accused of being a "Viennese Libertine" who engaged in "mental masturbation" and encouraged perversity and illegitimacy (Gay, 1988). It did not take long before the same straight-laced society that denounced Freud would also accuse Schiele of a crime.

---

[1] The content of this chapter first appeared in Knafo, D. (1993). *Egon Schiele: A Self in Creation: A Psychoanalytic Study of the Artist's Self Portraits*. Rutherford, NJ: Fairleigh Dickinson University Press.

Schiele's oeuvre is replete with depictions of androgynous, masturbating Lolitas, emaciated trees, uninhabited towns, and people in bizarre poses. Even more telling are his convulsing, gyrating, amputated, castrated, nude self-portraits. Schiele's work can easily be understood as containing a statement about the culture in which he lived. It mirrored *fin-de-siècle* Vienna's sense of fragmentation and doom, and unmasked the hypocrisy of its superficial values. Karl Kraus, the fierce Viennese polemicist, described *fin-de-siècle* Vienna as "an isolation cell in which one is allowed to scream" (Comini, 1974, p. 3). Schiele's numerous portraits depict him and others in an environment akin to Kraus's isolation cell, and his images were very much a response to and a symptom of his social reality. As one of the first to cultivate an art centered on the self, Schiele, like his contemporary Sigmund Freud, revealed the face of modern man. Just as a number of Freud's major discoveries grew from his self-analysis (*The Interpretation of Dreams* discussed in the previous chapter), so did Schiele's art become a vehicle for self-expression and self-exploration. Through his confessional self-portraits, Schiele laid his life out on canvas and embarked on an analysis as deep and ruthless as Freud's analysis of himself. The individual, the subjective, and the psychological became the focus of Schiele's work, as well as the vehicle through which he achieved that focus. His compelling explorations of his own psychic depths, primarily through repeated, merciless confrontations with his identity, sexuality, and mortality, paralleled the growing concerns of psychoanalysis at that time.

Yet, when one carefully analyzes Schiele's art, with particular emphasis on his self-portraits, one readily discerns its intimate relationship to his life experiences as well as the historical period to which he belonged. Two sets of events were crucial to Schiele's life and art. A failed mirroring experience with his mother during the formative stages of his self-development led to his anguished sense of fragmentation and disintegration and the subsequent obsession with his own image. (He produced more self-portraits than Rembrandt and Van Gogh combined.) Additionally, his brooding preoccupation with sex, death, and masculinity were shaped by the sexual origin of the disease responsible for family deaths, including those of his four siblings and, most important, that of his syphilitic father, who perished paralyzed and completely insane.

As a consequence of these adverse childhood experiences, Schiele struggled throughout his life to find his lost parents in himself and his lost self within his art. Art substituted for the missing and needed objects, and his perpetual employment of self-portraiture constructively attempted to master his losses. In his quest he underwent a regression that eventually aided reintegration, by deconstructing his self-image in order to reconstruct it anew (see Chapter 2 on regression in art). Schiele employed his art as a corrective emotional experience (Alexander & French, 1974), whereupon he repeatedly nurtured, and ultimately repaired, a battered psyche.

THE MIRROR

The mirroring experience provides the child with his first sense of identity, which initially means body identity (Lichtenstein, 1977, p. 215). The mother as primordial mirror interacts with the infant, especially in its feeding and nurturing experiences. As Winnicott (1971b) viewed it, the infant, by looking into the mother's eyes, experiences the first awakenings of identity; he emphasized "the mother's role of giving back to the baby the baby's own self" in early visual contacts (p. 118). Decades of microanalytic research (Beebe, 2003, 2000; Beebe & Lachmann, 2002; Stern, 1985, 1995) examining face-to-face patterns of interaction confirm the importance of visual interplay between mother and child in the child's social and cognitive development. Specifically, mother's attuned gazing, smiling, and cooing reflect back to the baby a positive image/feeling of self. Affectionate, need-oriented, and timely communication locates the baby in a happy and safe space that becomes synonymous with his own body and sense of self. A mother's loving mirroring literally *assembles* the child's self and prepares the child to self-regulate emotion and attachment on his own.

Interestingly, Freud (1912/1958b) compared the analyst to a mirror: "The doctor should be opaque to his patients, and, like a mirror, should show them nothing but what is shown to him" (p. 118). Winnicott (1971b) and Kohut (1971, 1977) further emphasized the importance of mirroring in psychoanalytic psychotherapy. Kohut cited mirroring as an invaluable source of transference for the narcissistic patient. By acting as a confirming reflection of the patient's own grandiose infantile fantasies and needs, the analyst validates the patient's self-esteem and, gradually, by means of a selective process involving the development of increasingly tolerable frustration, restrains these fantasies within more reasonable limits. Kohut also believed that the patient might experience the analyst as part of himself or as a twin or alter ego, sharing similar thoughts and feelings. Alternately, he might experience the analyst as a separate person but seek to become the gleam in his analyst's/mother's eye. Finally, the analyst often becomes idealized by the patient, and the patient, in turn, internalizes these idealized features through association. We shall see that all of these types of transference are evident in Schiele's use of his parental figures or their substitutes in his art.

As noted in previous work (Knafo, 1993) and in Chapter 2 of this volume, the same search for self that takes place in the mirroring reciprocity between mother and infant, and between analyst and patient, is often undertaken by artists in the creation of their works. The structure of art, by establishing preordained limits within which the artist must work, provides a more concrete dimension to the mirroring experience. In particular, the self-portrait is an apt, almost self-evident, means by which an artist acts as a mirror to himself, simultaneously reflecting his need for self-definition and his attempt to achieve it. Like the witch in the story of Sleeping Beauty

("Who's the fairest?") or Alice peering into her looking glass, Egon Schiele repeatedly searched in his mirror for the answers to a series of questions aimed at knowing himself.

When the mirroring experience is unempathic, distorted, negative, or absent, or if there is, in Spitz's (1965, p. 134) words, a "derailment of the dialogue" between mother and infant, then the child's own existence becomes negated, and he develops a disturbance in his primitive self-feeling. According to Lacan (1949/1977), a failure in the mirror phase results in the infant's sense of body fragmentation, which he calls *le corps morcelé* (the dissected body). Faulty mirroring may result from the mother's own self-involvement or her depression.

Schiele's mother simply could not give him what he so desperately needed. She was too miserable and depressed and in deep need of parenting herself as revealed by her own statements: "I suffer—I did not deserve this! ... because of the children I am forced to lead such a miserable life ... I need somebody, who will firmly take care of me" (Nebehay, 1979, p. 133). She had little appreciation for her boy's talent, becoming enraged at him for using up an entire sketch pad in one day and then burning his drawings in the oven. He wept over the destruction of his creations, which he had proudly displayed, and his mother's obvious contempt for his work (p. 39).

Schiele's statements are full of references to his mother's absent or negative responses: "[My] mother is a very strange woman ... she doesn't have the least bit of understanding for me and unfortunately not much love either" (Roessler, 1948, p. 21); "My mother, every time I saw her, gave me reproaches, nothing else" (Nebehay, 1979, p. 64).

Schiele tried his hand at poetry and, unsurprisingly, titled many of his poems "Self-Portrait." Seeking verbal expression for what his paintings portrayed, he painfully reiterated the stunting effects his early experiences had on him (as cited in Whitford, 1981, p. 95):

> I, eternal child—
> I sacrificed myself for others ...
> who looked and did not see me ...

His poetry abounds in mirroring imagery (Schiele, 1988, p. 18):

> Everything was dear to me—
> I wanted to look at the angry people
> with loving eyes,
> to make their eyes do likewise; ...
> and the children
> who looked at me with big eyes
> and rewarded my looking back with caresses ...

Schiele is known to have had a unique relationship with mirrors. He never passed one without stopping to closely examine his reflection, and the single piece of furniture he took with him everywhere he went was a large mirror that, ironically—because in a sense it became a substitute for her—originally belonged to his mother. To repair the damage he felt, Schiele turned to his mirror, which, as a transitional object, facilitated his separation and individuation from his mother. It was no longer she whom he needed; now he had an object that was both mother and not-mother. Thus, through his mirror (and the mirror of his art), he would express himself and heal himself *all by himself*. He once wrote to his mother, "I have only myself to thank for my existence" (Nebehay, 1979, p. 266). Clearly, such a statement, though flying in the face of biological fact, nonetheless expresses a psychological truth; he felt profoundly neglected by her and had only himself to heal himself.

Finally, Schiele made numerous portraits of his mother in which her glance noticeably turns downward or to the side, always avoiding eye contact; many of these portraits are in profile and most show her either blind or dead (see Plate 23). Thus, in his art he reenacted her absence and neglect while providing himself with the feedback of his own past, a feedback that he later shaped and controlled. As artist in control of his craft, he attempted to convert passive grief into active mastery.

MOURNING

Because the child's early self-image is structured through the mental representations of key figures in his world, the loss of one (or more) of these figures is often experienced as actual body loss. To lose a loved one, especially early in life, is to lose part of one's own being, both in its mental and physical dimensions. Psychoanalysts have investigated the effects of parental loss on depression and creativity. Melanie Klein (1929/1979a) viewed the reparative work of the infant's depressive struggle as the source of all artistic creativity. Anzieu (1986) and Pollock (1975) address the long list of artists, writers, and scholars who were orphaned or abandoned as children. Pollock explains how the mourning process serves as an avenue for self-creation: "Through the immortality of the … aesthetic creation, the mourning process can come to conclusion" (p. 338). The mourned object is never relinquished but, rather, remains immortal in psychic life and is reincarnated in the manifold transformations of art.

As I have already noted, Schiele's father's syphilis physically devastated family members, and the sight of his father's progressive mental and physical deterioration over his final 3 years haunted Schiele throughout his brief life. His survivor guilt with regard to his siblings' deaths created additional problems, including fear for his own death and a feeling that his life was purchased at the cost of others. More important, his longing for his father never disappeared, and his hunger for object replacement took the form of an unending series of father surrogates. His relentless self-searching (and searching for the father in himself) is evident in his art—whose major motifs are sexuality, insanity, and death.

Despite the continuous nature of Schiele's self-obsession, his depictions of himself varied in important ways, evident in both his style and subject matter. In fact, his self-portraits reflect the changes that took place in his psychic organization, particularly in the development of his sense of self and object relationships. To better understand these alterations and transitions, I have divided his career into four phases. Each phase expresses an important shift in Schiele's relationship with his past, particularly with his losses incurred through his neglectful mother and syphilitic father, and beautifully illustrates the coping strategies expressed in his art. Before we look at these phases, however, it is necessary to review some aspects of Schiele's childhood.

CHILDHOOD

Egon Schiele was born in Tulln, a small provincial town on the Danube River, about 18 miles west of Vienna. His father was a stationmaster of the town, and the family lived over the railroad station, which proved to be a convenient location for young Egon, who spent his early years intently gazing at, sketching, and recording the comings and goings of the various trains he observed. His paternal grandfather had been a railway builder and inspector, and his uncle and godfather Leopold Czihaczek, who later became his guardian, was also a railway engineer. Of course, Egon was expected to follow in the footsteps of the men in the family. That his mother desired this is evident from a short biography she wrote of her son in 1927, in which she recalls her dislike for what she thought was a waste of her young son's time, his constant drawing, "because Egon should have studied instead to become an engineer one day, our most ardent wish" (Kallir-Nirenstein, 1966, p. 47). Indeed, Schiele loved trains, and it is notable that the only picture of him smiling is one in which he holds a toy train; later in life he even enjoyed riding trains with no particular destination in mind. Egon did not become an engineer or a railway official or, for that matter, anything remotely connected with railways. He longed only to be an artist and revealed a prodigious drawing ability from early childhood. An introverted child with dark, penetrating eyes and unruly hair, Egon spent every waking moment drawing. If his family was unprepared to acknowledge his gifts, he seemed desperate to nurture his own personal assessment of himself as a *Wunderkind*.[1]

---

[1] Biographical information on Schiele's life is taken from Alessandra Comini (1974) unless otherwise indicated.

On examining photographs of Schiele's family during his early years, one is struck by the fact that no one smiles. Furthermore, there is a sense of sadness and disconnectedness among all family members, who are in physical proximity but apparently worlds apart, each looking in a different direction, and all showing signs of inward reflection.

While growing up in Tulln, Egon's preferred companion was his younger sister, Gertrude ("Gerti"), born in 1894. The siblings watched the family hens together and kept exact records of their breeding times. This voyeuristic activity reflects something of the erotic nature of Egon's relationship with his beloved sister, who eventually modeled nude for him. At a time when Freud was busy formulating his theory of infantile sexuality (1905/1953c), Schiele wrote of the painful feelings his sexuality caused in him:

> Have adults forgotten how they themselves were incited and aroused by sex impulses as children? Have they forgotten how the frightful passion burned and tortured them while they were still children? I have not forgotten, for I suffered excruciatingly from it. (Roessler, 1948, p. 33)

For 4 years Egon attended elementary school in Tulln, where he remained friendless. Since Tulln had no secondary school, he was sent to the nearby town of Krems to complete his studies. Separated from his family and his cherished trains, the 11-year-old boy was entrusted to the care of a strict landlady who rarely permitted him to leave the house. His despair over this situation probably contributed to his eventual departure, when he went to live with an army officer's widow. The solitude, loneliness, and alienation that he experienced at that time soon permeated his early self-portraits. He naturally sought within for that which he was unable to find without.

In 1902, Adolf Schiele's syphilis entered its terminal phase, gradually turning him into an invalid. This state of affairs worsened over the last 3 years of his life, forcing him into an early retirement and creating a dismal financial plight for the family. Consequently, the family moved to Klosterneuberg, where Egon joined them. Deepening economic difficulties and embarrassments related to the father's increasingly bizarre behavior resulted in four more moves in Klosterneuberg. Comini (1974) describes the deteriorating mental condition of Egon's father and the family's reaction to it:

> The family had to adapt to the unpredictable presence of imaginary visitors—railroad inspectors and other dignitaries whom the father often produced, introduced and invited to stay for dinner. Out of compassionate complicity the family entertained these invisible guests and ceased to show surprise. (p. 11)

Like the Vienna they lived in, the Schiele family remained steeped in denial, refusing to openly acknowledge the destructive and uncontrollable forces at work. Instead, they all became actors in a mad drama directed by someone who had lost touch with reality. The unstable and morbid atmosphere of illness and madness in which Egon lived produced a profound and long-term effect on him. His grades suffered; he was 2 years older than his classmates because he had to repeat classes. As he felt his father slipping away, Egon sought ties with the first in a long series of father surrogates. His art teacher in Klosterneuberg, Ludwig Karl Strauch, was the first to recognize and encourage his artistic talents.

PHASE I: TWO MEN (1905–1909)

It is significant that Schiele turned to self-portraiture following the death of his father and his change of status, as the only male in an otherwise female household. No longer having an adult male model with whom to identify—and his memories of his father were of an emotionally and physically handicapped man—Schiele needed to reaffirm his masculinity and intactness and grieve his losses; thus he turned to self-representation. Only days away from the 1-year anniversary of his father's death, he offered his first oil painting, a self-portrait, to a friend, Edward Weber; on that same day Schiele wrote a poem, originally to his father, in Weber's album (Leopold, 1972, p. 517). This initial self-portrait depicts Schiele in profile with his head lowered in contemplation or sadness. More than simply mourning his father's death, Schiele was mourning for himself.

Schiele painted this first self-portrait in 1905 and began his studies at the Vienna Academy of Fine Arts in 1906 when he was only 16 years old. His self-portraits during his early academy years attest to a manifest growth in his self-esteem, which was largely attributable to the pride he took in his newly legitimized identity as artist. Schiele's clothing, rather than his empty facial expression, conveys his identity. His quest for an inner psychological identity had not yet begun. The props (e.g., palette) and accessories (e.g., beret, cravat) stand in as "good enough" substitutes for him.

One such "prop" involved Schiele's adaptation of Klimtian techniques (e.g., *Jugendstil*'s emphasis on colorful ornamentation) in his art. Gustav Klimt was the greatest Viennese painter of that time and leader of the Secessionist Movement, one determined to break with Austria's prevailing conservative and traditional art. Klimt came to represent the opposite of what the Academy of Fine Arts stood for and Schiele, like Klimt before him, eventually abandoned his studies there. It is believed that Schiele sought out Klimt in his atelier to ask for his opinion on his work. Coming face-to-face with the bearded master who characteristically dressed in a long caftan and sandals, Schiele handed him a portfolio of his art and simply asked, "Do I have talent?" After inspecting the contents of the portfolio, Klimt is reported to have responded, "Yes, too much!" (Comini, 1974, p. 21). From that day onward, a deep friendship developed between the two men. Klimt, 28 years his senior, became Schiele's most significant father figure and, indeed, Schiele would enact with the grand painter the many struggles and conflicts he'd been unable to express directly with his own father.

In *Two Men with Halos* (1909), Schiele portrayed himself with Klimt, both men bearded and wearing long robes. Klimt is shorter and his caftan is decorated with circular scribbles, perhaps referring to his signature decorative style. Schiele, the taller of the two, is dressed in a long black robe as he presents Klimt with a large white sheet. Although he is paying homage to his mentor here by representing their first encounter, Schiele is also beginning to assert his dominance over Klimt. The heart-shaped halo surrounding the men's heads does not eclipse the ambivalent, Oedipal struggle and rivalry emerging in their friendship. Toward the end of this phase, Klimtian curves are replaced with Schiele's sharp angles, and dramatic poses are accentuated by sharp outlines. Schiele's "pretty boy" self-portraits begin to give way to deliberately unflattering, naked, and emaciated portrayals of himself. In this phase of his life Schiele is beginning to define himself as an artist and to provide himself, through his art, with an identity denied to him by his upbringing. That Klimt confirmed him as a talent enabled Schiele to press on with his most difficult journey of self-creation.

PHASE II: SELF-SEER (1910–1911)

The years 1910–1911 mark the development of Schiele's singular artistic idiom. He decided to leave his family's home in order to live alone, as well as leave the academy. Without the framework of his family, the academy, or Klimtian style, he was on his own both personally and artistically for the first time. The Klimtian style of portrait, which glamorizes, decorates, and disguises the sitter, gave way to Schiele's innovative and uneasy exploration and exhibition of a self laid bare. In his struggle to establish a separate identity, he experienced a profound crisis, reflected in the number of disturbed and disturbing self-portraits that he created during this period. When asked why he drew such ugly representations of himself, he responded,

> Certainly: I have made pictures which are "horrible"; I do not deny that. But do they believe that I like to do it in order to act like a "horror of the bourgeois." No! This was never the case. But yearning too has its ghosts. I painted such ghosts by no means for my pleasure. It was my obligation. (Comini, 1974, p. 51)

Indeed, most of Schiele's self-portraits were produced during this time, and they stand unremitting in their horror and ugliness and, therefore, remain the most interesting from the psychoanalytic perspective of his use of art as a mirror (see Plate 20). It is as if he were asking his spectators to engage in a reciprocal relationship patterned after the one he had with his mother, testing the limits of whether he is lovable even—or especially— with his wounds. Floating heads with expressions of angst and horror, clawlike hands, amputated limbs, emaciated torsos, skin transparencies, and human screams that get lost in a vacuum abound in Schiele's art from these years. The artist is utterly alone and thoroughly exposed, both phys- ically and psychically. There is no background in these works. Schiele's figure stands alone, and its body contortions and facial grimaces are inten- sified by the expressive force of his brittle, angular lines. His watercolor derives from these powerful linear rhythms; almost as an afterthought, colors follow, igniting the spaces opened by firm, black-chalked contours, producing independent forms that express mood and emotion. Purples and blues evoke a sense of spreading decay in a disintegrating body; oranges, reds, and whites produce the effect of fevered rage or passion about to flare up and explode.

Standing Nude, Facing Front (Nude Self-Portrait, Grimacing) (1910), a typical self-portrait of this period, shows Schiele's nude, gaunt, rib-exposed body posturing in the center of a void (see Plate 21). His face is contorted in a grimace; his eyes squint with terror and rage; and his mouth sneers, gnarled and twisted. His thick hair stands on end as if electrified. While his arms and hands are not amputated here, as they are in so many of the self-portraits of this period, they are nevertheless extremely long and useless; they only serve to exaggerate an already bizarre and unnatural pose. The elongated fingers form multiple V-shapes, suggesting vaginal symbolism. One hand's thumb is pressed together to gain entry into the other hand's V-shaped fingers, cre- ating a symbolic intercourse. The reddish-blue colors used for flesh tones produce the effect of raw meat and intimates underlying internal organs as well. He is castrated and yet filled with sexual anguish. A strong outer line delineates body boundaries and is surrounded in turn by white paint that creates a nimbus-like aura around him. By transforming himself into an ugly, hateful, yet radiant image, Schiele expresses his disgust toward himself as well as anger at the hated parts of his parents he internalized (Fairbairn, 1943/1952). And by manifesting this in his art—his psycho- logical state, his woundedness, and trauma—he could also separate himself from it while controlling its expression.

One might wonder why tortured works like this one are great art. Despite the self-destructiveness apparent in Schiele's art of this phase, his self-portraits always remain on the side of life. They are explosively potent and vital despite their fragmentation and castration. They are filled with energy, rage, and potential because they are uncompromising in their self- searching. In the name of his heroic task of self-recreation, Schiele spared neither himself nor his image. Although his art indicates an undercurrent of menace and disequilibrium, it never became psychotic art. One obvious aspect of his genius lay in his ability to visually combine diametrically opposed possibilities. Thus, whereas the content of a particular work may reveal malignant forces, its composition generally serves to unite those elements that have been destroyed. What is missing in one part of the painting is often found, if only symbolically, in another. For example, the absence of Schiele's penis is often compensated for by the representation of his entire body as a penis. Rigid and upright, armless and topped with a head, he becomes an enormous phallus, the penis he lacks—a *phallic man*. By showing damage and repairing it at the same time, Schiele was able to achieve a sense of psychological wholeness through even his most butchered self-portraits. Furthermore, he transformed a distressing personal reality by creatively reshaping it into a universal theme: modern man's search for identity.

Schiele's choice of the frontal position in most of his self-portraits of this phase is significant, since it is one rarely employed in artists' portraits. Francis O'Connor (1985) writes about the healing function frontal self-portraits possess for artists in times of crisis and transition. The artist faces the viewer in a direct and opened posture, one of maximum exposure, allowing the greatest degree of encounter and therefore containing the greatest possibility of reparation. Schiele's emphasis on the face, hands, and genitals in these works is also a sign of his desperate struggle to establish a separate identity at this time, since these three body parts are the most crucial for the development of a unique and differentiated body self (Greenacre, 1971b). Furthermore, the eyes and hands are indispensable to the visual artist who devours the world with his eyes and uses his hands to control and recreate what he perceives. In his self-portraits, Schiele's eyes both seek mirroring and invite punishment for what they have seen: mad decompensation and death of the syphilitic father and cold, dismissive eyes of the corpse mother. He often squints with one eye (the German word, *schielen*, means "to squint"), and his hands are elongated and manneristically posed to satisfy his needs, all of which help create an idiosyncratic signature for himself and his art.

Though terrified and overwhelmed by his sexual and aggressive impulses, Schiele desperately longs for human contact. He gazes with a rigidly fixed stare into the eyes of his painted face as well as the eyes of his viewers as he dares them to enter his self-created world and feel what it is like to be in his skin. Schiele certainly derives satisfaction from his ability to establish a connection with spectators by provoking in them strong reactions to his art. At times he attacks his viewers as he did himself, both demanding and receiving validation.

The Double

The fragmentation he experienced from 1910 to 1911 was so great that Schiele even began to draw split-off parts of himself in double and triple self-portraits. Setting himself free from Klimt's influence and feeling himself cut off by another father figure, his guardian/uncle Czihazcek (who refused to take further responsibility for Schiele owing to his unconventional lifestyle and demanding behavior), Schiele reexperienced the profound reaction to the loss of his own father. As a result he dealt with primitive yearnings in which he brought his father back to life as his double. Otto Rank's (1914/1971) study of the double shows how the "idea of death ... is denied by a duplication of the self" (p. 83). Schiele's double self-portraits, which he titled *Self-Seer*, illustrate Kohut's twinship transference as he faced his father's and his own death while simultaneously rendering them both immortal.

In these and other paintings, Schiele either glorified or gouged out his penis, the very physical appendage that caused him so much pain. The provocative hide-and-seek game with his genitals reflects the artist's power in treating reality as plastic material for him to shape as well as his ambivalence vis-à-vis his sexuality. Autoerotic excitement is transformed into guilt and shame and ultimately culminates with castration as its unavoidable punishment—again demonstrating the tension between unbridled sexuality and moral restraint. Touching and caressing himself on canvas with his phallic brush, Schiele transforms his art in 1910–1911 into a form of autoerotic masturbation. It is as if he realized that only by coming to terms with his sexuality could he achieve a true sense of identity.

The inevitable consequence of Schiele's revival of his father from the dead was the need to scrutinize his own identity, to question the ways in which he resembled his father, and to determine whether his penis was doomed to become a diseased death-dealer like his father's. Expressing his deepest anxiety, he exclaimed; "I carry the seeds of decay within me" (Nebehay, 1979, p. 263). Schiele's double self-portraits became vehicles through which he attempted to buttress his masculinity. But in the end the double became the enemy itself, the *doppelgänger*, the specter of death come to claim the living (see Plate 22). All that remained in Schiele's final double portraits of this phase was a mask, an x-ray, a skeleton of a self (e.g., *The Self-Seer/ Death and Man*, 1911).

Schiele's double portraits with his father as alter ego possess multiple meanings. The first, *Self-Seer* (1910), clearly emphasizes self-perception and self-awareness. The second, *The Prophet* (1911), displays a visionary and ghostlike quality. The third, *Death and Man* (1911), has a double meaning: his second self protects him from mortality but also becomes a persecutory object that both symbolizes and threatens death.

Dead Mother

Although he brought his father back to life as his alter ego in his double self-portraits, Schiele busily kills his mother in a series of "Dead Mother" portraits (1910–1911). Schiele felt the wrong parent had died, and one function of his art sought to correct this painful reality. Schiele's idealization of his father stood in inverse proportion to his demonization of his mother; she became a repository for all his bad feelings and projections. By killing off his mother, Schiele denies his need for her and asserts his independence. While reassuring himself that he will go on living if his mother dies—perhaps his greatest fear—he negates any need for communion. Nevertheless, Schiele's art denotes both impulse and defense; therefore, it is not surprising that his portraits of a dead mother also include a baby—himself—inside the womb in the ultimate state of unison, the need for communion nakedly admitted. Again we have the sign of his artistic brilliance in combining disparate, conflicting, and paradoxical themes. Schiele is engaged in a psychological working through of unconscious desire and conscious pain. Mother is unresponsive. She is dead. Nevertheless he needs her.

Arthur Roessler, Schiele's major patron, helped to convert the artist's troubled relationship with his mother to Schiele's advantage. On December 24, 1910, he suggested that Schiele create a series of paintings with motherhood as the theme. Very excited by the idea, Schiele spent that Christmas Eve riding a train and then painting *Dead Mother I* (see Plate 23). Having gone the entire night without sleep, he rushed to Roessler in the morning to proudly show him the painting that hadn't yet dried. Schiele had identified his mother with Mary and himself with Christ, born on Christmas day. This double portrait remained one of his favorites for the rest of his life. The painting shows a pregnant woman—his mother—whose body is transparent, allowing a view of her yet unborn fetus. Although the title implies death, the mother and baby appear to be sharing a moment of symbiotic repose.

In 1911 Schiele painted *Dead Mother II*, this time adding an alternate title—*The Birth of Genius*—which revealed the personal significance this painting held for him as well as his grandiose self-perception. It is clear that Schiele's second Dead Mother portrait is a continuation of the first. The mother in the second painting has enormous, darkened circles around her eyes, and her fingers have become unalterably stiff. The baby, on the other hand, has awakened to life. Terror is expressed in his widened stare and in his clawing hands, which tear at the mother's womb to be set free.

It seems that between the painting of these two pictures Schiele realized the danger surrounding his birth and sad childhood. Suddenly aware that his mother was dead—or as good as dead—and that he too could die *prematurely* shocked him into struggling for his life. These Dead Mother portraits express Schiele's fragmented and detrimental early mirroring experience and his determination to not be destroyed by it.

Additionally, Schiele further lost his mother's attention and interest at the beginning of his Oedipal attachment to her because she was consumed with grief over his older sister's death and had suffered the difficult birth of his younger sister. He experienced his mother's loss of vitality and interest in him as abandonment; she had become dead to him, instilling in him also a kind of death. In his paper "The Dead Mother," André Green (1986a) has written about the devastating effects of maternal depression on the child. He describes a type of mother who, while mourning the loss of one child, loses interest in a living child and leaves an indelible scar on the child's psyche. The child perceives the mother as psychically dead, transmogrified from a source of vitality into an indistinct, colorless, and practically inanimate figure.

Schiele's Dead Mother portraits are multifunctional, expressing and attempting to correct his psychic state: They kill her, thus enacting revenge; they display her as a kind of animated corpse, for her positions are those taken by living bodies; they display Schiele's inner state of moribund life-lessness while linking her directly to his condition; and they indicate the artist's determination to transcend his sense of inner deadness (the second painting, shows the fetus-Schiele-clawing his way to freedom).

Schiele had an intense longing for confirmation and validation of himself as a child, a need that was apparently too great for his depressed mother. Clearly his mother was overwhelmed by the deaths of four children, and the horror and betrayal she must have felt at the syphilis she had contracted from her husband. That the children's deaths were linked to the disease her husband passed on to her through procreation makes one wonder how she didn't go insane. If she, as the metaphorical breast, had dried up by the time her needy and demanding son had arrived, who could blame her? Yet Schiele had little sympathy for her and was too self-involved to show mercy for her plight. Nevertheless, Marie Schiele was not a silent sufferer and, despite the enormous tragedies in her life, she may have entertained a grim sense of humor; she frequently sent Egon postcard reproductions of Whistler's *Mother* to remind him of his filial responsibilities (Comini, 1974).

Schiele left Vienna in May 1911 to live in Krumau, his mother's native town in Bohemia; he was accompanied by his model/mistress, Valerie "Wally" Neuzil, a woman introduced to him by Klimt. Self-portraits during this time include scenes from Krumau, a place he called "Dead Town" (parallel to "dead mother"). Whereas Schiele loved Krumau, the city's residents actively disapproved of his lifestyle—that is, living in sin with his mistress and not attending church—and pressured him and Wally to leave. Disillusioned by his forced exile from Krumau, Schiele's suspicion of others grew. Krumau, his mother's town, had rejected him just as he felt she had.

In this second phase of his artistic career, Schiele had defined himself as an artist. Issues of fusion and separation became crucial, assumed life-or-death proportions, and were highlighted in his double portraits with both mother and father in his art of this time. Aside from their great contribution to art, these works provided Schiele with the means to begin working through his suffering and conflict.

PHASE III: PRISONER (1912–1914)

After leaving Krumau, Schiele did not wish to return to Vienna because he distrusted his colleagues there. "Everyone conspires against me. Former colleagues regard me with malevolent eyes," he wrote to his friend, Anton Peschka (Whitford, 1981, p. 69). Instead, he decided to settle in Neulengbach, a small village about 20 miles from Vienna. Wally accompanied him, and they rented a garden villa with a beautiful view. His new living situation was idyllic, and Schiele began to feel at peace and to create what he felt were some of his most important works. During the third phase of his artistic career, which lasted from 1912 to 1914, Schiele again tackled his relationship with his father. Idealization and merger would lead to punishment and purification.

Schiele began to depict himself as either monk or hermit. For example, in his double portrait, *The Hermits* (1912), Schiele is portrayed with Klimt in ascetic garb. Schiele's figure, wearing a Christ-like crown of thorns, stares straight ahead and leads the way while supporting Klimt's handless and sightless figure, which trails impotently behind him (see Plate 24). That Klimt functions as a substitute for Schiele's own father is illustrated in a letter he wrote to his patron describing this painting:

> This is a picture I could not have painted overnight. It reflects the experiences of several years, starting from my father's death; I have painted a vision ... This is ... a world in mourning ... the indefiniteness of the figures, which are collapsed inwards, the bodies of people tired of life, of suicides, yet men of feeling. Look at the two figures as though they represented a cloud of dust ... which seeks to grow but can do no more than collapse impotently. (Leopold, 1972, p. 511)

Schiele's statements help clarify the meaning this painting had for him: mourning his father's death through a process of identification and merger with him. Schiele had begun, perhaps for the first time in his life, to accept not only his father's death but also his father's limitations and weaknesses as a man. He wrote, "If you knew something of how I see the world and how people have behaved towards me so far—how treacherously, I mean; so I must retreat [to my world] and paint such pictures which have value only to me" (Leopold, 1972, p. 511). He signed *The Hermits* three times, as if to counter the effects of the thematic content of fusion and to reassure himself of his existence as a live and separate being.[1]

---

[1] Schiele signed another painting in triplicate, *Pregnant Woman with Death* (1911), in which he is the figure of death and his mother the pregnant woman who was plagued by dead babies.

Schiele's allegorical representations of himself during this phase are characterized by a lessening of his direct self-preoccupation, as are the large number of landscapes and townscapes he painted. However, these latter works can additionally be understood as reflections of his self-image, since his thin autumn trees are connected to supports and reveal the same frailty and isolation as his human figures; his townscapes, while colorful, are barren views of unpopulated cities. Schiele's erotic drawings, which constituted his major source of income, also proliferated at this time, perhaps due to the continued, sexually inspiring presence of Wally, who herself became the subject of some of Schiele's most sexually explicit drawings. An additional reason for the abundance of these drawings, however, is the presence of many local children who were attracted to Schiele's isolated home and whom he invited to model for him—sometimes in the nude and in quite seductive poses.

Prison

Schiele's Vienna was marked by an abundance of sexual taboos aimed at encouraging purity of thought and deed. In Stefan Zweig's autobiographical book of the period, *The World of Yesterday* (1943/1963), he describes prostitution as widespread and "constitut[ing] a dark underground vault over which rose the gorgeous structure of middle class society with all its faultless, radiant façade" (p. 83). Indeed, venereal disease was rampant and many, including Schiele's father, became its victim. Not surprisingly, many women were prone to hysteria, caused by repressed sexuality, in a society that tried to conceal sex in all its forms. At the same time, sexology, the scientific study of human sexuality, was born, and it descended into the "underground" with writers like Richard von Krafft-Ebbing, who published a pathbreaking treatise on sexual disorders (1922/1936). Freud also established sex as the guiding energy and principle determinant of human behavior and developed his controversial theory of psychosexuality (1905/1953c), which claims that sexuality begins at birth. Set in this context, Schiele's art provides interesting access into the sexual activities of *fin-de-siècle* Vienna, because he was among those who attempted to expose sexuality, even in its childhood forms. The consequences were grave.

Schiele was arrested on April 13 of 1912 and imprisoned briefly (24 days) on counts of "immorality" and "seduction of a minor"; more than 100 of his drawings were confiscated. Though the latter charge was dropped, the court found him guilty of immorality in the corruption of children, because he'd exposed them to his erotic drawings. Of the 13 watercolors he produced during his incarceration, four were self-portraits—the only ones he is known to have executed without the use of a mirror.

In one such self-portrait, *For My Art and My Loved Ones I Will Gladly Endure to the End!* (1912), the image of Schiele's isolated figure strapped in a Viennese straitjacket suggests an exquisitely tortured state of being. Cramped and imprisoned in his self-contained world, Schiele floats in limbo and faces us with an unflinching, open-eyed stare that desperately pleads with us to enter his space. Indeed, this painting resembles his 1911 *Dead Mother/Birth of Genius* portrait. In both paintings, Schiele looks like a newborn baby who claws through the amniotic fluid surrounding him while his strangulated screams become lost in the void. In his solitary world, in his mother's deadly womb, in his isolation cell, and, ultimately, on his canvas, Schiele articulates his estranged self-image and his violent fight for survival.

The public condemnation of Schiele's art (and himself), with its direct replication of a painful childhood experience (during his trial, the judge burned one of his drawings, just as his mother had done when he was young), proved humiliating and stressful for him and reinforced his paranoid attitude with regard to society. Schiele transformed his traumatic prison experience into Christ-like suffering in the last entry to his prison diary: *"Anyone who has not suffered as I have—How ashamed he will have to feel before me from now on!"* (Comini, 1973, p. 105). He thus entered the ranks of religious martyrs, and the ascetic and grandiose portrayals of himself as monk, hermit, and saint increased. In *Self-Portrait as Saint Sebastian* (1914), the figure in his self-portrait is penetrated by arrows, implying Schiele's new sense of vulnerability to outside forces.

Schiele departs from the nude, single self-portrait and begins to depict himself clothed and in the presence of another figure—either Wally (as mother substitute) or Klimt (as father substitute). While clothing himself in monks' garments, he provocatively undresses society. Schiele was determined to vent his frustration and reveal society's hypocrisy, and he now exposes *its* sexuality. In his painting, *Cardinal and Nun* (1912), a variation of Klimt's well-known *The Kiss* (1907–1908), Schiele shows a cardinal (himself) and nun (Wally) engaged in a sexual embrace. The fluid sensuality of Klimt's couple is replaced with the wooden, doll-like appearance of Schiele's figures. Both cardinal and nun express guilt as they sneak furtive glances to the side as if to detect someone about to catch them in their naughty encounter. Although the painting contains no nudity (except for the figures' legs), sexuality is implied both in Schiele's neck, which resembles the shaft of an erect penis, and his use of a flaming red hue to denote intense passion.

Apart from feeling victimized, Schiele seems to have unconsciously equated his incarceration with punishment for his sexual feelings (whether he was actually guilty of sexual misconduct is unknown)—most likely his early incestuous feelings.[1] As a result, he mentions his fear of being castrated

---

[1] After his father died, Schiele repeated his parents' honeymoon with his younger sister Gerti. Later, he would marry his wife on his parents' wedding anniversary (Comini, 1974).

several times in the diary he kept while in prison: "Well, they certainly are not going to castrate me, and they cannot do that to art either ... Castration, hypocrisy! ... He who denies sex is a filthy person who smears in the lowest way his own parents who have begotten him" (Comini, 1973, p. 62).

Up until that point Schiele's need to be punished for his sexual feelings is suggested in his castrated penis or amputated limbs found in his self-portraits. Now finding an objective, external punishment—which he equated with castration—not only caused him pain, but also served the function formerly taken by his art. Thus, Schiele welcomed his punishment on some level for its aid in absolving his guilt. It is not in sarcasm, therefore, that he exclaimed in his diary and in the title of a self-portrait drawn in prison, "I feel not punished but purified!" (Comini, 1973, p. 45).

In this third phase of his career, Schiele matured as an artist and began coming to terms with his own sense of failure and disappointment. His work, a project of self-exploration and self-exhibition, reflects his developing maturity and suggests his progress in creating a unique and distinctive self.

PHASE IV: LOVE AND DEATH (1914–1918)

In order for Schiele to join society, there needed to be a victim, and this time he wanted to be certain it wasn't him. In *Death and the Maiden* (Man and Girl), he paints the sacrifice of Wally (see Plate 25).[1] She is depicted as a forlorn, desperate woman who clutches the apparition of death. Indeed, it is Schiele who appears as Death in the form of a lifeless monk who sucks blood from her head like a vampire. His features are fossilized to match the boldly rugged background landscape. Each of his hands creates a V-shape, while both figures stare vacantly and aimlessly into space. Although their relationship is dead, they are locked in an embrace and refuse to part. In *Death and the Maiden* (1915), Schiele continues his reworking of Klimt's *The Kiss* and extends it to its final resolution: the encounter between Eros and Thanatos. *Death and the Maiden*, painted at a time of personal and political transition, signifies more than a farewell to Schiele's faithful paramour. Following the outbreak of World War I, on August 4, 1914, Austria became engaged in a complete rupture with its past. War meant the dismemberment of the Habsburg rule that had by that time become ossified and powerless. Vienna was the European city that would suffer most from the war. Like the corrosive setting in *Death and the Maiden*, Vienna's radiance had

---

[1] Wally (Valerie) Neuzil had been Schiele's companion, lover, and model since 1911. In 1915 he suddenly developed a sense of urgency to marry "most advantageous, perhaps not W[ally]." Yet he proposed he and Wally take a yearly summer vacation together. Wally was hurt by Schiele's inconsiderate behavior and she left him and they never saw each other again. She volunteered for the Red Cross at an army field hospital where she died of scarlet fever in 1917 (Comini, 1974, p. 143).

been extinguished and her façade was rapidly crumbling. Neither Vienna nor Schiele would ever be the same again.

In a letter to his sister Gerti on the eve of her wedding in November 1914, Schiele wrote, "We are living in the mightiest period the world has ever seen ... whatever happened before 1914 belongs to a different world" (Comini, 1974, p. 143). Schiele's words refer not only to the war but also to his own life, which had taken a dramatic turn after 1914. Having received a draft notice in February 1915, Schiele discovered that he would become eligible for improved benefits as a married soldier; therefore, he made plans to wed Edith Harms, the younger of two sisters he was courting. He began his military service four days after his wedding. By becoming both husband and soldier, Schiele strove to unite love and death.

The fourth and last phase in the development of Schiele's self-portraits began with the war and ended with his premature death in 1918. This phase shows Schiele at his most mature. No longer alone and deformed, his image becomes increasingly real, whole, and connected to the world around him.

Love

During their first year of marriage, Schiele made a series of double portraits with Edith in 1915 that he titled *Embrace*. These portraits reveal information about the early stages of the couple's relationship. The two figures are usually half-clothed and locked in an embrace that creates a circular movement and a lack of distinction between one body and the next. The stripes in Edith's dress (which she made from Schiele's curtains) dizzily rotate as the two bodies squirm more with agitation than desire. The merging of bodies, as well as the position of the two figures (Schiele's head is meaningfully situated at Edith's breasts), indicates that these embraces resemble those between a mother and child more than between a grown man and woman.

Turning to double portraits, now with a woman, Schiele felt compelled, as he had in his Dead Mother portraits, to render one of them dead. In all of these drawings one figure is endowed with a realistic face while the other resembles a lifeless puppet. Afraid of intimacy with Edith, a woman who, unlike Wally, reminded him of his mother, Schiele needs to create distance between them. He accomplishes this by rendering either Edith or himself as an inhuman, doll-like creature and by using clothing as a protective barrier between them. The simultaneous portrayal of love and death, symbiosis and depersonalization, in these double portraits is indicative of Schiele's difficulties with intimacy. In *Seated Couple (Egon and Edith Schiele) (Embrace III)*, Edith is shown panicking, perhaps as she attempts to keep up with her husband's demanding sexual appetite; she clutches him from behind as he masturbates while staring vacantly at his mirror image (see Plate 26). "We are in bed all the time," she wrote in her diary, where she kept track of the time and place they had sex. "We are pressed against one another as closely as possible so as to forget the world around us" (Kallir, 1990, p. 195).

Although the number of self-portraits decreased drastically during this period, Schiele did not entirely abandon the genre. For example, drawing realistically, he demonstrates a new sense of maturity in a series of squatting self-portraits where he is portrayed alone and nude. With increased recognition of (and financial stability gained from) his art, his view of himself as an isolated and misunderstood artist diminishes. This is reflected in the introduction of background objects and scenery into his final self-portraits. From a stylistic viewpoint, his brittle line, previously employed as an outer contour to emphasize strong body boundaries, softens and begins to work together with his increasingly realistic use of color. His self-portraits also reveal the emergence of a more naturalistic self. He is no longer depicted as a conglomerate of parts that do not always fit (often because they are incomplete); the man as a whole, rather than his feelings of angst and despair, is portrayed in his final self-portraits.

Schiele's mirror in which he once saw reflected a hateful, fragmented self becomes in the end a benevolent and true-to-life interpreter of reality. A most striking instance of this is Schiele's final portrait of his mother, painted in 1918. This portrait differs dramatically from his previous mother portraits. Most important, his mother is portrayed naturalistically rather than blind or dead. Her head is turned to the side and her eyes are filled with sadness; her arms join together to form a circle. She is alone. Further blurring the identities of the two women in his life, Schiele depicts his mother wearing a dress with stripes, a characteristic feature in most of the portraits he painted of Edith. The most remarkable part of this drawing is the absence of stripes in the middle of the figure, which produces the effect of a missing object. The gesture she makes in conjunction with this vacant space reminds one of a mother cradling an infant. Nevertheless, one is acutely aware of the baby's absence. Here is a woman who directs her eyes away from the observer (and the baby) and who merely goes through the motions of a nurturing mother, but ironically, her gestures are empty. Yet in his final mother portrait, Schiele no longer castigates her for what she failed to give him. For the first time, he shows his mother and her limitations with humanity and acceptance. Later portraits of his wife reveal similar facial expressions and arm movements. Schiele, too, forms a circle with his own arms symbolically creating a womblike encasement for his family in *The Family*. The child in this painting looks up with a glimmer of hope. Indeed, when he painted *The Family*, Edith was pregnant. The painting remains unfinished.

Coming to terms with his mother allowed Schiele to go through the final passage toward adulthood and to relate to a woman as more than a sexual object, thereby accepting real intimacy with her. Only then was he able to make the transition from being a son to being a lover. He assumes the role of lover in his final self-portraits and is once again shown in the act of embracing a woman. In his painting, *The Embrace* (*Lovers II*; 1917), he holds a voluptuous woman in his arms, marking an important shift in his conception of himself as lover as well as of the type of woman he is now capable of loving (see Plate 27). A nude Schiele turns his back to the viewer—a stance his paranoid suspicions had prevented since his incarceration. No longer afraid to join a woman and embrace her with sensitivity, Schiele reveals a newfound trust. Neither of his figures is depersonalized or inhuman. In her nudity, the woman is far from being one of the countless prepubescent, androgynous-looking girls of Schiele's earlier drawings. Instead, she is voluptuous, well-developed, and feminine, with cascades of dark, wavy hair. The colors Schiele employs in this painting produce naturalistic flesh tones that further enhance its sensual effect. Yellow, his favorite color, surrounds the figures and embraces their passion. The theme of this painting is not sexual torture but love, and this time the love appears mutual.

Schiele was elated by his flourishing artistic career and the fact that he replaced Klimt (after he died of Spanish influenza in February 1918) as the leading Viennese artist. As a result, Schiele reverts to religious themes in his art and grandiosely assumes the role of Christ. For example, in his 1918 poster for the Secession Exhibit, *Round the Table* (*The Friends*), there is a direct allusion to the *Last Supper*, and it is Schiele himself who sits at the head of the table. Schiele regards himself as a man who, like Christ, has suffered from social injustices and reemerges with a higher level of human understanding and acceptance. In the poster, Schiele is no longer isolated; he is surrounded by men who, like himself, believe in the spiritual leadership of artists.

Death

Events took an unexpected turn for the worse in October 1918. Edith succumbed to Spanish influenza, an epidemic that ravaged Vienna in the winter of 1918 and ultimately took more lives than did the war; she was six months pregnant when she died. Three days later Schiele lay on his deathbed. Within a few days of Schiele's death, an armistice was signed marking the formal dissolution of the Habsburg monarchy. The war was over. It was the end of an era.

For Schiele, life and death were forever linked with birth and his mother. Throughout his life, endings brought about beginnings and beginnings endings. His birth had been associated with death—that of his siblings—and now his death, following that of his wife and unborn child, brought him back to his origins. There is some controversy over what Schiele's precise dying words were. Among the various versions, Comini cites, "The war is over ... and I have to go. Mama!" (1974, p. 187). His brother-in-law recalls Schiele's parting words as "Mother, give me oxygen!" (Kallir, 1990, p. 245, n. 71). Coming full circle in death as he had in his life and art, Schiele expressed the unrequited cry for his mother's love and attention one last time.

A SELF IN CREATION

Schiele employed self-portraiture not only to express himself but also to create a self. When viewed chronologically, Schiele's self-portraits display the emergence of an evolving self. Unlike many artists, like Alexander Pope, Toulouse-Lautrec, or Frida Kahlo (see Knafo, 2009b), who are known to have dealt creatively with physical handicaps, Schiele had no such problems. His self-image derived instead from a faulty and immature sense of himself. His art, and particularly those self-portraits in which he is depicted as a hideous caricature of himself, served multiple functions, the most obvious of which was the unburdening of powerful emotions and subsequent catharsis. Over and over again, Schiele showed himself in the roles of both victim and executioner as he engaged in relentless self-assaults. The butchered figure we observe in his early self-portraits is the end product of these venomous attacks on the self and his internal objects. Although he was strongly attached to the image he had of himself as a *monstre sacré*, he simultaneously struggled to purge himself of it, to destroy it so it could not destroy him.

Schiele's self-portraits reveal his transformation from a solitary adolescent tormented by his sexuality and morbid fears of body damage and psychic dissolution into a man with a more integrated character structure. Consequently, although his career was brutally cut short by his premature death at the age of 28, Schiele's oeuvre possesses a sense of completeness and resolution.

As we comprehend the underlying motivations in Schiele's art, we can better appreciate not only the meaning his art held for him, but also the fascination it continues to hold for us. It may initially seem surprising that an artist's personal struggle could possess such widespread appeal. Yet, we discover that Schiele's problems are merely an exaggeration of problems found in all of us. As spectators, we are repulsed by the emotional turmoil expressed in his art and, at the same time, attracted to the release of powerful feelings. The image in his self-portraits holds us spellbound, and we cannot look away; his penetrating eyes haunt us and invite us to ogle his gesticulating, ravaged body, to embrace his burning, raw flesh. It is impossible to escape, for the feelings he expresses also exist within us.

Through his art Schiele succeeded in repeating the mother–infant dyad with its mutual gazing reciprocity. Creating his double in his self-portraits, he not only became his own spectator; he became his own mirror. At least in his art, Schiele reached a state of forgiveness and reconciliation with his mother, because he guaranteed not only that his image would live on, but also that it would forever be mirrored. Thus, spectators who come face to face with Schiele's painted figure have taken over the artist's role by unceasingly mirroring his image. It is in this manner that Schiele created a radiant art, a better mother, and a deeply engaged audience. By creating a self, and eliciting reactions to it, Schiele recreated the birth experience. And giving birth—this time on his own terms—was his ultimate creative act.

Chapter 8

At the Limits of the Primal Scene

Revisiting *Blue Velvet*[1]

The thing is about secrets.

—David Lynch

The final mystery is oneself.

—Oscar Wilde

David Lynch has achieved a curious blend of notoriety and fame as one of the most eccentric yet innovative artists today. His films are evocative and known for their kinky, grotesque, violent, and weird themes. He has been called the "czar of the bizarre" and a "pornographic fabulist." His work disturbs and disorients the viewer as it revels in the portrayal of violence, perversion, deformity, and insanity.

In the created world of Lynch, things are never what they appear to be. He inverts the American dream—the idealized vision of a comfortable, orderly, secure, and moral life—and shows that behind the thin veneer of normality lurks an underworld permeated by evil, corruption, and disorder. Lynch undermines the illusion of goodness that bolsters one's security and comfort.

An interesting facet of Lynch's films is the way in which the viewer becomes implicated in the corrupt underworld that is revealed. The unfolding of the stories and the use of cinematographic images and techniques shape the spectator's experience, participation in the film, fantasies, and identification with its characters. Throughout his films, Lynch employs sounds and visual images to engage the viewer's voyeuristic and associative processes, which makes the experience of watching his films interactive and dreamlike. This chapter will show how Lynch employs the primal scene fantasy in the content and context of his best known and arguably most

---

[1] An earlier version of this chapter appeared in Knafo, D., & Feiner, K. (2005). *Unconscious Fantasies and the Relational World*. Hillsdale, NJ: Analytic Press. I have rewritten it for this book with Rocco Lo Bosco.

evocative film, *Blue Velvet* (Caruso & Lynch, 1986). In this examination, the appeal and power of Lynch's work will become clear, as will his ability to simultaneously excite and unsettle the viewer. The movie, layered with the primal scene, casts the audience as Peeping Toms who experience conflicted excitement, gratified curiosity, and gnawing guilt, with the implication that beneath their voyeurism seethes dangerous impulses and illicit desires. More important, *Blue Velvet* points to the limits of seeing and knowing in light of the primal scene and thus radicalizes and recasts this important psychological concept in an existential framework.

THE PRIMAL SCENE

Lynch's typical hero is often an average, innocent, untried young man from an idyllic small town. During the course of his films and his *Twin Peaks* TV series (Frost & Lynch, 1990), the hero is required to undergo a moral education that involves facing his capacity for violence and perversion. The confrontation with his own darkness is accomplished through an emphasis on secrets and their revelations. It is not surprising, then, that primal scene fantasies—fantasies about what parents or other adults are doing to and with each other behind closed doors—inform Lynch's films, as well as organize and give shape to their images, characters, plots, and relationship to the viewer. This is especially true of *Blue Velvet*.

Freud (1892–1899/1966; 1900/1953b; 1905/1953c) considered primal scene exposure (seeing or hearing parents or adults engaging in sexual behavior) to be inherently traumatic, because he thought the child would be over-stimulated and tend to interpret the sex as a sadistic act. Later writers (Arlow, 1980; Green, 1986b; Ikonen & Rechardt, 1984) emphasized the blow to the child's self-esteem and narcissistic injury at being excluded from primal scene events. The concept of exclusion, of being forbidden to enter a charged domain, has since been central to literature on the primal scene fantasy. The fear of exclusion resonates in so many daily scenes and holds all kinds of dreaded threats: missed opportunities, betrayals large and small, cold and bitter exile and, worst of all, death. Death is the final and most bitter of all exclusions, because deep inside one must know that the whole scene will go on without us. Kurt Vonnegut, in *Deadeye Dick* (1982), famously described being born as having one's "peephole" opened and dying as having one's "peephole" closed and thus cast the entirety of life as a kind of primal scene.

Others (Edelheit, 1967; Esman, 1973) have wisely pointed out that the impact of the primal scene depends on the quality of parental relationships. Primal scene exposure seems most likely to be traumatic in situations in which it either confirms or symbolizes preexisting, conflict-laden wishes, fears, or anxieties (Arlow, 1980; A. Freud, 1967). The sensitivity a given individual may have developed due to such exposure notwithstanding, the primal scene fantasy figures largely within the traumatic context of human life.

Despite the focus on negative and pathological consequences of primal scene exposure, Freud (1925/1961e) was the first to point out the stimulating effects the primal scene can have on the child's curiosity, intellectual activity, and emotional development. He implied that interest in mysterious parental activities forbidden the child will incite a generalized curiosity about other mysteries. Pederson-Krag (1949) connected curiosity with the primal scene in her intriguing paper on detective stories. Early curiosity, deeply impassioned, generalizes to a broader intrigue that is projected onto the world and its objects. Blum (1979) cites the primal scene's function in sex-role rehearsal and sexual-identity formation. I have argued (Knafo & Feiner, 1996) that children construct multiple identifications that shift in conjunction with dynamic changes in perceptions of their relationships to the parents and to the self. Thus, the primal scene fantasy, though positioning the child on the outside of the action, also allows the child to be in the scene by identifying with all of the characters involved. Through these multiple, shifting identifications, the child develops an internalized working model for what relationships—particularly intimate and passionate ones—consist of and what is worth exploring about the world, human life, the other, and most of all oneself.

Having both an ontological and epistemological function, the primal scene helps to situate the self in reality—by defining the self in relationship to the other, by marking the dynamic and semipermeable boundaries between the self and its objects, by establishing the possibilities of both legitimate and transgressive boundary crossing, and by announcing the fact of mystery, the possibility of knowledge, and the creation of meaning.

THE PRIMAL SCENE AS CONTENT
AND CONTEXT IN *BLUE VELVET*

Blue Velvet is a coming-of-age story that centers on the efforts of its protagonist, Jeffrey Beaumont, to solve the mystery of a crime he uncovers. Jeffrey is first seen following a visit with his father who is hospitalized after having suffered a heart attack or stroke (as with so much in the film we can never be sure). While dawdling on his way back home from the hospital, Jeffrey discovers a bug-infested severed ear in a field, which he delivers to Detective Williams. Later he visits Williams at his home because he wants to know more and is dissuaded by the detective from further pursuit. But as Jeffrey leaves Williams's home, the detective's daughter, Sandy, steps out from pitch-black darkness to tell Jeffrey what she overheard her father saying about the case, and Jeffrey becomes further intrigued and enlists her help to solve the mystery. Similarly to Oedipus, whose need to penetrate the riddle of the Sphinx leads him to commit his crime, Jeffrey sets off on an investigation into a dark underworld that will lead him to darkness within himself. Through our role as titillated spectator and excited voyeur, we too will be made to face the darkness within us. In the process of his sleuthing, Jeffrey becomes involved with two women: Sandy, the young, virginal blonde, and Dorothy Vallens, the "blue lady," a beautiful, exotic woman who is being sexually and emotionally savaged by a psychopathic villain, Frank Booth, who has kidnapped her husband and son for the ransom of sexual favors.

In sharing with viewers the revelation of clues, overheard parts of private conversations, mumbled and murmured intrigues, and the scenes that take place behind closed doors, Lynch recreates in the audience the mental state of the primal scene witness and participant. Lynch links the child's curiosity and the detective/protagonist's compulsion to delve beneath the surface with the viewer's effort to make sense of the film. At all levels, there is a revival of unconscious primal scene fantasies that include repressed desires, fears, and guilt. These fantasies are partially gratified and contained but, most of all, they are manipulated by the film. Furthermore, they all function to goad the viewer into working to make sense of what is taking place. And although at a surface level the movie tells us a story that culminates in a denouement, its ironic subtext is the erasure of meaning that is embedded not merely in the images that pass before our eyes but in the very structure of the film itself. The viewer is left with ambivalence, uncertainty, and opposition. Reality and fantasy, the substantial and the ephemeral, are wrapped inseparably into one grand illusion. *Blue Velvet* is to traditional story what an Escher drawing is to traditional objects.

Blue Velvet opens with a long and unvarying shot of a shimmering blue velvet theater curtain. Bobby Vinton's velvety voice croons the words to his 1960s hit song: "She wore blue velvet ... bluer than velvet was the night ... Softer than satin was the light ..." Our curiosity is aroused and our anxiety heightened during the prolonged view of the curtain swaying and the accompanying music. This soppy shot dissolves into a slick and brilliant pastiche of small-town America, where blood-red roses and dark yellow tulips, so perfect that they look fake, undulate in front of a white picket fence under an azure sky. Idyllic scenes in hyper-realistic color go by lazily in slow motion: a fireman waves at us from a passing fire truck; a female crossing guard walks children across the street to safety; an overweight citizen waters his pretty lawn. This is Lumbertown, the innocent, brightly lit American dream world, rendered in parody and serving as the bookends of Jeffrey's descent into the underworld. Several times throughout the movie we see a quick image of a truck transporting fallen trees, an apt symbol of castration and of the darker aspect of human nature vehemently denied on the surface of culture.

The scene shifts to a television program, a film noir that Jeffrey's mother and aunt are watching. The close-up of a hand gripping a gun on the indoor television screen parallels the man (who turns out to be the protagonist's father) holding a hose to water the grass. The hose is knotted and the water is backing up. Suddenly the man grabs his neck and falls to the ground. The hose, still clutched in his hand, sprays water wildly from near his crotch area and is playfully snapped at and lapped up by a dog. Tragedy and comedy merge, as do reality and fantasy, to create suspense and elevate curiosity.

The camera then zooms in on green blades of grass. As we are brought closer to the dark, chaotic world of busy insects crawling beneath the surface, colors turn brown and black, and unnerving gobbling sounds become progressively louder. We suddenly find ourselves in a nest of sickening beetles, thrust in the midst of a frenzied violent activity, a move that will periodically repeat itself throughout the film. Initially, we are outside observers viewing scenes from a distance. But gradually, we are invited, and more often compelled, to participate in the action, lured by curiosity and excited and repelled by what we encounter. The insect underworld is dark, and all the key scenes of this film take place at night. Lynch hijacks our attention and brings us into a world of perversion, sex, and violence, the underbelly of the adult world normally idealized in sanitized scenes. He takes us into the dark where dreams speak to us of their buried secrets, and he also leaves us in the dark by transforming the familiar into the strange, by mixing psychological truth and fantasy, and by creating a structure which itself is an insoluble labyrinth.

Blue Velvet begins with the removal of paternal authority. The generational hierarchy is reversed, boundaries between adult and child are easily crossed, and the idyllic world of childhood (and the American dream) is destroyed. The surface order—security and morality of the tranquil scene—is shown to be illusory, perhaps even a dream. Lynch's film illustrates Chasseguet-Smirgel's (1985) premonitory comment that the removal of paternal authority initiates a reversal of the value system, the first stage in a process whose outcome is the destruction of all values.

In much of the film's opening scenes there is little dialogue, and many of the images are so fleeting that it is difficult to follow the thread of the action. We observe a pair of scissors cut through tape marked "Police Crossing" at the crime scene; immediately after we hear the coroner's report that the ear was probably cut off by scissors. Despite the fact that Jeffrey is warned by Detective Williams to say nothing about the ear he has brought to the police station, the injunction serves only to heighten his (and our) curiosity. Jeffrey's need for "knowledge and experience" and his resolve to uncover the mystery seem to know no bounds. He identifies with the detective's fact-finding mission and quickly becomes involved with his daughter, thus insinuating himself into the detective's family.

As spectators, we are led to attempt to discern what is happening. The juxtaposition of the ear, the coroner's comments, and the close-up image of the scissors create a threatening (castrating) atmosphere. Viewers experience a heightened sense of danger as they link the threat and the injunction together, and as they watch Jeffrey blithely disregard all limits.

With the help of a few clues given to him by Sandy, who suggests a primal scene enactment when she tells him she overheard her father talking about the case, Jeffrey is led to Dorothy Vallens about whom he says, "I bet someone could learn a lot by sneaking into that woman's apartment." He justifies his desperate pursuit when he tells Sandy, "There are few opportunities in life for gaining knowledge and experience. Sometimes it's necessary to take a risk." Jeffrey's quest expresses his wish to gain entry into a mysterious adult world and to uncover its secrets. His curiosity, as well as his tendency to arrogate the prerogatives of grown-ups and to ignore parental injunctions, reveals his effort to deny the intolerable loss of narcissistic omnipotence associated with acceptance of parental authority and his exclusion from the primal scene. He has already ignored the detective's admonishment to say nothing about the ear, and he refuses to heed his mother's warning to avoid Lincoln Street, located on the bad side of town. Later on, he is oblivious to the fact that Dorothy is married when he becomes sexually involved with her, and he pursues Sandy without giving much thought to her having a boyfriend.

Jeffrey's need to solve mysteries is fueled by his search for a good paternal authority figure to help emancipate him from the bondage of his maternal tie. Instead of Lincoln, the symbol of freedom from slavery, he finds Frank Booth (presumably an allusion to Lincoln's assassin), a brutal, dangerous, criminal.

As the film unfolds, Jeffrey becomes an Oedipal member of still another family, a dark and seedy triad composed of Frank Booth, Dorothy Vallens, and himself. The Williams family and his own, two clans reminiscent of the families found in the sitcoms of the 1950s, provide the denouement for Jeffrey's quest. His eventual pairing with the detective's daughter lands him in the simulated happy ending of the American dream. But Jeffrey's membership in these two groups pales in contrast to his self-injected inclusion in the Booth "family." This family reflects his dark side, his night side; it harkens to the beasts that walk in his dreams and the insects that crawl underground. Though his involvement with the Booth family may be only a dream or a fantasy (the question of what really happens, as we shall see, remains undecidable), its visceral and frightening potency renders it the story's central reality.

Jeffrey gains entry into Dorothy Vallens's apartment in the guise of an exterminator, during which time he steals a spare key for future incursions. Once again bugs become symbolic not only for the dark under/inner world, but also as a metaphor for his spying on adult activities, which should otherwise be off limits. The obvious irony is that an exterminator's aim is to eliminate unwanted intruders.

During a second "visit," Dorothy suddenly returns while Jeffrey is searching in her apartment for clues connecting her with the severed ear. With no time to escape, he retreats to the closet, peeking through the slatted door while he (and the viewer) watches Dorothy undress. Hearing Jeffrey, Dorothy pulls him from the closet and is transformed into a phallic, castrating maternal figure, identifying with her own tormentor as she sadistically taunts Jeffrey with a knife. She forces Jeffrey to undress, telling him she wants to "see" him, and begins to touch and fondle him. While offering Jeffrey the possibility of sexual initiation, enlightenment, and, of course, Oedipal triumph, she simultaneously kisses him and threatens to kill him. Dorothy thus represents both the desire to transgress and danger of doing so.

At the moment of his sexual initiation (she begins to fellate him), Dorothy's persecutor, Frank Booth—the menacing psychopath and lead "bug" who rules the sadomasochistic criminal world at the center of the film—bursts in, and Jeffrey is cast out. Hurriedly, Dorothy sends Jeffrey back into the closet, where, through the louver doors, he helplessly witnesses Frank's brutal sexual attack on her. The scene is filmed primarily from Jeffrey's perspective and so, like Jeffrey, we (the viewers) are cast out and forced to passively witness Dorothy's violation.

Riveted in horror, fascination, and excitement, we watch through our eyes but also through Jeffrey's as the camera restlessly moves back and forth between him and the scene unfolding before him: the primal father savaging the helpless mother, who submits for the safety of her kidnapped child. In this scene, beginning with Jeffrey's hiding behind a door, Lynch evokes the most archaic fears and forbidden desires around the issues of exclusion, seduction, possession and control, rape and violation, and the threat of impending death. Wallace (1997) notes, "The camera's ogling is designed to implicate Frank and Jeffrey and the director and the audience all at the same time" (p. 206). This scene, the first of two key psychological climaxes of the film, is a bone-chilling and spectacular primal scene enactment, and it refers as much to the audience as it does to the characters.

When Frank enters the apartment, Dorothy greets him by calling him baby. (On the phone she called him sir.) Frank yells, "Shut up, it's Daddy," and demands his bourbon and oxygen mask. Inhaling an unknown drug (Blue Velvet is also the street name for a drug, and Dennis Hopper, who played Frank, claimed in an interview it was amyl nitrate), Frank looks at Dorothy and whines, "Mommy, Baby wants to fuck. Get ready to fuck, you fucker's fucker!" Enraged by her eye contact, he punches her in the face and growls, "Don't you fuckin' look at me!" Dorothy places part of her blue robe into his mouth to soothe him, and he begins to maul her briefly before throwing her down while snarling obscenities. Removing a pair of scissors, he cuts the air above her menacingly, evoking a brutal and frightening image of castration and again warns her not to look at him. He then stuffs the end of her robe's belt into her mouth and the other end into his own. "Don't you fucking look at me. Daddy's coming home. Don't you fucking look at me ..." After violently probing her genitals, he throws Dorothy to the ground and while still dressed, he mounts her until he climaxes. During this time, he continues to warn Dorothy against looking, a sanction that resonates in viewers, since we have, in spite of ourselves, been watching closely in perverse fascination.

The warning against looking is directed at Dorothy, Jeffrey, and the viewer all at the same time. Shame is rarely possible without the gaze of the other, and even if one shames oneself when alone, another is imagined as watching the shameful act. We want to be seen and we fear being seen.

> Look at me, please look!
> Don't you dare fucking look at me!

In Frank's scenario, he enters in the role of a punitive father—Daddy—interrupting Jeffrey's initiation. However, he quickly is transformed into the savage id-driven Baby who wants to fuck Mommy. He then reverts to the primal Daddy fucking Mommy, bringing her ruin and the ever-present threat of death for her and her family. In this searing visual and auditory film passage, which threatens castration as a punishment for invading the primal scene, Jeffrey's witness to Booth's actions insinuates him in a reversed, perverse, and demonic family romance where his imagined parents of origin exist not in celestial realms but in insectoid caverns. His position in the closet forever connects him to Frank and Dorothy. Later when Sandy says to Jeffrey, "I don't know whether you're a detective or a pervert," and he answers, "That's for me to know and for you to find out," the viewer must wonder if in fact he knows anything of the sort. The fact that 25 years later the scene is just as shocking and disturbing as it was in 1986 is a testament to the power of unconscious fantasy and the repressed murmurings of the psyche's darker impulses and desires.

At the demented heart of the movie is Frank Booth, who is quite insane, riddled with boundless perversity and rage. Even if we understand him through theory, the mystery of his darkness eludes us, for who can imagine a mind like his? And even as he causes so much suffering, we see that he too is involved in his own pathetic struggle as he rages from scene to scene with his manic twitching and anxious unease, with his little fetish objects—the blue velvet cloths that he strokes for comfort and his oxygen mask that he uses for courage—and with his tears as he watches Dorothy sing "Blue Velvet" in the Slow Club. But what the actual nature of his struggle is we cannot know. And so our eyes remain riveted to the scene that remains not only primal but a primal mystery even after analysis. Watching that scene, however many times we can bear to, we get the sense that we are still missing something. We can still say with legitimacy, "What just happened?"

And yet because we are linked to Jeffrey, who is linked to Frank, we too are tied to him, the maniacal and savage Baby-Daddy-Fucker. Later Frank will remind Jeffrey that he is with him in dreams; so, too, in our dreams he walks—not merely as the dangerous and unknown other who may threaten us from without, coming to ruin life and meaning, but as the unknowable destroyer abiding within, tainting our most sincere efforts with a sense of falseness and charade, mocking the lie of ourselves that we present to the world. Frank Booth is the worm at the core of being and knowledge.

After Frank leaves, Jeffrey emerges from the closet offering solace to Dorothy. The camera moves in, and we watch Dorothy and Jeffrey as she asks him to hold her. For moments of long duration, we observe the two together, viewing them from the outside. Then the camera zooms to an ultra close-up of Dorothy's face, in particular her reddened lips and teeth, a front one chipped, most likely by Frank's fists. The audience is brought into the clinch as we see Dorothy from the proximity we know we could only gain if she were literally in our own arms. Once again, Lynch has moved us from outside observers to insiders and participants, making us see and feel the primal scene from both outside and inside.

Dorothy offers Jeffrey her breast and tells him, "You can feel it, touch it." Then, shifting the mood and creating palpable conflict, she asks him to hit her. Trying to sustain an innocent, moral self-image, he refuses, telling Dorothy that he wants to help her. At this moment, he retreats from the dark world of adult sexuality.

Yet at a later time, Jeffrey is again drawn to Dorothy's apartment. During his subsequent visit, he and Dorothy lie together on her sofa. Once again, Dorothy asks Jeffrey to hit her. Jeffrey starts to back away, exclaiming, "No, no!" When Dorothy says, "Then go," Jeffrey relents, hitting her lightly. Following this, he glares at her and slaps her violently, realizing that the condition for his sexual initiation entails the acceptance of his sadistic impulses. As he hits Dorothy, we hear the sound of a roaring animal and see a burning flame, both symbols present at the time of Frank's climax when he attacked Dorothy. Jeffrey's identification with Frank is solidified. He finally leaves the apartment feeling shaken and tainted, as do members of the audience.

The power of these scenes is found in the voyeuristic relationships that Lynch creates. Throughout the film he plays with questions of looking and being looked at and with the power relationships that are constituted by these different positions. Kernberg (1994) recognized the ability film has to enable the viewer to realize in fantasy the invasion of the primal scene. Indeed, film, the most voyeuristic of art forms, allows the promiscuously curious viewer who willingly enters a darkened theater to passively wait to be stimulated and shocked, and to voluntarily engage in the most deviant kind of voyeurism. "Everyone is a detective," says Lynch. "All of us want to know what's going on" (as cited in Knafo, 1991).

The film engages emotions associated with exclusion from the primal scene. Lynch makes the most of this possibility by inciting the viewer's curiosity as well as evoking a sense of guilt and helplessness. Like Jeffrey, we too become voyeurs against our will. Along with Lynch's characters, we too shift from one perspective to another. Here, we identify with the voyeur; there, with the aggressor; and there, with the victim. Lynch's camera (and our eye) moves back to Jeffrey (and his perspective) 19 times during the 5-minute scene in which Jeffrey first encounters Frank.

In an earlier article, along with Feiner, I (1996) proposed that primal scene fantasies are constituted by multiple identifications that shift in conjunction with dynamic changes in the child's perception of his relationship to the parents and the self. These identifications involve being in several places at once, as both the observer and the observed (Myers, 1973) and as included in and excluded from relationships with each parent as well as the parental dyad (Klein, 1940/1979b). Lynch depicts a primal scene that engages these shifting identifications in his protagonists and viewers alike in this key scene.

Wallace (1997) points out the similarity between Frank's mask and the oxygen mask Jeffrey's father wore in the hospital. This object, along with the repeated use of Mommy and Daddy, clearly link Jeffrey's father with Frank. Dorothy becomes the Oedipal mother who is perceived to be with the father by force rather than preference. To Jeffrey, Frank is the menacing, castrating father (scissors in hand) who has evicted him and reclaimed the mother for himself—the father who has come home and who is about to come. This sadomasochistic version of the primal scene (as if written by Freud himself!) allows Jeffrey to cast himself as the mother's rescuer, and to take the place as the preferred male over this cruel and violent paternal figure. However, this self-image proves to be unsustainable because Jeffrey comes face-to-face with his own darkness.

For Frank, the scenario of his rape of Dorothy represents the enactment of an Oedipal triumph. Frank whines, "Mommy, Baby wants to fuck—you fucker's fucker." The "fucker's fucker" is the mother possessed by the father, with Frank as the baby. Frank *becomes* Baby with Mommy. Yet, by taking the father's place, he too becomes the "fucker's fucker." Frank's triumph is felt as he invokes the castrating father's return at the moment of orgasm.

At one point in the film, Frank catches Jeffrey with Dorothy and forces them both to accompany him and his "friends" to a house of prostitution called THIS IS IT. The house is run by Ben, a thoroughly weird and pompous pimp and drug dealer who affects a slimy suaveness tinged with madness. It is in this house, this nest of ugly insects, that Dorothy's child is being held for sexual ransom, though we hear her speaking to her boy only from behind a locked door. In an iconic scene still getting thousands of hits on YouTube, Ben, using an industrial droplight as both a prop microphone and an improvised spotlight illuminating his creepy face from below, lip-syncs Roy Orbison's song, "In Dreams." Frank, completely enraptured, first weeps with what seems like a mixture of passion and sorrow, and then becomes so enraged that Ben is forced to cut short his performance.

We are again witnessing a primal scene that both eludes and implicates us. Many elements enrich this scene with suggestive nuance implying substitution, boundary loss, sudden reversal, and rupture with reality. Orbison's innocent song of lost love is recontextualized as a forbidding ode to darkness. The uncanny drama enacted by Ben and Frank, two men so bound by a common vision of homoerotically charged malevolence that each one might be the other's *doppelgänger*, suggests that there will always be things that can happen that we would never expect, let alone be prepared for. "Goddamn, you are one suave fucker!" Frank tells Ben. In this nest of insects, in this underground space where Frank and Ben raise a toast to "fucking," one thing can become another in the wink of an eye: Fucking can become killing; desire can become death; a droplight can become a microphone; a cheap lip-sync of a sappy love song can incite emotions far more powerful than those incited by the original; a pimp can be transformed into a prophetic messenger; a cold-hearted killer can weep tears in recognition of some unbearable memory or actuality. In the moment of Ben's performance, when rapture, grief, and fury dawn on Frank's face, we realize that perhaps Ben is conveying a terrible truth—and that this truth is at the heart of this scene (THIS IS IT) and the film itself.

This truth seems to be deeply coded into the very next scene. Frank, his cohorts, and his victims pile back into the car and leave Ben's house, racing down the highway at over 100 miles per hour. Angered because Dorothy looks at Jeffrey, Frank swerves the car off the road and screeches to a halt at the deserted lumber mill where Dorothy's kidnapped husband is being held. After Frank takes some deep snorts from his mask, he tells Jeffrey (and us) with glee, "You're just like me!" He then begins to degrade and molest Dorothy, and Jeffrey punches him in the face. Frank then has Jeffrey torn from the car, and he kisses him forcefully, smearing the lipstick he has placed on his own lips onto Jeffrey's face. He threatens him with a bullet ("love letter") straight to the heart. The tape of Orbinson's "In Dreams" is again playing, this time from the car stereo. Before beating Jeffrey, Frank looks him intently in the eye and assures him that *in dreams* Jeffrey belongs to him:

> In Dreams I walk with you
> In Dreams I talk to you
> In Dreams you're mine
> All of the time ...

In this scene, Jeffrey is forced into the role of male aggressor as well as that of woman, nicely illustrating the shifts in perspective and identification Lynch has his characters (and viewers) assume in the primal scene configuration. In the end, Frank and his cohorts beat up Jeffrey and leave him wounded and stranded in the dirt. By virtue of our identification with the foolhardy kid who wants to see what goes on behind the curtain, and has transgressive desires and repressed perversions, we also walk with Frank as well. He is the crack in the pretty façade, the stain spreading beneath the surface, the insect feeding on the flesh, the madness denied in ordinary life, the justification for every death. He is always denied and disavowed, existing between the dream and waking life—a place neither fully inside nor outside that is also symbolic of the undefined space between the objective and the subjective, between cultural normalcy and unconscious madness, between the mask and the faceless darkness beneath it.

Afraid that "things got a little out of hand," Jeffrey allows himself to be persuaded by Sandy to tell her father, Detective Williams, what he has learned. For the first time in the film, Jeffrey appears to accept his limitations. Yet, a final reversal in the primal scene occurs when he is on a date with Sandy, having finally won her over. Spirituality and innocent romance are highlighted by lighting and (church organ) music. But this too is ominous. Sandy's boyfriend, whom she dumped for Jeffrey, follows them in a car chase that is so dangerous Jeffrey is convinced it is Frank at the wheel of the car. Once again, Jeffrey is interrupted—this time by Sandy's boyfriend who seeks to avenge the injury of losing her.

When the cars stop, an incoherent, naked, and bruised Dorothy appears like a ghost. Jeffrey runs to her and holds her in his arms as she sobs. "Jeffrey, is that you?" she calls, recognizing her intruder and lover. We see and feel Jeffrey's anguish as the two women in his life come together, forcing him to choose between colliding worlds. As Jeffrey stands with Dorothy, he becomes the perpetrator of Sandy's painful exclusion. Sandy, now the outsider, is shocked and aghast and cannot stop looking and crying. It is she who now witnesses the intimacy between Jeffrey and a naked woman who could be his mother. It is she who now feels horrified by the implied sexuality and brutality and by her sudden exclusion from Jeffrey's arms. Part of the power of this scene, as with those that came before it, is the camera's movement back and forth between the couple and the observer, which forces us to identify now with one and now with the other. Sandy's gaping mouth and sense of helplessness are palpable and moving in their reminders of the shock value that the primal scene has on its observers. She later exclaims, "I love you but I couldn't watch that." An ambulance arrives and Dorothy is given an oxygen mask, reminiscent of Frank's and Jeffrey's father's masks.

Surely the most visceral and gripping part of *Blue Velvet* is what takes place in the underworld, in Frank's world, and in the space between two ears, and yet, upon reflection, many events occur throughout the film that would ordinarily be difficult to believe. What young man would take such repeated risks and dare to punch a crazy, violent maniac in the face while surrounded by the maniac's criminal friends? What woman would want to have sex just after having been brutally assaulted and raped by a weeping, whining psychopath who threatens annihilation in every interaction? How could a woman in this situation take up with a second invader who she finds in her closet? Certainly such a woman might use sex to enlist the aid of her second intruder, but it is hard to imagine she would enjoy it while her abducted husband bleeds from a gaping wound after his ear is severed and her traumatized child waits in mind-numbing terror in the house of a drug-dealing, crazy pimp. It is also hard to believe that Sandy, an innocent girl, quickly forgives her lying boyfriend for sleeping with an older, more experienced and seductive woman while he uses her to gain access. And yet it all works.

Sensing more danger, Jeffrey embarks on his final mission to Dorothy's apartment. He finds a policeman with a bullet hole in his head, standing upright as his radio continues to blast. Who would ever hope to find a man shot in the head still standing on his feet? All of this works because the grip of fantasy suspends the audience's disbelief. The fact that such unrealistic occurrences work so well is testimony to the power of unconscious fantasies to shape our perception of reality. One might even argue that Lynch hijacks our unconscious, subjecting us to a kind of hypnosis by provoking fantasy elements that have such power we hardly notice the contradictions.

Jeffrey also discovers Dorothy's husband, dead and sans ear, with a blue velvet cloth stuffed in his mouth. Jeffrey begins to leave when he hears a car stop and glimpses Frank in disguise hurrying up the stairs. He hides in the same closet from which he had first witnessed Frank rape Dorothy. This time, armed with a gun that he lifts from the policeman's pocket, he waits in the closet. As Frank approaches the closet, Jeffrey shoots him in the forehead. Detective Williams and Sandy burst into the apartment. "It's all over, Jeffrey," the detective assures him. Even though we never doubt that Jeffrey is on the side of the good, it is clear that he has learned to be sexual, duplicitous, and violent, not unlike his nemesis, Frank.

As Sandy and Jeffrey kiss in the hallway to the sound of police and ambulance sirens on their way to the carnage in Dorothy's apartment, the scene shifts to a close-up of an ear—this time Jeffrey's. The beginning of the film had us enter the ear of a doomed man, and the end of the film has us exit the ear of a live one. Two ears, bookends of the film, create boundaries delineating what goes on between them, in the mind of one person: the filmmaker, Jeffrey, the viewer.

When the camera finally exits Jeffrey's ear, he seems completely unfazed by all he has been through. He has embarked on a seeming hero's journey, weeping and crying out in anguish along the way, but passing through unaffected, bereft of any of the wisdom and knowledge we might expect him to gain in this strange and extreme coming-of-age story. He ends up with Sandy, and one of the last images we have is of him stupidly smiling at a mechanical robin and nodding to Sandy's proclamation that true love has returned. He and Sandy are intentionally dissolved back into actors, stranded in a silly parody. We are returned to the ground of the story— Lumberton and its inhabitants—and the things that happened in the dream space have lost all ontological meaning. In the end Sandy sums it all up with the movie's repeated refrain: "It's a strange world, isn't it?"

So what does Jeffrey know? What do we know? And what does it all mean? These questions cannot be answered to our satisfaction when the very framework of the film is like a Möbius strip, its world both inside and outside *and* simultaneously neither inside nor outside. If there is a denouement in *Blue Velvet* it occurs in the space between the two ears and is of a decidedly metaphysical nature that situates the viewer in the mystery of the self and the real. We have looked behind each door, and yet we are not entirely sure what we have seen. We definitely saw something, but something key also seems to be missing. It is as if some central truth must remain hidden in order for everything we saw to have taken place. Indeed, we have encountered an inherent limit of seeing and knowing expressed in an insidious and highly suggestive manner. Even when we look behind the door— and as Lynch points out, everyone wants to know what's going on—we are still not sure what's going on, what it means, or what part of reality it contains. In this sense *Blue Velvet* speaks to the very heart of human uncertainty. There is almost nothing we can be certain about, and no meaning we make is absolutely secured against rupture.

Lynch is establishing the primal scene not merely as a personal psychological encounter, but rather as the very context of human discovery and ontic assignation. *The primal scene*—looking behind the closed door and wanting to know and understand what is on the other side—*is the human scene*. It is the tragic element of human knowledge, that of inherent limitation and ontological insecurity. When people say they have seen too much, don't they mean that they haven't been able to make sense of what they have seen? Knowledge of the world falls short; self-knowledge is nearly a beggar. The door to oneself always leads to another door and perhaps one may be, after all, only a series of endless doors opening upon scenes whose meanings are ambiguous and multidetermined. Indeed, to be human is to suffer a kind of inherent alienation, an exclusion from certainty, completeness, and the mystery of one's existence. Eventually, when one dies, it is an exclusion from life itself. The limits of the primal scene structure our lives going forward (What, if anything, is behind the final door?) and going backward (What still lives in hiding behind closed doors?).

The harrowing, hair-raising tale between two ears always takes place at night. It is graphically visual and grips us with its visceral invasion of our sensibilities and its provocative resonance with shadowy and ominous aspects of our unconscious. *Blue Velvet* takes place in an unconscious dream space where we are brought to ourselves in a most uncomfortable way.

As spectators, we leave the film with our metaphysical questions still unanswered and the sense of having encountered unsavory and perverse aspects in ourselves. Within the film the real was unreal (Lumberton) and the unreal was real (Frank's world). We do not understand all of what we saw or what exactly to make of it. There's so much we would make of it, but as with the Möbius strip and the Escher drawing, each profile taken returns us to the paradox and collision of two self-contradictory realms. But somehow the journey has imbued us with the kind of self-knowledge we might like to avoid. Indeed, Lynch poses the possibility that the entire film might simply have been Jeffrey's dream, or a product of *our* unconscious primal scene fantasies, projected onto the screen. Therefore, the major character in *Blue Velvet* might very well be the viewers who must, like all "real" characters, find their truth in darkness and their darkness in truth.

Chapter 9

Ana Mendieta
Goddess in Exile[1]

I know how those in exile feed on dreams.

—Aeschylus

Exile is ... the unhealable rift forced between a human being and a native place, between the self and its true home: Its essential sadness can never be surmounted.

—Edward Said

Torn from her mother and her motherland at an early age, Cuban-born Ana Mendieta (1948–1985) used her art to come to terms with maternal loss. The attempt to master the painful fissure of separation and loss was the raison d'être of her art. In her best-known, self-titled Earth-Body Works, Mendieta created sculptural pieces that blend into the natural landscape (see Plate 28). Though her art deals with matters of loss and death, it exhibits a transformative power derived from the artistic gesture that breathes life into natural materials. Mendieta created a ritual that she repeated time and time again: creation, destruction, death, and regeneration.

Making art became a spiritual act for Mendieta. She saw herself as a dynamic conduit, the willing shaman who left a talisman to work its magic with the elements. In creating her earth-body sculptures, she created her own rituals, usually working alone, claiming her territory, preparing the land, and rendering it sacred before fashioning fetish objects that in her mind possessed magical and spiritual powers (see Plate 29). Appropriating the healing imagery from Santeria—a New World synthesis of Yoruban, Roman Catholic, and Native American religious beliefs created by the descendents of Nigerian slaves brought to Cuba in the 16th century—Mendieta drew on ceremonies and symbols that affirmed social bonds and connected her to

---

[1] An earlier version of this chapter appeared in Knafo, D. (2009b). *In Her Own Image: Women's Self-Representation in Twentieth Century Art*. Rutherford, NJ: Fairleigh Dickinson University Press.

the past. Ultimately she sought to overcome the limitations of time, place, and separation, as is evident in the following poem she wrote:

Pain of Cuba
Body I am
My orphanhood I live.

In Cuba when you die
The earth that covers us
Speaks.

But here, covered by the earth whose prisoner I am
I feel death palpitating underneath.

And so,
As my whole being is filled with want of Cuba
I go on to make my mark upon the earth,
To go on is victory.

(Cited in Katz, 1990, pp. 169–170)

The ephemeral quality of Mendieta's earthworks reflects her subject matter: the dissolution and fragility of our ties to people and places. An artist in exile, Mendieta claimed space after space only to create a powerfully felt absence within them. She reproduced her form by shaping her silhouette into the earth; yet that very form, so fragile and delicate, susceptible to weather changes and the forces of nature, gradually vanished, leaving only a trace of what once was. Mendieta's physical body became, in the end, a numinous presence. Although her art, like a child's sandcastle, was not protected against change and dissolution, its restoration was ironically guaranteed through its gracious return to and merger with the surround that furnished its existence.

The "disappearance" of Mendieta's earth-body sculptures begs the question of what the actual artwork is and where it belongs. Indeed, many of her pieces were never seen by anyone but herself and the photographer. All that remains of them are 35-mm slides, Super 8 films, and color or black-and-white photographs. These are images of a fleeting art, simulacrums expressing the tension between time and timelessness and the profound anxiety attending the encounter with the transitory nature of all things. Mendieta repeated her own private trauma in these performative dramas and, at the same time, introduced a powerfully evocative aesthetic language to express the universal problem of exile, dislocation, identity, and transcendence.

BEGINNINGS

Ana Mendieta was born into a well-to-do, politically connected Havana family in 1948, a family dominated by her maternal grandmother, Elvira, the daughter of General Carlos Maria de Rojas, a leader in Cuba's war of independence (1895–1898). Her grand-uncle, Carlos Mendieta, had been president of the nation in the 1930s (Rauch & Suro, 1992).

Following a difficult pregnancy, the last three months requiring complete bed rest, Mendieta's mother, Raquelin, gave birth to Ana, her second daughter, a sickly child who suffered from anemia and chronic bronchitis. She received three transfusions of her father's blood during her first year of life (Katz, 1990). Consequently, she was overprotected and indulged, and developed a particularly close attachment to her mother. Though young Ana got a great deal of attention, warmth, and nurturance from a large extended family and from a variety of maternal figures, including her mother, grandmother, nannies, and older sister Raquel, she also suffered numerous painful separations from all of them.[1]

Mendieta's mother, a professor of chemistry and physics, worked full time and left much of the daily caretaking responsibilities to nannies who came and went, including Mendieta's favorite, a Chinese-African nanny who left for the United States when Ana was eight. The two Mendieta sisters along with their two female cousins spent every summer and holiday at their beloved grandmother's house in Cárdenas, and Ana always cried when it was time to leave.

Mendieta's father, Ignacio, a lawyer by profession, worked as an attorney for the police department during World War II and identified members of the Communist party for the CIA. The only way to later redeem himself and obtain employment was to join the Communist party. He refused. Unemployed and blacklisted, he engaged in Cuba's counterrevolutionary struggle.

After the United States had severed ties with communist Cuba, political events became even more frightening for many Cuban families. Catholic schools were closed, and members of the religious community were advised to leave the country. Families feared governmental influence would weaken their ties with one another. Along with many other families, Mendieta's parents decided to send Ana at age 12 and Raquel at age 15 to the United States through Operation Peter Pan, a program created in 1961 by the Catholic Church to encourage emigration and preserve the children's Catholic upbringing. Although Mendieta's parents believed the separation would last only one year, it extended far longer. Mendieta's mother and younger brother, Ignacio, joined the girls after 5 years. Her father was arrested in 1965 for

---

[1] Biographical information is taken from Katz (1990), Herzberg (1998), and from my interview with Ana Mendieta's sister Raquel, which took place on January 13, 1996.

his CIA spying and not permitted to leave Cuba until 1979, 18 years later (Herzberg, 1998).

Cast out of their homeland, Ana and Raquel lived for several months in a camp in Miami before being sent to an orphanage in Dubuque, Iowa. Although initially thrilled by what she perceived as an exciting adventure, Ana cried incessantly when she realized the grave reality of her situation. The orphanage housed many adolescent delinquent girls, and the nuns often separated and mistreated the Mendieta sisters (Montane, 1991). From the orphanage, the sisters were shuttled from foster home to foster home, and soon Mendieta began to regard herself as an orphan (Spero, 1992). When her sister left for college, Mendieta again endured an agonizing separation, now from the person who had become the sole constant companion in her life and her primary mother figure. Mendieta's pain was exacerbated by the fact that her high school classmates teased her with racial epithets (Horsfield, Miller, & Garcia-Ferraz, 1988). At that point, she stopped eating and became so depressed that her foster family sought psychiatric help for her. The tearing apart of her family began to tear her apart. Later in life, she understood the need to make art that used her own body to express the concrete as well as the symbolic aspects of her trauma.

MOTHER EARTH

Mendieta's oeuvre is multifaceted, consisting of body art, performance pieces, and well-known earthworks made of twigs, grass, mud, sand, stone, clay, snow, and ice built up on riverbanks, beaches, archeological sites, trees, and limestone caves. Most of her art uses her body or its silhouette to express an exquisite relationship with the elements and her longing for merger and (re)union. She also made delicate petroglyph-like drawings and carvings on fig leaves and paper. "Art must have begun as nature itself," she wrote, "in a dialectical relationship between humans and the natural world from which we cannot be separated" (Clearwater, 1993). Mendieta saw deeply and correctly that humanity emerged from nature, and the two exist in reciprocal connection.

The many natural elements embodied in Mendieta's art are laden with both cultural and psychological meaning. Her oeuvre is linked with that of a group of artists who emerged in the late 1960s and 1970s, "land artists" who wished to challenge the museum and gallery spaces by creating art in outdoor sites. Mendieta described the shift in her artmaking:

> The turning point in my art was in 1972 when I realized that my paintings were not real enough for what I wanted the image to convey— and by real I mean I wanted my images to have power, to be magic. I decided that for the images to have magic qualities, I had to work

directly with nature. I had to go to the source of life, to mother earth. (Katz, 1990)

In contrast with the large-scale, mostly abstract, monumental, and often invasive, works executed by Michael Heizer, Robert Smithson, and Walter De Maria, Mendieta created more personal pieces and nearly always left the natural elements undamaged. She said: "I have thrown myself into the very elements that produced me, using the earth as my canvas and my soul as my tools" (Clearwater, 1993).

Even though most of her figures reveal few, if any, distinguishing feminine features, Mendieta's oeuvre is undeniably concerned with the female form and its cultural history. In fact, some of her earthworks are carved into the ground rather than superimposed on it. With their dark, oval crevices, these works suggest a mysterious inner space, the creation of vaginal forms. Unsurprisingly, then, in addition to the land art movement, the feminist movement had a profound effect on Mendieta's self-portrayals and performances. Influenced by fellow artist Mary Beth Edelson, Mendieta joined the feminist art movement, Reclamation of the Goddess, whose primary aim was to find and use historical images of powerful female forms (Orenstein, 1994). Yet, prior to this Mendieta knew that the mythical projection of the feminine onto nature served as a chief metaphor for the source and sustenance of life. Indeed, the earth is often associated with the womb and birth— the word *nature* comes from the Latin word *natura*, which means "birth or character"—yet the earth is also connected to death, as it is the most frequently used burial site. Life and death unite in Mendieta's earthworks as they bring together the most powerful forces with which we contend.

Mendieta's strong need to merge with the earth and to repeat its natural cycles by creating "living" artworks is illustrated in a highly evocative and powerful earth-body performance she executed in 1974 and documented on a film lasting three minutes and fifteen seconds. At the beginning of *Burial Pyramid*, Mendieta's hardly discernible body is buried beneath a pile of large stones at a temple structure in Yagul, Mexico. We watch as she takes deeper and deeper breaths that cause her torso to swell and the stones to rise and fall, eventually dropping from her body. Mendieta slowly emerges as if excavated from among the archeological ruins. Her naked body then begins to undulate, simultaneously miming the act of birth and the act of sex. Both acts revive her from a deathlike state and reconnect her to life forces. Literally breathing life into what appeared to be dead and buried matter, Mendieta leaves us awed by the power of her interaction with the universal forces of nature and her ability to endow them with human form. Reminiscent of Freud's famous archeological metaphor for psychoanalysis, Mendieta exemplifies his statement that "stones talk" (Freud, 1896/1962a).

In her ongoing reverential and intimate dialogue with nature, Mendieta expresses a sacred perspective: that the earth is vibrant, creative, and everlasting, a modifiable source of life to which we owe our existence. And, like the early psychoanalytic assertion of a sex and death drive to explain human behavior, Mendieta exclaimed: "All of my work is about two things … it's about Eros and life/death" (Montano, 1988). In a performance piece from 1975, *On Giving Life*, she placed her naked body on top of an adult human skeleton that lay on the grass and kissed its mouth. The image is shocking and provocative; she engages in what resembles mouth-to-mouth resuscitation and nakedly embraces death, daring to breathe life into dead bones and to show the natural yet discomforting intimacy between sex and death.

Since prehistoric times, women have been identified with the earth (Mother Earth and Mother Nature). For Mendieta, the earth became a surrogate mother with which she played out her issues of separation, loss, and creation. She treated the earth as if it were her mother's body and used it to simultaneously repeat and repair her trauma of exile. Mendieta accomplished this through a continued exploration of the concepts of figure and ground. She literally grounded herself in each new site, thereby becoming not only a figure within the ground, but also, a grounded figure. Mendieta's need to remain grounded was so intense that she suffered from a crippling fear of heights throughout her life. She blurred the boundaries between self and object by joining figure and ground, thereby representing the longed-for symbiotic reunion of mother/ground and child/figure. Few artists have expressed their psychological idiom as concretely as did Mendieta; her psychic trauma and her determination to transcend it are literally engraved in her body of art.

Freud's concept of repetition compulsion as a defensive attempt to master trauma helps us comprehend the reasons Mendieta returned to her silhouette hundreds of times in a relatively brief period (Freud, 1920/1955; Chapter 4 of this volume). Psychologically, Mendieta's art expresses both a reaction and response to the forced exile she experienced as a youth. She was traumatized by the loss of a protective mother, someone who could contain her sense of disorganization and dissolution. Metaphorically repeating her merger and extraction from her mother's womb in her art, she attempted to master these feelings. With its dissolution of boundaries, Mendieta's art stresses the importance of loss and the attendant hunger to reunite with the lost object (Klein, 1978/1979a), as well as the need to preserve and remember the past not merely through recollection but, perhaps more poignantly, through repetitive action.

The impermanence of most of the materials Mendieta used (soil, sand, fiber) and also their volatility (gunpowder and fire) demonstrates the sudden, powerful, and ever-present forces of nature and the fragility of form as it is ever altered by wind, rain, and time. Perhaps most important, the materials reflect the transient nature of the primary subject of her work: the ephemeral bonding with the mother and its vulnerability to unexpected and even explosive change. Mendieta was clearly aware of the psychological sources of her artwork when she wrote the following:

> I have been carrying on a dialogue between the landscape and the female body (based on my own silhouette). I believe this has been a direct result of my having been torn from my homeland (Cuba) during my adolescence. I am overwhelmed by the feeling of having been cast from the womb (nature). My art is the way I re-establish the bonds that unite me to the universe. It is a return to the maternal source. Through my earth/body sculptures I become one with the earth ... I become an extension of nature and nature becomes an extension of my body. This obsessive act of reasserting my ties with the earth is really the reactivation of primeval beliefs ... [in] an omnipresent female force, the after-image of being encompassed within the womb, is a manifestation of my thirst for being. (Barreras del Rio & Perrault, 1988)

Mendieta's longing to recreate the "oceanic feeling," discussed by Freud as "an indissoluble bond, of being one with the external world as a whole" (Freud, 1930/1961a) which derives from the mother–infant merger, is granted concrete expression in one of her early performance works in which she floats naked in the ocean. She deliberately executed this piece and several others in Florida's southernmost points to be as physically near to her homeland as possible. Striving to reconcile the painful psychological distance between the United States and Cuba, and between her mother and herself, the artist laid her body in the sand facing in the direction of Cuba and allowed the tide to wash it up. Mendieta's "aesthetics of disappearance" movingly recreate the tragedy of exile (Blocker, 1999). They also represent her way of mourning her losses.

In contrast with classical psychoanalysis, which views the mother–child relationship as solely influenced by the mother, recent research on the mother–infant dyad emphasizes the reciprocal influence that mothers and infants have on each other (Beebe & Stern, 1977). Mendieta, too, was aware of the mutuality of the mother–infant bond, the reciprocities and resonances that mirror, echo, reverberate, and transform both parties. Although she chose the sites of her earth-body sculptures and the materials she used to make them, she could not control what happened to them. Nature was left to take its course and acted on her as much, if not more, than she acted on it.

Silueta

Mendieta's *Silueta* series, produced in the 1970s, best illustrates the artist's dialogue with her lost mother by way of her art. These earth-body sculptures are distinguished by the lingering shape of Mendieta's body, which is literally hewed into landscapes, traced in sand, etched in dirt, carved in rock, and at times covered with blood (see Plate 30). Freud (1917/1957b) wrote of how the "shadow of the [lost] object" falls on the ego of the person in mourning and leaves a trace of its existence. Mendieta's title *Silueta*, or silhouette, can be understood as referring to this shadow, or in her own words, the "after-image" of her mother whose imprint had invariably remained in her life and art (see Plate 31). Incorporating the lost object through a process of identification, she tries to reestablish her place in the world.

In her first silueta executed in 1973 in an ancient Zapotec stone grave at Yaagul in the Valley of Oaxaca in Mexico, Mendieta calls attention to the convergence of life and death forces. She converted the rock-hard burial site into a womblike cavity in which she laid her soft, live body and covered it with fresh, white blossoming flowers (see Plate 32). This work nicely demonstrates the manner in which she made art by using her body to bring back to life what, for her, had seemed dead. After all, exile is a kind of death from which one must strive to emerge again as a new being. Furthermore, exile is itself a kind of womb, a container of isolation, a merger from which one must leave to embrace life and find a future. As she did when she mimicked making love with a skeleton, Mendieta here literally faces death and her fear of it.

Mendieta's exile separated her not only from her mother, but also from her father, whom she was prevented from seeing for 18 years. Ignacio was a frustrated artist who had created wood carvings in a studio attached to the family home (R. Mendieta, personal communication, January 11, 1996). Mendieta identified with her father by becoming an artist herself, a choice that allowed for a release of emotional expression, a mastery of trauma, and a means by which she kept him close to her. The first man she found to replace her father was Hans Breder, her art teacher at the University of Iowa, married and 13 years her senior. Mendieta and Breder had a 10-year relationship that proved romantically and professionally fertile. A self-imposed exile from Germany, Breder most probably had an implicit understanding of Mendieta's displacement issues. Breder's influence on the evolution of Mendieta's artistic idiom is unmistakable. He exposed her to a wide variety of performance artists who employed their bodies in their work, and actively encouraged her to use her body in artmaking (H. Breder, personal communication, January 15, 1996). Breder watched approvingly as Mendieta joined her body with Mother Earth, and he filmed her during the creation of most of her siluetas (H. Breder, personal communication, January 15, 1996). Consequently, Mendieta's works incorporate a male gaze of awe and reverence rather than chauvinistic appropriation.

Mendieta sought out various sites in Iowa and Mexico for her silueta works and visited Mexico with Breder every summer in the 1970s. In Mexico she discovered a culture similar to her own. She liked that the Mexican people were short and dark, like her, and she appreciated their commemoration of death in their annual Day of the Dead celebrations. She adopted several elements from Mexican iconography, like the posture she frequently assumed with upraised arms (Viso, 2004). Most important, she used the land to explore her relationship to her lost tribe. In essence, Mendieta, the self-proclaimed "orphan," created a family romance with Mexico as her new mother/land. "There is above all the search for origins" (Mendieta, 1996, p. 216), she wrote in 1983. She also said, "Plugging into Mexico was like going back to the source, being able to get some magic just by being there" (Fusco, 1992, p. 61).

Mendieta chose to work in Mexico's archeological sites due to her fascination with ancient civilizations and indigenous societies. Since Freud's time, archeology has been employed as an apt metaphor for psychoanalytic excavations into buried (repressed/unconscious) memories of one's individual and collective past. Mendieta, too, perceived her goal as that of mining societies that had been lost and forgotten, misunderstood and hidden, to keep their memories and customs alive and to prevent their total obliteration. Clearly, her attempts to revive these lost civilizations acted as a way of symbolically reconnecting to the land, people, and life that she had lost. Mendieta seemed never to tire of resuscitating the dead.

Blood

Influenced by Santeria, Mendieta used animal blood or red tempera paint as a symbol for sacrifice and rebirth (see Plate 30). In many of her siluetas, she also added these elements to represent the blood of Christ in transubstantiation. Mendieta mixed Christian and Pagan symbols in her art, since both held deeply sacred meaning for her. She traced her body's outline in blood, placed a bloody animal heart on top of her naked body, and made repeated prints of her bloody hands (see Plate 35). In one performance piece, she wrapped herself in a white bedsheet and lay in various poses while Breder sprinkled blood onto the sheet that covered her body. The result was a bright, blood-stained silhouette of her form. Recalling Christ's Shroud of Turin, Mendieta established her role as symbolic of eternal themes of martyrdom. The bloody outline of her body, and the bright silhouette on the sheet are the essential traces she leaves of her body and her life. Mendieta's blood, the invisible fluid coursing in her darkest depths, is made visible while Mendieta herself is absent, as if to say "Mendieta is here and yet not here at all."

On a more personal level, it is important to recall that Mendieta came close to dying in infancy. It was her father's blood, transfused into her body, that revived her and kept her alive. Incorporating blood in many of her works recreates the act of sacrifice and resurrection present in Catholicism, Santeria, and her own childhood. By smearing or dripping blood onto her body or its silhouette, Mendieta creates a ritual of sacrificial healing and rebirth. She thus becomes one with her absent father.

Fire

Mendieta once said, "Fire has always been a magical thing for me ... fusion ... its transformation of materials" (Mereweather, 1996). By incorporating candles, gunpowder, and fireworks into her art, Mendieta infused fire with multiple meanings. The light produced by the fire invokes a sense of ritualized spirituality or enlightenment. Mendieta's use of fire in her art is also symbolic of awareness, existence, and sacrifice, and suggests consciousness of the human situation, inherently poignant and tragic. She favors the powerful posture of the human form with arms upraised, beckoning upward for release, recalling the Catholic priest raising his arms during Mass, the Catholic tradition of a soul burning in purgatory, or the innocent and holy witch's surrender to the fire while being burned at the stake. Few things shock us more than a body on fire. We are life and yet life devours us. We are the fire and what it consumes; we burn and our smoke rises to the heavens. Small wonder Mendieta revived alchemy and created her own recipe for gunpowder using sulfur (representing the soul), sugar, and saltpeter (Brett, 2004). Some of her figures were set in mounds or raised "containers" of earth resembling volcanoes waiting to erupt (see Plate 33). In contrast to the slow changes the siluetas underwent when left to natural decaying processes, gunpowder and fireworks siluetas were transformed rapidly, dramatizing the suddenness of change we sometimes experience in life.

And yet Mendieta always returns to the land, not merely because she loved it, but also because she raged against her exile, the expulsion from her mother's bosom, the gnawing sense of rejection that she attempted to overcome. Her love for what she missed and her fury at losing it while still so innocent permeates her art. She once remarked, "Art for me has been a way to sublimate rage. In fact it has been necessary to have such rage to free myself from confinement and the fury of confinement" (Herzberg, 2004). This statement casts further light on her use of explosives in some of her silhouettes. After becoming one with the elements, a number of her forms were set on fire and left to smoke and smolder until all that remained was a blackened cavity filled with the ashes of what had once been a benign union.

Santeria

Santeria became a major source of inspiration for Mendieta, showing her a way to use natural elements to enact her spiritual quest. Derived from the Spanish *santo*, Santeria connotes the worship of saints. Mendieta preferred the teachings of Santeria, with its view of the earth as a living thing from which one gains power, rather than Catholicism's emphasis on distant, heavenly entities. Catholicism, the religion in which she was raised in Iowa orphanages, reminded her of the pain of exile and difference while Santeria connected her to the natural and spiritual realms. Santeria also brought back fond memories of her lost childhood because it was the religion of the Black servants and nannies with whom she grew up. She is known to have spent many afternoons with these women listening attentively to their tales of the powers and magic of the *orisha* gods, each of whom is identified with a force of nature (Spero, 1992). In her exiled adulthood, Mendieta sought to reestablish connections with some of her secondary maternal figures from early life. She found affirmation and comfort in Santeria's holistic belief in the harmony of the universe, which, in turn, found expression in her art. She once said:

> It was during my childhood in Cuba that I first became fascinated by primitive art and cultures. It seems as if these cultures are provided with an inner knowledge, a closeness to natural resources. And it is this knowledge which gives reality to the images I have created. The sense of magic, knowledge and power found in primitive art has influenced my personal attitude toward art-making. (1996, p. 186)

Santeria influenced Mendieta's transition from the personal use of her body in art to the creation of more generalized female archetypes. In 1975 she replaced her actual body with the arrangement of natural elements in the shape of her silhouette (Clearwater, 1993). Later she used a cardboard form of her body to make the contour of her silhouette. In the 1980s, she abandoned her body shape entirely and replaced it with universal feminine forms. The movement from body, to natural element, to cardboard form, to archetype suggests the gradual disappearance of Mendieta's immanence from her work, a soft and slow exile of her flesh gradually replaced by symbols. Again Mendieta is addressing the trauma of exile and loss, but now from a transcendent viewpoint as if to say, "I am the mother I seek whose home is everywhere." Her fade from view is thus all the more poignant, and the delicate beauty of her journey toward the ephemeral generates a continuum of artistic self-representation that speaks to the longing for transcendence inherent in the human condition for which exile, loss, and grief are guaranteed. Thus, her psychological journey inevitably becomes transpersonal. The personal issues she works through in her art and the therapeutic subtext of her work take her beyond her own individual estrangement, exile, loss, and mourning. Inevitably her work speaks to us as players in a grand cosmic drama, telling us of the universal aspects of transience, separation, change, death, and rebirth. We, too, are comprised of the forces of nature—forever created and dissolving forms. Personal pain led Mendieta to spiritual union and cosmic depersonalization.

GODDESS

As Mendieta's art evolved over the years, the theme of her work remained closely tied to the mother; however, her focus eventually became the universal Mother. Because they were once worshipped for their powers of fertility, fecundity, and agricultural bounty, goddesses supplied the perfect catalyst for Mendieta's movement away from the personal to more universal themes. She first employed the Mayan goddess Ixtel as inspiration for several pieces she made in 1977; however, it was not until the 1980s that she created plentiful goddess images.

Interestingly, psychoanalyst Otto Rank (1924, 1932) believed that all artistic forms, from the primitive to the modern, can be traced to the maternal vessel. He argued that the human need for form originates from the will to overcome the first separation from the mother, the trauma of birth. Rank believed that birth was our first major trauma because it represents death of unity with the mother. Mendieta's goddess works use minimalist lines to represent the female form. They are delicate images in which the lone figure is carved or burned into the surface of cave interiors, tree trunks, paper, or leaves. Some divide the female form into three oval limbless shapes; some include large breasts; some have a deep gash denoting the vagina. Several have mud coils that curve about inside the body to create a labyrinth effect with no discernible beginning or ending. In one, Mendieta carved a goddess shape around a thick vine that moves through its entire body. Using the mother–child metaphor, with its "umbilical cord" attaching the woman to the earth, she shows the obvious connections among goddess, mother, and earth (see Plate 34).

Goddess mythology embraces notions of fertility, creation, and symbiosis, and glorifies the universal female principle. The goddess mythology is at odds with patriarchal hero mythology in which the hero's journey involves transcending boundaries along the path *away* from the mother. Through acts of heroism, the hero completes his differentiation and distinction from the female mystery; he stands alone and apart, becoming his own man, an entity who may have emerged from the female, but now transcends her. Goddess mythology does not have this aim: rather, one becomes whole by seeking to merge with the "Great Mother," by becoming the willing form through which her creative principle is expressed. This mythology is highly sensitive to the cycles of Mother Nature and the mysteries of her creations. Destructive forces, in addition to creative and nurturing ones, are necessary elements in goddess mythology. Mendieta was naturally drawn to goddess lore because it helped her apply universal symbolism to convey her personal experiences and gave her the elements necessary to express her need and desire for transcendence. In the end, she seemed to be saying that while art is temporary, earth and sky (nature) seem everlasting and we belong to them—they are our true home; they are our primordial parents.

This unification of the personal and the cosmic with immanence and transcendence, with time and the eternal, is what makes Mendieta's oeuvre essentially spiritual. She once wrote that "the greatest value" of art is the "spiritual role" it plays (R. Mendieta, personal communication, January 11, 1996).

For years Mendieta was obsessed with returning to Cuba. Between 1980 and 1983, she took seven trips to Cuba and was once even invited by the Castro government.[1] Her best known goddess earthworks were executed in her native land (see Plate 34). By making works in the Cuban landscape, she claimed that she was bringing her Silueta series back "to its source" (Viso, 2004). In 1981 Mendieta carved what she called her *Rupestrian Sculptures*, feminine images of Taínan goddesses, into the limestone rock of the womblike caves of Jaruco, a mountainous region west of Havana. Mendieta's choice of the "Cavern of Lost Space" was significant because it had served as a refuge for runaway slaves and independence fighters as well as a hospital site during the battle of 1895. The cave became a symbol for freedom and healing in Mendieta's art.

Mendieta named her images for the pre-Columbian goddesses in the language of the Tíano Indians. Her attraction to the Tíano is clear: She identified with this extinct people whose culture was lost because they had been overpowered by the Spanish and decimated by hunger and disease (Clearwater, 1993). Once again Mendieta employed her art to give life to what had formerly been destroyed. Unsurprisingly, in her motherland—the land of her mother(s) and the place where she had once been mothered—many of her titles refer to the Mother Goddess (e.g., *Mother of Waters*, *Old Mother Blood*, *First Woman*, or simply *Mother*).

EXILE

Our world has increasingly become one teeming with exiles, refugees, and émigrés. In fact, much of modern Western culture (think of Joyce, Nabokov, Beckett, Pound, Einstein, Marcuse, or Conrad, to name only a few) has been shaped by those who were estranged from their homes in one way or another. Therefore, exile and displacement might easily be considered the tragedy of our time (Said, 2000). Adorno (1974) wrote in his memoir, *Minima Moralia: Reflections on a Damaged Life*:

> The house is past … The best mode of conduct, in the face of this, still seems an uncommitted, suspended one: to lead a private life, as far as the social order and one's needs will tolerate nothing else, but not to

---

[1] In 1983, Mendieta went to Rome, a city that for her was a viable compromise between Cuba and America. She quickly adapted to Rome, made many friends, and showed her work.

attach weight to it as something socially substantial and individually appropriate. "It is even part of my good fortune not to be a house-owner," Nietzsche already wrote in *The Gay Science*. Today we should have to add: it is part of morality not to be at home in one's home. (p. 38–39)

The exile's anxiety unequivocally embraces homelessness, orphanhood, dislocation, and alienation. I believe this anxiety is largely responsible for the postmodern emphasis on multiple, shifting identities and perspectives. The notion of a decentered self in a fragile home that is vulnerable to a largely indifferent, and often destructive, environment has become the norm for many of us. Self-invention and reinvention, popular tools of the contemporary art scene, develop naturally from such a precarious scenario.

Like anyone forced into exile, the artist has the option, and more often the necessity, to use her exile as inspiration and muse for her work. Mendieta sought to replace a fluid existence with a stable one, a rootless life with rootedness, and wandering with a home. Her work involves compromises made between her native land and that of her hosts; it creates an intermediary place to live on the hyphen between Cuban and American. She wrote:

> There is an African custom which I think ... is analogous to my work ... The men from Kimberly go outside their village to seek their brides. When a man brings his new wife home, the woman brings with her a sack of earth from her homeland and every night she eats a little bit of that earth. The earth will help her make the transition between her homeland and her new home. (Blocker, 1999, p. 84)

Interestingly, Freud used a land metaphor when referring to women as "the dark continent." He admitted to having a blind spot with regard to the significance of the mother in early development when he wrote that "everything in the sphere of this first attachment to the mother seemed to me so difficult to grasp ... so grey with age and shadowy and almost impossible to revivify ... it was as if it had succumbed to an especially inexorable repression" (Freud, 1931/1961b, p. 226).[1] In fact, women analysts, most notably Melanie Klein and Margaret Mahler, have shifted the psychoanalytic focus from the Oedipal father to the mother by uncovering and elaborating the insufficiently explored territory of pre-Oedipal (mother–infant) relations, with the emphasis on early maternal bonding.[2]

---

[1] See also André Green (1987), Heinz Kohut (1977), Hans Loewald (1960/1980), and Janine Chasseguet-Smirgel (1986). All have discussed Freud's blind spot regarding female sexuality and motherhood.

[2] Otto Rank and Sándor Ferenczi were among early male psychoanalysts who were alert to the importance of the mother. Interestingly, Freud broke off with both men over his differences with them.

In both art and psychoanalysis, it has taken the work of women artists to recover and represent the "shadowy" stage of early development that Freud found so impenetrable. It is difficult to find an artist who has done more than Ana Mendieta to represent the archaic union between mother and child, or what Mahler called the *milieu interieur*. Mendieta's art surfaced and underscored the crucial significance of early states of merger with the mother for the development of one's body ego. She thereby captured the indissoluble yet fragile nonverbal bond with the mother in the form of artmaking.

VIOLENCE AGAINST WOMEN

Mendieta considered colonization violent, claiming that ruling classes uproot persons from their traditions and beliefs, and greedily exploit them (Mendieta, 1996). She also moved easily between the orbits of culture and gender and, therefore, felt troubled by cultural violence and violence against women. In 1973, college student Sara Ann Otten was brutally murdered on the campus of the University of Iowa where Mendieta was an art student. Soon afterward, Mendieta staged a performance to which she invited an unsuspecting audience of fellow students. When they entered her apartment, whose door was left ajar, they were aghast to discover Mendieta's bloody, motionless, half-naked body tied to a table amid a panorama of disarray. She later explained that she had conceived this work, the first in a series of rape pieces, in reaction against the idea of violence against women.

Mendieta staged additional tableaux of rape and violence that year. She did not announce these works but, rather, left them to be discovered by unsuspecting passers-by. In one tableau, she spread animal blood on the sidewalk next to a door and sat in a nearby car filming the pedestrians, who invariably noticed the blood but did not stop and inquire about it in a demonstration of casual voyeurism and indifference to violence. One of Mendieta's rape performances (1973) shows her half-naked body, lying exposed and bloody on a tree trunk, her pubis elevated for all to see. This work is reminiscent of Duchamp's *Etant Donnés*.

Continuing this theme, Mendieta created a powerfully economical piece, *Blood Writing* (1973), in which she faced a white wall with her back to the camera. She left traces of her blood-stained hands on the wall as she leaned against it and slid down to her knees from a standing position. Two wide lines of blood move toward her body and onto the floor. When she finished marking the wall, Mendieta left the pair of hand prints to stand alone in supplication, surrender, and testimony (see Plate 35).

Mendieta's signature handprints as well as the numerous siluetas with hands upraised were the perfect symbol for her helplessness, on the one hand, and for her victory on the other. In one unforgettable piece in which she departed from the familiar horizontal pose, Mendieta mounted the figure vertically high on a pole.[1] *Anima, Silueta de Cohetes* (*Soul, Silhouette of Fireworks*), created in Oaxaca, Mexico in 1976, shows the Goddess with arms raised toward the sky on a burning pyre (see Plate 36). The piece, made of bamboo armature, was constructed with the help of a local fireworks maker and set on a vacant expanse of land with a mountain view. The periphery of the figure and its heart were ignited to create a burning effigy that assumed the shape of a cross. Yet here it is not a man who is being sacrificed but Mendieta—Woman, Mother, Artist, Goddess. The heart continued to burn when the flames encircling the body were extinguished, leaving ash falling back to the earth. This work is one of the most sublime in Mendieta's entire oeuvre, its aesthetic form revealing a simple beauty and natural elegance.

In the 1980s, Mendieta's career was on the rise. She was exhibiting in the United States and in Rome, a city she lived in and felt more at home in than New York. Her confidence grew, and her future seemed promising on all fronts except for her stormy marriage with well-known Minimalist sculptor Carl Andre, who, like Breder, was 13 years her senior. Clashes were fueled by alcohol abuse on both sides and by Andre's infidelities. At age 38, Mendieta became the possible victim of an infamous and unresolved murder resulting from a fall from the 34th-floor balcony of the apartment she shared with her husband. Andre was tried and acquitted of her murder.

Mendieta's martyrdom, so powerfully articulated in her "Fireworks Silueta," was used against her 12 years later during her husband's murder trial. Andre's defense attorney referred to Mendieta's art, especially its use of blood, its affinity for death and martyrdom, and, in his words, "the wedding of the human body with the earth," to justify his claim that she had committed suicide and had not been murdered by her husband (Katz, 1990). The attorney went so far as to suggest that the flattened shape her body had assumed after the 34-foot fall was, after all, no different than her death-enamored siluetas and, in fact, could have been her final—fatal—work of art.

Surely, Mendieta's art showed a fascination and ease with the forces of death. The countless images of her body positioned flat on the ground readily call to mind burial rites and undoubtedly relate to Mendieta's working through deathlike processes in her art. The outrageously shocking allegation that Mendieta's art exposed her suicidal tendencies, however, neglects the very obvious connection Mendieta always had to life. In addition, suicide by leaping out a window would hardly be the choice of

---

[1] After 1984, Mendieta began to create vertical sculptures, mostly freestanding, upright tree trunks with fire engravings. She also began making transportable sculptures that lent themselves to exhibition in gallery spaces.

someone terrified of heights. Death to her was an inseparable part of the life cycle, a cycle in which all of nature and humans invariably partake. Mendieta confronted loss, decay, abandonment, and exile by showing these processes in her repetitive cycle of creation, death, rebirth and regeneration. In fact, her attempts to *master* loss, exile, and death are the most pronounced messages in Mendieta's oeuvre. She regenerated herself again and again like the legendary phoenix, and she brought the dead back to life by reviving even the most buried civilizations. Mendieta's spirit continues to live on through her art in defiance of its ephemeral quality and in defiance of her own death.

Chapter 10

Bruno Schulz
Desire's Impossible Object[1]

> I tried to describe to a stunned audience that indescribable thing, which no words, no pictures drawn with a trembling and elongated finger could evoke. I exhausted myself in endless explanations, complicated and contradictory, and cried in helpless despair.
>
> —Bruno Schulz

Though the opening quotation refers to the narrator's anguished quest for *The Book*—envisioned as the foundational myth underlying human experience—it also indicates the plight of Polish author and artist Bruno Schulz (1892–1942), who created a world in which beauty coexists in exquisite tension with arbitrariness and absurdity. Entering Schulz's voice and vision, the reader is left stunned by the brilliance of a sensorium fully attuned to the mysterious allure of the childhood world, articulated by a narrator whose dazzling command of lexicon strains the boundaries of language itself.

> And then as the knives and forks began to clank softly above the white tablecloths, the violins would rise alone, now suddenly mature although tentative and unsure just a short while before: slim and narrow-waisted, they eloquently proceeded with their task, took up again the lost human cause, and pleaded before the indifferent tribunal of stars, now set in a sky on which the shapes of instruments floated like water signs or fragments of keys, unfinished lyres or swans, an imitatory, thoughtless starry commentary on the margin of music. (Schulz, 1989, "Spring," p. 146)[2]

Who in the pantheon of literary giants writes like Bruno Schulz, perfectly poised in the undefined space between the dream and the waking state,

---

[1] This chapter was written with Rocco Lo Bosco.
[2] All quotations of Schulz's writing are taken from Schulz, B. (1989). *The Complete Fiction of Bruno Schulz* (C. Wieniewska, Trans.). New York: Walker & Co. Titles of his stories are inclued in the parentheses.

between the condition of transcendent and ecstatic psychosis and a bracing, quotidian rationality? Schulz wrote poetry that is fiction and fiction that is poetry, song-stories born aloft in the fevered chambers of an imagination that hungered for a primal sense of meaning, the unassailable Logos, only to come up against the impossibility of its attainment. In the sublime tension generated by the conflict between desire and the impossible object that it seeks, his art was born—the real and the unreal dancing freely together with neither one in the lead:

> At last, at the city boundary the night gives up its games, removes its veil, discloses its serious and eternal face. It stops constructing around us illusory labyrinths of hallucination and nightmare and opens wide its starry eternity. The firmament grows into infinity, constellations glow in their splendor in time-hallowed positions, drawing magic figures in the sky as if they wanted to announce something, to proclaim something ultimate by their frightening silence. (Schulz, 1989, "A Night in July," pp. 211–212)

Schulz created *the event of a language* flooded with connections between primary and secondary process thinking, imaginative reconstructions of temporality that subverts the notion of linear time. His adroit and synesthetic imagery enflames objects and nature with mystery and danger, and his use of irony undermines certainty and provides a fresh perspective on conventional literary themes. Indeed, in a radical sense, the language itself is Schulz's main character, and it demands entrancement from the reader. Only when inebriated with the innumerable possibilities of the Schulzian lexicon—which means surrendering to the unconscious flow of his narrative and fully steeping oneself in his vision—does the reader enter with Schulz the fantastic streets of his reimagined hometown of Drohobycz, where every character is both more and less than what he seems to be. Even his most beloved character, Schulz's father, Jacob, appears both as a grand heresiarch and a perfect fool.

Despite their hypnotic beauty, Schulz's stories are difficult to read and resistant to facile interpretation. His stories bespeak a world radiant with humming, enlivened surfaces that appear as theater and stand for both a throbbing, subterranean realm and a transcendent beyond. And yet those very possibilities are ruptured and foreclosed by dross, by *tandeta*[1] in the form of cheap and shoddy goods, weedy and insidious overgrowth, huge cockroaches, painted birds that disintegrate into junk, white spaces on a map indicating forbidden and lurid neighborhoods, broken and melancholic characters, and transgressive forms of time and space (Schöndle, 1991).

---

[1] *Tandeta* is a Polish word for cheap material, worthless junk, low culture, and trumpery.

Rarely are the plenum and the void so equally and eloquently represented as they are in Schulz's work:

> Dizzy with light, we stepped into that enormous book of holidays, its pages blazing with sunshine and scented with the sweet melting pulp of golden pears. ... Everyone in this golden day wore the grimace of heat—as if the sun forced his worshipers to wear identical masks of gold. (Schulz, 1989, "August," pp. 3–4)

> It was at a moment when time, demented and wild, breaks away from the treadmill of events and like an escaping vagabond, runs shouting across the fields. Then the summer grows out of control, spreads at all points all over space with a wild impetus, doubling and trebling itself into an unknown, lunatic dimension. (Schulz, 1989, "Pan," p. 46)

This chapter explores the nature of Schulz's idiom, paying special attention to the unique manner in which unconscious thought potently and persistently informs both his writing and drawing, and gives rise to a vast masochistic vision. Schulz wrote in a letter, "I know what happens is not altogether unconscious, but you don't realize how much of it is the action of more profound forces, how much is the doing of a metaphysical puppetry in you" (Ficowski, 1988, p. 206). Schulz's oeuvre, especially his literature, relies on regression, fantasy, condensation, and the spatiotemporal plasticity of the unconscious in the service of his art and his grand vision. His stories dance with the family romance fantasy, and his drawings dance with the primal scene fantasy, both loaded with unconscious power. In art and writing, Schulz strongly expressed the intense allure and sublime impossibility of attaining the object(s) he desired.

SACRED MASOCHISM

During his lifetime Schulz published two books that were compilations of loosely connected stories: *Cinnamon Shops* (translated as *The Street of Crocodiles* in English) and *Sanatorium Under the Sign of the Hourglass*. He was working on a third book, *The Messiah*, which was lost, along with other writings, paintings, and drawings, when the Nazis came to power. Shortly thereafter Schulz died at the age of 50, his life ended by Karl Günther, who shot him twice in the head to even a score with fellow Gestapo officer Felix Landau. Landau "owned" Schulz, a "necessary Jew," because he painted murals and other commissioned art projects for Landau in exchange for bread and supplies. Interestingly, Landau's stepfather had been Jewish. He was assigned to the employment of Drohobycz Jews but, in actuality, was responsible for their mass killing. Schulz obtained "Aryan papers," which he had received to defy his "protector," but he was afraid to use them to escape Drohobycz, the provincial Galician town he had lived in his entire life.[1] There is a bitter irony to Schulz's enslavement by his Nazi master, since Schulz spent much of his life entertaining sadomasochistic fantasies and scenarios. His writing positions the narrator, and the male in general, as a masochist, and his drawings are replete with images in which he and other males are depicted slavishly worshipping women, crawling at their feet, displaying the sweet pain of subjugation and humiliation. The foundation for this position was established early in his life and poignantly rendered in a dream he related in a letter to psychologist, Stefan Szuman:

> … my truest and profoundest dream, which I dreamed at age seven, a dream that foretold my fate. In my dream I am in a forest at night, in the dark; I cut off my penis with a knife, scoop out a little cavity in the earth, and bury it there. This is the antecedent, as it were, the part of the dream without emotional tone. What follows is the real dream: I come to my senses, bring my conscious mind to bear on the atrocity, the horror of the sin I have committed. I refuse to believe that I really committed it and keep finding to my despair it is so, that what I have perpetrated is irrevocable. I seem to be already beyond time, *sub specie aeternitatis*, an eternity that cannot be anything else for me now but a dreadful consciousness of guilt, awareness of irreparable loss down through the eons. I am condemned forever, and the form this takes is public confinement in a glass retort, from which I shall never escape. The feeling of interminable torment, damnation through ages uncounted, I shall never forget. How is one to explain, at such an age, the symbolic charge, the semantic potential of this dream, which I have been unable to exhaust to this day? (Ficowski, 1988, p. 37)

The young Bruno dreams that he severs his penis, his connection with his biology, and buries it in an earth cavity, a kind of womb. But these acts within the dream carry no emotional tone; it is as if they are fated, deeds predetermined by forces outside his will. They express his desire to return to the mother, the source, while simultaneously rendering him extraordinary, beyond time and circumstance, a kind of damned angel or sacred freak trapped in a glass cage. The guilt-ridden rejection of his gender burden and his unwillingness to differentiate from the mother masochistically imprison him in "a state of spellbound suspension within a personal solitude" (Ficowski, 1988, p. 37).

---

[1] Biographical information on Schulz's life comes from Ficowski (1988, 2003), unless otherwise indicated.

Yet there are benefits to Schulz's isolation. He gets to stand outside of time, independent of arbitrary, contingent, temporal realities, and sing his own creation. Like the father in his stories, he too becomes a heresiarch, but of a much higher order. Unlike Jacob's painted birds that fall to pieces or Jacob's "Treatise on Tailors' Dummies" contemptuously dismissed by a maid's naked foot, Schulz's artistic embodiment will burn with inexhaustible "semantic potential." For his sacrifice he receives the rarest of all muses, one who will play his self-condemned eunuch like a celestial harp. Yet how mighty will Bruno's severed penis seem when it reappears in his stories, inseminating his writing with mythopoetic glory and pyrotechnic splendor!

Though Schulz will long for the biological and emotional connection to the woman, his profound masochism will ensure that she remain an object he can approach only on his knees. He will conjure up magical perceptions from the innocence of childhood, but he will live the hard realities of having to support his family after his father dies. And although he will deeply hunger for mystical knowledge, an indestructible and eternal meaning and sense, he will find a silent cosmos calling for his words, a world far less beautiful than the one he imagines. He will be agonizingly and forever separated from the object of his desire, but that agony will bring forth an ecstasy, found in both his stories and pictures.

Schulz seemed fully conscious of his masochism, which covered the widest possible spectrum of human existence, when he wrote:

> My creativeness differs ... from the stereotyped creativeness of perverts like Sacher Masoch or de Sade ... It doesn't represent direct imaginative satisfaction of a perverse drive but reflects rather my entire inner life, the focal center of which is formed about a certain perversion. Creatively, I express this perversion in its loftiest, philosophically interpreted form as a foundation determining the total *Weltanschauung* of an individual in all its ramifications. (Wegrocki, 1946, p. 164)

Schulz saw in the sadomasochistic structure the defining relationship between himself and existence and between the cosmos and its inhabitants, played out in particular as sadomasochistic theater between men and women. In the most general sense, Schulz places nature in the role of sadist. Nature looms large and threatening, and people tremble before its power, as it subjugates them to its whim and fancy. In "Night of the Great Season," a treacherous and poisonous dusk makes rotten all that it touches, causing people to flee in panic, "but the disease always caught up to them and spread in a dark rash across their foreheads. Their faces disappeared under large, shapeless spots" (Schulz, 1989, p. 87). In "The Gale," darkness reaps an "enormous, hundredfold harvest" (Schulz, 1989, p. 78). What surrounds human beings towers above them and commands their lives with its awesome power.

> The sky was swept lengthwise by the gusts of wind. Vast and silvery white, it was cut into lines of energy tensed to breaking point, into awesome furrows like strata of tin and lead. Divided into magnetic fields and trembling with discharges, it was full of concealed electricity. The diagrams of the gale were traced on it which, itself unseen and elusive, loaded the landscape with its power. (Schulz, 1989, "The Gale," p. 79)

The Mistress—in the form of Mother Nature symbolically connected to his own mother—is mysterious and incites endless pondering. One must approach Her with humility and hope; one must court Her with astonishing poetry:

> A night in July! What can be likened to it? How can one describe it? Shall I compare it to the core of an enormous black rose, covering us with the dreams of hundreds of velvety petals? The night winds blow open its fluffy center, and in its scented depth we can see the stars looking down on us. (Schulz, 1989, "A Night in July," p. 210)

But however deeply She is courted, She ultimately discards Her forms and colors, continually shaping "something out of chaos" and ultimately "rejecting every shape" (Schulz, 1989, "A Night in July," p. 210). One lives at Her feet only so long, for "beauty is a disease ... it is the dark forerunner of decomposition" (Schulz, 1989, "A Second Fall," p. 221); it is a world that stands above human beings as a master stands above a slave. In this world *tandeta*, or junk and overgrowth, is inherent in every being and object, for all things eventually decompose and all beings must die. Dross and loss are built into the proliferation and spoil the hope for perfect unity and meaning. Yet the entire show has a sacred quality because forces beyond comprehension are at play and these very forces inspire and drive the writing itself.

Schulz's language is imbued with a terrific power of description and suggestion in which extraordinary connections and relations abound. A sneeze is described as punctuating a day's events with "witty commentary" (Schulz, 1989, "The Age of Genius," p. 139). Half-witted cousin Touya has a face that "works like the bellows of an accordion" (Schulz, 1989, "August," p. 6). Even silence comes to life in Schulz's poetic prose as it "talked ... yellow, bright ... delivered its monologue, argued, and loudly spoke its vulgar maniacal soliloquy" (Schulz, 1989, "August," p. 7). Such language continually speaks in the voice of the unconscious as it joins images that aren't ordinarily found together, creates new symbols, and renders an overwhelming and mysterious world of profound and threatening beauty. No wonder Schulz saw his vision as existing beyond mere perversion. He viewed himself and others as instruments of vast, inchoate forces and powers. Life lived its people; people did not live their lives. For him human beings are not only subjected to the mysteries of nature, to the infinite surround they incarnate, but also to the forces of mind, as they embody experience of irreducible complexity: "Yet what is to be done with events that have no place of their own in time … events that have been left in the cold, unregistered, hanging in the air, homeless, and errant? Could it be time is too narrow for all events?" (Schulz, 1989, "The Age of Genius," p. 131).

Linear time cannot account for the parallel events taking place in the world or the unconscious, the endless connections, compressions, and disseminations of meaning that play the underground fugues. Schulz's temporal creations of multitrack, cul-de-sac, and demented time point to the timelessness of the unconscious so apparent in dreams. Multiple time frames may be condensed into a single image. Events may be absurd or follow an absurd course. Effect can antecede cause, or cause and effect may be dispensed with altogether. We find these kinds of unconscious inventions throughout Schulz's stories—for example, when we discover that a "second autumn" is caused by the "miasma exuded by degenerate specimens of baroque art crowded in our museums" (Schulz, 1989, "A Second Fall," p. 221), or we realize his father is simultaneously both dead and alive in *Sanatorium Under the Sign of the Hourglass*.

The Street of Crocodiles and especially *Sanatorium Under the Sign of the Hourglass* can each be read as a tour of the author's mind, especially its unconscious dimension. In *Sanatorium*, father, although dead, is brought back to life and, through his multiple states, time becomes reversible. "Here we reactivate time past, with all its possibilities … including the possibility of recovery," says the doctor at the sanatorium (Schulz, 1989, p. 246). Schulz writes: "everybody is asleep all the time … it is never night here" (p. 245), yet sleep is not confined to the bed. A parcel never ordered is delivered to the father's shop, despite its just opening and not even having a sign. In the parcel is a folding telescope through which the narrator sees the back of the sanatorium. In other words his mind provides him with a magnifying instrument with which to further examine itself. A chain of endless solipsistic self-references is set in motion. "I stood in front of the mirror to fix my tie … it secreted my reflection somewhere in its depth" (p. 250).

Time begins to "indulge in crazy clowning" (Schulz, 1989, p. 259), and so his father may be in two places at one time, behaving foolishly at a restaurant while also being sick in bed. In this "town" the narrator tries to conceal things from himself, things "quite fantastic in their absurdity," one of which is that his mother appears and offers him a "pleading smile." He asks her, "Where am I? What is happening here? What maze have I become entangled in?" (p. 264). And, of course, in this town of the mind, in which his dead father still lives, conflict must reign. Packs of dogs run the streets, and an enemy army invades the town. (What prescience!) The narrator meets the embodiment of his perversion and lust in the form of a dog beast who then appears as a man, "given to dark, sudden passions" (p. 269) and with whom the narrator fakes a short lived and "terrible friendship" (p. 270).

But the narrator cannot bear the connection with his bestial side, and so abandons the dog-man, leaving the enraged beast with his sick father—again an act of self-castration and a rejection of the sexual burden and responsibility of being a man. He is left at the story's end as he is left in his childhood (self-castrated) dream, wandering and damaged. He lives now on a train and becomes the very conductor with a bandaged face that he encountered at the beginning of the story. The story's framework couldn't be clearer: he has encountered only his own mind through the course of the story.

In Schulz's world ordinary space is not large enough to contain events across the total spectrum of meaning and implication. As with time, space is altered in his stories and becomes a kind of outlaw space, concealed within space itself, rooms hidden within rooms or hidden in the mind, rooms like the kind one finds in dreams. In his "Treatise on Tailors' Dummies," Jacob speaks of

> old apartments [where] there are rooms which are sometimes forgotten. Unvisited for months on end, they wilt neglected between the old walls and it happens that they close in on themselves, become overgrown with bricks, and, lost once and for all to our memory, forfeit their only claim to existence. The doors, leading to them from some backstairs landing, have been overlooked by people living in the apartment for so long that they merge with the wall, grow into it, and all trace of them is obliterated in a complicated design of lines and cracks. (Schulz, 1989, "Treatise on Tailors' Dummies," Conclusion, p. 37)

The dreamlike and arbitrary events that occur in Schulz's stories are often tinged with a gentle and humorous cruelty as they express the sheer power of life over its creatures. The spatiotemporal labyrinths therein and the multidimensional images that fill those labyrinths indicate an order of being that most of us would do best to forget. *Existence itself positions the human being as a masochist. Existence drives the being. Its meaning eludes the being. Its necessity forces the being to toil without end. Consciousness of it taunts the being. Its desire uses up the being. And its time eventually discards the being as a corpse, as tandeta.*

Even if one, with whip in hand, takes up the sadistic cause, it is only a small imitation of that Grand Mistress. And should one prefer the pen or the brush to the whip, fancying oneself a heresiarch of sorts, a second-order demiurge possessed of great semantic or graphic fire, still one always falls short of the "real thing" in which even the smallest and most insignificant event "when drawn close to one's eye ... may open in its center an infinite and radiant perspective because a higher order of being is trying to express itself" (Schulz, 1989, *Sanatorium Under the Sign of the Hourglass*, p. 130). And even the "real thing" may be only a simulation; man and his tailor's dummy might be interchangeable after all.

However cosmic or deeply psychological he renders the sadomasochistic scene, Schulz's position grows out of his "nature" and personal history. His childhood dream, an archetype of sacrifice and submission, indicates his early stance within a system of guilt allayed by punishment and self-castration that nevertheless elevates him to the position of an artist possessed of unique vision and creative ability. He was overly sensitive and sickly from childhood on. His mother once found him feeding sugar water to flies to help them with the coming winter (Ficowski, 2003). Much later he admitted that, "My great enemy is lack of self-confidence and *amour propre*" (Ficowski, 1988, p. 136). He perceived himself as weak and lacking "the necessary strength and conviction" to fight for what he wanted (p. 98). He complained bitterly about being forced to work at a job as a high school arts-and-crafts teacher that was not to his liking and that left little time for his own art: "I submitted to the demands of a school routine alien to my temper and how much I suffered under this yoke" (p. 100). His elder brother died suddenly in 1935, after which his semi-invalid sister, her son, and a cousin depended entirely on him for their livelihood. They were poor and lived in cramped quarters that left him longing for solitude to create: "This substantial quiet, positive—full—is already itself almost creativity" (Ficowski, 2003, p. 48). Schulz wrote of the strain and disgust his teaching job created in him: "Every day I leave that scene brutalized and soiled inside, filled with distaste for myself and so violently drained of energy that several hours are not enough to restore it" (Ficowski, 1988, p. 99). These living conditions clearly fed Schulz's masochistic leanings.

The housemaid dominated his own father, and his mother appeared cold and aloof. Mother's ghost, as we shall see, haunts his work and lends great poignancy to his vision of unanswered desire and masochistic longing and pain. Additionally, the young Bruno had a punitive and harsh nanny who humiliated him. In Schulz's world women possess confidence, *savoir vivre*, and unquestionable excellence, while men are often portrayed as doglike, down on all fours, or cowering near the curbs and gutters. They are pathetic and haunted creatures who, however learned or talented, cannot measure up to women's natural perfection:

> Each girl seems to carry inside her an individual rule ... Walking thus straight ahead, with concentration and dignity ... they so conscientiously carry within themselves ... an *idée fixe* of their own excellence, which the strength of their conviction almost transforms reality ... an untouchable dogma, held high, impervious to doubt. (Schulz, 1989, *Sanatorium Under the Sign of the Hourglass*, p. 260)

Women do not question their right to exist, "the heroism of womanhood triumphing by fertility over the shortcomings of nature, over the insufficiency of the male" (Schulz, 1989, "August," p. 9). Schulz wrote that women "had everything within themselves, they had a surfeit of everything in themselves" (Schulz, 1989, "Tailors' Dummies," p. 28). Even Touya, the "dark half-naked idiot girl" in *Cinnamon Shops*, is described as satisfying herself physically as she "rises slowly to her feet and stands like a pagan idol" (Schulz, 1989, "August," p. 7). Men, on the other hand, are dependent on others in order to feel alive:

> You blossom forth for a moment. You rub against somebody, attach your homelessness and nothingness to something alive and warm. The other person walks away and does not feel your burden, does not notice that he is carrying you on his shoulders, that like a parasite you cling momentarily to his life. (Schulz, 1989, *Sanatorium Under the Sign of the Hourglass*, p. 298)

REGRESSION IN THE SERVICE OF ART

A great difference existed between Schulz's fantasy life, so vividly depicted in his stories and drawings, and the harsh and ultimately terrible reality he was forced to live. In fact, his memory, imagination, and artistic talent temporarily saved him not only with the Nazis but throughout his life. Schulz wrote that the "universal disillusioning of reality" was "unbearable unless it was compensated for in some other dimension" (Ficowski, 2003, p. 83). The "other dimension" is of course implied in his stories as a unitive primal sense and purpose, but in concrete terms he is referring here to the dimension of art. Art for him was the Real that transformed the barren wasteland of ordinary events into a vivid landscape of wonder, terror, and beauty. Such a transformation requires regression to a freer form of thought, an imagination unconstrained by the analytic and parsing mind, an earlier era Schulz called the "age of genius," a time in childhood when imagination and reality remain undifferentiated. He compared ordinary books to meteors because each has "a moment when it soars screaming like a phoenix, all its pages aflame," but soon turns to ashes (Schulz, 1989, "The Book," p. 126). Books whose origins stem from the age of genius, however, deal with "things that cannot ever occur with any precision. They are too big and too magnificent to be contained in mere facts" (p. 129). In a story titled "The Age of Genius," the young Joseph (his fictional alter ego), overwhelmed by fiery inspiration, discovers drawing and the visionary possibilities of creative imagination:

> I sat among the piles of paper, blinded by the glare, my eyes full of explosions, rockets, and colors, and I drew wildly, feverishly, across the paper, over the printed or figure-covered pages. My colored pencils rushed in inspiration across columns of illegible text in masterly

squiggles, in breakneck zigzags that knotted themselves suddenly into anagrams of vision, into enigmas of bright revelation, and then dissolved into empty, shiny flashes of lightening, following imaginary tracks. (Schulz, 1989, "The Age of Genius," p. 133)

Schulz drew before he could talk, covering "every scrap of paper and the margins of newspapers with scribbles" (Chmurzyński, 1995, p. 36). In time, he turned to writing, a medium he felt allowed him a greater range of expression:

> If I am asked whether the same thread recurs in my drawings as in my prose, I would answer in the affirmative. The reality is the same; only the frames are different ... A drawing sets narrower limits by its material than prose does. That is why I feel I have expressed myself more fully in my writing. (Chmurzyński, 1995, p. 36)

Yet, because of the oppressive duties of his life, Schulz was unable to dedicate much time to his artistic pursuits. Therefore, however childlike his imagination, his artistic expression is essentially dark and melancholy. The primal sense and unity he seeks elude him. Junk and ruinous excess triumph. It is hardly promising that Jacob, Schulz's literary father, is reborn as a roach, a crab, and part of a wall. People can even be transmogrified into "the rubber tube of an enema" (Schulz, 1989, "Treatise on Tailors' Dummies," p. 39).[1] There are no real denouements in his stories; strange and often seemingly random events carry a soft-spoken dread, and the characters appear and fade like smoke, drifting through dark and ephemeral worlds on the way from nowhere to nowhere, encountering each other like figures in a dream. In 1937, he wrote to a friend, "What I lack is not so much faith in my own gifts but something more pervasive: trust in life, confident acquiescence in a personal destiny, faith in the ultimate benevolence of existence" (Ficowski, 1988, p. 148).

Still his art allowed him to return to his childhood and imagination, a happier time when he felt close to his father, and the world was filled with bright wonder uncorrupted by *tandeta*.

> It seems to me that this kind of art, the kind which is so dear to my heart, is precisely a regression, a returned childhood. Were it possible to turn back development, achieve a second childhood by some circuitous road, once again have its fullness and immensity—that would be the incarnation of an "age of genius," "messianic times" which are promised and pledged to us by all mythologies. My ideal goal is

---

[1] This absurd image functions perfectly as an apt metaphor for actual and frightening human possibilities. Think of a person in a hospital bed kept alive by machines.

to "mature" into childhood. This would really be a true maturity. (Ficowski, 2003, p. 72)

Engaged in veritable "regression in the service of the ego" (see Chapter 2 of this volume), Schulz employs his art as a return to childhood to bring his beloved father back to life, to work through his early conflicts, and to tap into the richness of the child's perspective and experience.

He admitted his bizarre stories were autobiographical. "To what genre does *Cinnamon Shops* belong? How should it be classified?" he asked once and then replied, "I think of it as an autobiographical narrative" (Chmurzyński, 1995, p. 37). The town he described is of course his hometown, Drohobycz, and the "cinnamon shop" is Jacob's, his merchant father's, shop. His image and that of his father are sprinkled throughout his drawings, and his books are written in the first person. Family members, friends, and even the household servant play major roles. Yet, though highly autobiographical, Schulz was aware of the myth-making involved in his work:

> Just as the ancients traced their ancestors back to mythological unions with the gods, so I have attempted to establish for myself a mythic generation of forbears, a fictional family from which I derive my real origins. In some sense such "histories" are real; they represent my way of life, my particular fate. (Ficowski, 2003, p. 92)

Rarely do we find such an obvious admission of an artistic mythology consisting in essence of a family romance fantasy. This has been an important feature of the Schulzian oeuvre and is entirely overlooked in the critical literature.

THE FAMILY ROMANCE OF JACOB AND JOSEPH

The family romance fantasy refers to the child's notion or fantasy that his parents are not his real parents and that his actual parents are of a more exalted stature (Knafo & Feiner, 2006). This fantasy unconsciously compresses solutions to many needs. It expresses the child's curiosity concerning origins and the effort to reveal them. The fantasy also functions to relieve guilt from incestuous impulses by distancing the child from the parent(s). It replaces devalued parents with idealized ones, again aiding the separation process. It also revives the nurturing, all-powerful parents of early childhood before disillusionment in them set in (Knafo & Feiner, 2006). Finally, it justifies the child's sense of being a unique and irreplaceable being, for if the parents are of an exalted nature, so then must be the child. The family romance fantasy is an excellent example of how the unconscious condenses motivation and meaning.

In Schulz's writing, the family romance has his father in an elevated position and his mother in a devalued one, in that the father is ever-present and powerful, whereas the mother is barely visible, though her absence infuses his stories with melancholy. In his drawings he reverses this position, elevating the woman and debasing the man. It is the woman who is the central figure of his art, whereas the man frequently huddles in the shadows. Yet, there is a deep sadness conveyed in both mediums since the woman, both as the concrete and symbolic object of desire, is forever out of reach. When his writing and art are taken together, we have a more complete picture of Schulz's family romance fantasy. Its psychological ramifications notwithstanding, this fantasy imbues Schulz's work with creative potency.

In his stories, Schulz's family romance replaces the small Galician town he lived in with one more ancient and grand, "swept by hot winds like a biblical desert" (Schulz, 1989, "August," p. 4). He transforms his elderly, ailing, and probably demented father, the central character besides himself in his prose, into an Old Testament prophet; he is Jacob, named after the biblical patriarch and compared to Old Testament Jacob, as well as Moses and Noah. (See Plate 37.) In the story "Dead Season," he even wrestles with a strange character all night as did the biblical Jacob with an angel. Like the biblical Joseph, Schulz's fictional alter ego, also named Joseph, is the youngest and favorite son of Jacob. Schulz confesses in his story "Spring," "I committed an unconscious plagiarism of another Joseph ... but no one held it against me" (Schulz, 1989, p. 149). It is hardly a coincidence that Schulz's favorite novel was Thomas Mann's *Joseph and His Brothers* or that he, like his biblical counterpart, was adept at interpreting dreams. In his 1937 essay, "The Republic of Dreams," Schulz wrote, "No dreams, however absurd or senseless, are wasted in the universe. Embedded in the dream is a hunger for its own reification, a demand that imposes an obligation on reality and that grows imperceptibly into a bona fide claim, an I.O.U. clamoring for payment" (Ficowski, 1998, p. 221).

Schulz's choice is significant, too, because the biblical story of Joseph is a family romance in its own right. The *Book of Genesis* tells us that Joseph's brothers threw him into a pit to die because they envied him for being their father's favorite. Joseph overcomes great odds by escaping to Egypt and being adopted by the exalted family of the pharaoh, only to become the second most powerful man in Egypt after the pharaoh. Biblical Joseph forgives his brothers and brings his family to Egypt to save their lives. Despite the fact that he was not wealthy or powerful, Schulz must have identified with the biblical Joseph because he too saved his family by sacrificing and providing for them. Furthermore, he possessed the special gift to transform an oppressive reality into resplendent art.

Whereas the real Jacob took to his bed and could no longer work while Schulz was still young (he was 46 when Bruno was born), the author magically transforms his father's mental and physical frailty. Jacob is set apart from others as "an incorrigible improviser" and "fencing master of imagination" (Schulz, 1989, "Tailors' Dummies," p. 24), and his madness only renders him more interesting. He alone "waged war against the fathomless, elemental boredom that strangled the city" because he alone "was defending the lost cause of poetry" (p. 24). His mad tirades become novel experiments; his collection of rare birds becomes his kingdom; his lectures on matter are dense and beyond everyone's comprehension. Father is "infecting everything with his dangerous charm" (p. 30), wrote Schulz in his story "Tailors' Dummies." The world and Schulz's life turn colorless and empty when his father dies. And one purpose of his art was to cope with this tragedy because "one thing must be avoided at all costs: narrow-mindedness, pedantry, dull pettiness" (Schulz, 1989, "Spring," p. 170). To this end, Schulz resurrects his father again and again, and turns this "broken man" into an "exiled king" (Schulz, 1989, "Birds," p. 23).

In "The Night of the Great Season," which takes place on a "thirteenth freak month ... a hunchback month, a half-wilted shoot, more tentative than real" marked by "crab days, weed-days ... white days, permanently astonished and quite unnecessary" (Schulz, 1989, p. 84), Jacob appears as an Old Testament prophet seated on a high stool with a bird's-eye view of his shop, taking stock of his colorful cloths. But nature's power ascends as the "great season" approaches, "beautiful yet evil," (p. 87) and everything turns into a "black night, saturated with dreams and complications" (p. 89). A mob advances toward father's shop and the vain housekeeper Adela is amused and smiling, impervious to the danger that surrounds them, as she is chased by the shop's assistants. Father loses control and grows purple with anger at the approaching crowd entering his shop. He leaps onto his shelves of fabric and blows the shofar, the Jewish horn of atonement. The crowd is unmoved and demands that he engage in commerce. In response, Jacob hurls the bales of material at them, "unfolding in the air like enormous flags, the shelves exploded with bursts of draperies, with waterfalls of fabric as if touched by the wand of Moses" (p. 90). Like Moses who is forced to deal with pagan worshippers as he descends Mount Sinai with God's commandments, Schulz's father "wandered among the folds and valleys of Canaan ... hands spread out prophetically to touch the clouds, and shaped the land with strokes of inspiration" (p. 91).

In keeping with the family romance fantasy, the father is much larger than life, truly imposing and yet also debased. Joseph asks in *Sanatorium*, "what could one expect of Father, who was only half real, who lived a relative and conditional life, circumscribed by so many limitations!" (Schulz, 1989, p. 252). One of father's limitations is that he is ruled by the maid Adela whose "power over Father was almost limitless" (Schulz, 1989, "Birds," p. 20).

Adela was able to walk up to Father with a smile and flip him on the nose (Schulz, 1989, "Tailors' Dummies," p. 29), putting him in his place with the smallest of gestures. Like his birds, father floats above everyone or he is near the ground, under the floor, in the dark, alongside roaches, even sharing his chamber pot with the animals. He is a magician, a mesmerist, a man who defies death by returning again and again in new forms. But he is also a man who is old and sick, and puts his head into a chimney shaft of the stove, a man who shrinks daily "like a nut drying inside a shell" (Schulz, 1989, "Visitation," p. 17). "How do I reconcile this?" asks Joseph, "Are there two fathers?" (p. 258). The answer is yes: In the family romance fantasy, the sublime and the devalued coexist side by side.

Schulz believed that each artist is allotted a few images, what he called "the iron capital of the spirit," with which to create: "It seems to me that all the rest of one's life is spent interpreting these insights ... artists ... do not discover anything new after that, they only learn how to understand better and better the secret entrusted to them at the outset" (Ficowski, 1988, p. 110). One of the images Schulz recounts as his iron capital is that of "a child carried by his father through the spaces of an overwhelming night, conducting conversation in darkness" (p. 110). The father caresses the child and tries to shield him from the natural elements, but, in the end, "there is no escape." The origin of this image seems to refer to Goethe's ballad *Erkling*, read to him by his mother, about an evil spirit that threatens children, especially he who is held in his father's arms at night. Schulz refers to this motif in his story "Spring": "There goes that man who hugs the child in his arms ... that refrain, that pitiful motto of the night" (Schulz, 1989, p. 166). Curiously aware of its family romance properties, he writes: "The story is about a princess kidnapped and changed for another child" (p. 166). Schulz found inspiration and sought protection in his father— whether he was real or a product of his imagination. He explained that as a small child, "I liked to stand between my father's legs, clasping them from each side like columns" (Schulz, 1989, "The Book," p. 118).

So powerful is the father's presence that the narrator identifies him, and not the mother, as the source of life. In "The Book" Joseph says that: "My mother had not appeared yet. I spent my days alone with my father in our room, which at that time, was as large as the world ... Then my mother materialized, and that early, bright idyll came to an end" (Schulz, 1989, p. 118). That the narrator claims the ruination of the magic world of childhood came with the appearance of his mother suggests a profound derailment with the maternal source. No wonder her appearances are rare and rather mysterious. One might say there is simply not enough of her to encounter. There are mere scraps of her to interpret. Mother is ever elusive and puzzling, unattained and unattainable, ever out of reach, perhaps nothing more than a vapor. As the element of a fantasy that supposedly elevates the imagined parent over the real one, she somehow seems paltry, described as unheroic and possessing a "simple and uncomplicated mind" (Schulz, 1989, "Dead Season," p. 227). When she is mentioned, it is often with anger because she disturbs the close tie Joseph has with Jacob, and she never seems to address her son honestly or directly. After Jacob's metamorphosis into a cockroach in which "he merged completely with the black uncanny tribe" (Schulz, 1989, "Cockroaches," p. 76) and is lost to his family, Joseph expresses the feeling to his mother that his father has not become a cockroach but a condor. The sense given in this short scene is that Joseph is begging his mother for some kind of reassurance, longing for her to affirm the nobler of the two transformations. *My father has become a condor, not a cockroach, right?* She looks at her son from "under her eyelashes" and asks that he not "torture" her, claiming that Jacob has become a "commercial traveler" who "comes home at night and goes away before the dawn" (Schulz, 1989, "Cockroaches," p. 77). That she asks her son not to torture her implies that he has sought help from her before and has been rebuffed. Coldly aloof and unconcerned with his travail, she neither denies nor affirms his speculation but dismisses both alternatives and replaces them with a third. In effect she denies his sorrow and his hope. Her response to his plea poignantly expresses the disconnect between them.

Joseph, as Schulz's alter ego, blames his mother for recovering too rapidly from his father's death and holds her responsible for the father's madness because "she had never loved him ... father had not been rooted in any woman's heart, he could not merge with any reality and was therefore condemned to float eternally on the periphery of life, in half-real regions, on the margins of existence" (Schulz, 1989, "Cockroaches," p. 73). Schulz is saying here that he believes a man becomes rooted in reality through his connection to a woman. He also seems to be referring to his own relationship to his mother as well as his father's. In his story, "My Father Joins the Fire Brigade," Schulz as narrator writes, "I never could learn from my mother how real were the things that I saw ... through my closed eyelids ... and how much of it was the product of my imagination" (Schulz, 1989, p. 216). Mother's failure to nurture her son and help him distinguish the inner and outer worlds is again implied. In the story, "The Age of Genius," Joseph literally shouts at his mother to assist him with his struggle: "Wake up ... come and help me! How can I face this flood alone, how can I deal with this inundation? How can I, all alone, answer the million dazzling questions that God is swamping me with?" (Schulz, 1989, p. 133). She does not answer. She offers no comfort whatsoever to his fevered heart. He quickly realizes that she will not help him, that he must help himself, and that the only way to accomplish this is through his art. And to be sure his art, in whatever form it takes, will always seek and fail to find her.

Schulz's final story in the volume *Sanatorium,* "Father's Last Escape," paradoxically tells of his father's death and refusal to die. "By dividing his death into installments, Father had familiarized us with his demise"

(Schulz, 1989, p. 311), observes Joseph. Jacob metamorphoses into a shameful and exposed crab found by the mother and then shows up at family meals. Father as crab "obstinately and indefatigably" appears to be "looking for something." Could it be the love of his wife? One day, Joseph discovers that his mother cooks Father/crab in a pot of boiling water. "How could you have done it?" he asks her in despair (p. 315). She wrings her hands but provides no answer. *She never answers her son.* If we take Schulz at his word that his fiction is autobiographical, then he is telling us that he believed his father lived a loveless and unfulfilled life that greatly diminished and eventually killed him. The mother cannibalized the father in stages and implicated the family in the deed. But the thought is too unbearable and so the father crab rallies even after death, "boiled and shedding his legs on the way," dragging himself "somewhere to begin a homeless wandering," never to be seen again (p. 316).

The mother's silence and marginal presence throughout Schulz's stories function to deepen the narrator's melancholy and enhance his isolation. Whereas the father plays a direct role in so many of the stories, the ghostly mother, nevertheless, infects each one of them with a sense of bleak loneliness and disconnection. But her person, unlike the father's, is neither elevated nor debased, for she lacks substance for either exaggeration. She is incorporated into the father (and the narrator) in the form of a profound sense of isolation, a derailment making it necessary to remake the world. Her inaccessibility drives the fictional father and the author/son to "fence" with the void by making something beautiful—to adorn birds with paint and trinkets, to make a fetish of a maid's foot, to ignite the female body with a radiance that appears to emanate from within, to breathe sad but wildly imaginative life into a sentence, to imagine a scene with a language that attains a talismanic power capable of endowing the world with transcendent mystery. The physical mother's absence creates a cruel and cold world for father and son. Schulz reinscribes that cruelty in the symbolic form of Mother Nature, a towering power driving her subjects forth with the whip of her seasons and the gales of her fancy. Mother/woman/bitch is out of reach, above them, detached, a bemused smile on her lips, her eyes looking elsewhere, ignoring their hunger and need—like the females in his drawings, like Bianca in his only love story.

We meet her in "Spring," a young woman dressed in white who looks like "she had just left the zodiac" (Schulz, 1989, p. 148). Bianca is perfection itself: "with every step, light as a dancer, she enters into her being and … with each of her movements she unconsciously hits the target" (p. 159). Joseph desires her and imagines that "to touch her body must … be painful from the sheer holiness of such contact" (p. 171). The sweet pain causes him to stalk her so he may catch a glimpse of her in her "flimsy white dress" from the window. He is "excited, almost demented from contradictory feelings" (p. 176).

It is in this story, his longest, where all the failures of the narrator's desires intersect in a convoluted and absurd plot whose course is dictated by his feverish passion inspired by a stamp album. The album of course stands in for The Book, the text of immutable truth and infinite possibility, and of course it must fail to deliver what it promises; the text of spring falls into hopeless ambiguity; the narrator's attempt to regress the reader to the origin of the world dissolves into a mindless tangle of "unborn tales ... lamenting choruses among the roots" (Schulz, 1989, p. 163); and Joseph's love, Bianca, is lost to Rudolph, his friend and owner of the stamp album. Confronting his castrated fate, the narrator compares himself in the last pages of the story to Abel, and the envious and plotting Rudolph to Cain. "There was a moment when my sacrifice seemed sweet and pleasing to God, when your chances seemed nil, Rudolph. But Cain always wins. The dice were loaded against me" (p. 203). Like Abel whose pure offering results in his murder, the narrator's sacrifice gains him no real favor. He relinquishes his competitive desires and hands Bianca over to Rudolph: "I am abdicating completely. I am dissolving the triumvirate. I am giving up regency in favor of Rudolph" (p. 204). In the end the narrator is led away in handcuffs for the crime of dreaming "the standard dream of the biblical Joseph" (p. 206).

The unattainable Bianca is also Schulz's unattainable mother. Her destructive power is in her profound absence and what that absence signifies: a broken connection, a breach of motherhood's promise of sense and sustenance, enlightened depravity, an arid world where one can never be worthy of love and is forever rendered a lowly beggar. The mother need not make too many actual appearances in his stories after all; the sense of her ruptured maternal connection and unavailability informs nearly every scene in Schulz's writing. Her unconscious shadow falls upon every object he sees. The fragmented body of her motherhood is the very context of the Schulzian literary cosmos and is reformed in his drawings as the decentered idol around which they revolve. A powerful shadow in his literature, she becomes a glorious goddess in his art as she incites unbearable longing in unworthy male beasts.

IDOLATRY

Schulz closely associated the Bible and the Zohar, the Jewish book of mysticism, with an early collection of his drawings that he called The Book of Idolatry (Xięga in Polish), created during the years 1920–1922. On several occasions, Schulz compared what artists do with God's creation. His father, another alter ego, was also a grand creator, moved by divine inspiration. In his "Treatise on Tailors' Dummies," Father defies God by announcing that there should be no monopoly on creativity. He therefore animates dummies, his golems, and argues for their equal rights. Schulz takes after him by bringing to life wax figures of famous world leaders in "Spring." Father, the heresiarch, creates his own belief system in which "even if the classical methods of creation prove inaccessible for evermore, there still remain some illegal methods, an infinity of heretical and criminal methods" (Schulz, 1989, "Tailors' Dummies," p. 60). In his "apologia for sadism," even homicide is defensible in cases in which "forms of existence … have ceased to be amusing" (p. 59). Father's numerous metamorphoses, as well as his theories on the endless possibilities of matter and time, reveal the complex nature of imagination and creativity and the many layers of existence. Everything is possible when one creates; there is no beginning or end, and time and space cease to follow physical laws.

In his *The Book of Idolatry,* Schulz substitutes the masculine, paternalistic, capricious god with women (and their feet) as sacred objects, thereby overturning and even mocking the Old Testament ban forbidding idols. Perhaps the idol is a necessity in a world where god makes little or no appearance. Erotically infused with imaginative power, it is the primary fetish, defending against anxiety while containing the pain and ecstasy of unanswered desire. So powerful an idol is the female foot and shoe for Schulz that in *Sanatorium Under the Sign of the Hourglass,* he claims that "God broke down" on the seventh day of creation. Rather than propose a day of rest, Schulz's God discovers the shoe, "the lustrous eloquence of that empty shell of patent leather" (Schulz, 1989, "The Age of Genius," p. 141). In his own words, then, the "authentic Book, the holy original" becomes "degraded and humiliated" (Schulz, 1989, "The Book," p. 126), yet much more exciting than the real thing: "How dull all my other books now seemed!" exclaims Schulz as protagonist in his story, "The Book" (p. 126).

When viewed alongside his writing, Schulz's drawings provide important insights into his complex psychology and echo his literary themes in simpler form. Through its images, *The Book of Idolatry* (1920–1922) tells the story of animal men huddled at the feet of indifferent women (see Plate 38). Originally comprised of various unique portfolios, each including a different selection of *cliché-verre* prints, the bookends always remained identical.[1]

The first print is a realistically drawn self-portrait of Schulz titled "Dedication." Hunched over, Schulz glances up at the woman (and the viewer) whom he approaches with extreme deference and carries a tray on which lies a golden crown. Clearly he is displaying his dedication to the women he is about to deify in the pages that follow. He appears shy and embarrassed, and several faces of men in the background jeer at him. In his

---

[1] Cliché verre, one of the earliest forms of reproducing images, is a technique in which an image is drawn with a sharp instrument onto a blackened glass plate. The plate is then brought into contact with light sensitive paper.

story "Loneliness," Schulz wrote, "Sometimes I see myself in the mirror. A strange, ridiculous, and painful thing! I am ashamed to admit it: I never look at myself full face … I stand inside the mirror a little off center, slightly in profile, thoughtful and glancing sideways" (Schulz, 1989, p. 309). Unlike Schiele's frontal self-portraits, most of Schulz's self-portraits depict him at this angle.

The final print is his drawing "The Book of Idolatry II," which portrays Schulz meekly approaching a half-clad woman whose face is shaded by a large chapeau and who carries a whip in her right hand. Schulz holds an opened book before her, most probably his very *The Book of Idolatry*, creating the motif of a book within a book. The woman is characteristically uninterested.

The image of a book is also a feature in his drawing, "The Book of Idolatry I." Here Schulz bends over as the woman steps on his back with high-heeled shoes. Behind them is a very large book whose pages are opened. It is as if the woman has emerged from between the book's pages to help live out Schulz's fantasy. In another drawing, "Undula with the Artists," Schulz stoops at the feet of his idol as she unresponsively glances at his artwork, allowing the pages to drop on the floor beside his humbled figure. Other dejected male artists' faces emerge from the darkened background. Books—the Bible and his *The Book of Idolatry*—are poor substitutes for the woman's body, especially her feet and shoes, objects so deeply invested with power that they take on sacred overtones.

Women in *The Book of Idolatry* are centrally placed in the drawings, often brightly lit as they emerge from a dark background. Some renderings take place out of doors against the backdrop of buildings from Drohobycz. Women walk, either naked or clothed, heads held high, seemingly indifferent to the men scrambling at their feet. The men are labeled in Schulz's titles as "pilgrims" and belonging to a "tribe of pariahs" in "procession" to gain proximity to the venerated female goddesses.

There is a spatial and emotional divide between men and women in Schulz's art that cannot be bridged. One print shows a despondent looking man who gazes through a window at a woman who is out of reach while his distorted, flattened face is pressed against the pane. He is thus separated from the woman he spies on, powerless yet desperate to enter her world. The crushed face is a repeated motif in Schulz's drawings. Often it is his face that is mashed by a woman's bare foot, which throws his body backward to form an arc of ecstasy.

Schulz's foot fetishism can be understood as a masochistic substitute for the encounter with women or, at the very least, an aid to it. It is also the final link in a sadomasochistic chain running through the cosmos. Men toil and spend their lives writhing beneath the woman's foot, a loaded, fleshy symbol of male subjugation. However many books he writes, however pious the company he keeps with other men, man is still a beast compelled to crawl on his knees to follow the woman's scent. His lofty aspirations are mocked by his unbearable lust, the *tandeta* that deprives him of true nobility. However castrated he feels, he cannot successfully banish the animal in him.

Focusing on the foot reduces the woman's body to more manageable terrain. It provides a kind of bridge between Schulz and the woman, a walk-up ramp to the awesome and frightening vagina. That the overwhelming quality of existence, the mysteries of the cosmos, the haunting of unbearable and unfulfilled desire, can be symbolized by the woman's foot and contained by that very symbol is indeed an act of creative magic.

The drawings that take place indoors display women lying on couches or beds, nearly always elevated above clusters of cowering men. Schulz is alone or in the company of others, some of them bearing the likeness of friends and acquaintances. He not only kneels at the women's feet; he sometimes drinks from their chamber pots filled with urine. In "The Beasts," one of the most striking fetishistic drawings from his *The Book of Idolatry*, a blushing yet self-possessed woman leans forward in a chair with her legs spread apart (see Plate 39). One leg is lifted to show off a black stocking and shoe while the other is naked as it catches the light. This leg is strategically placed in the center of the drawing, a vertical column beckoning Schulz to it. A whip emerges from the woman's hand positioned at her genitals. On the floor, Schulz crawls beside the phallic woman and approaches with an abject expression combining terror and desire, mouth agape and hands groping toward the single shoe planted in front of him to bait him like a beast. The woman's leg, foot, and shoe are the heart of the drawing. The high-heeled shoe is masculine and phallic, yet the foot's slender, delicate form is essentially feminine. Schulz's phallic women are complete in their combination of both genders, and they contrast with the men who are depicted as castrated, crippled, and dwarfed.

Who are the women in Schulz's drawings? Surely he was influenced by Sacher-Masoch's writings, especially *Venus in Furs*, published in Polish in 1904. But Undula is the name he chose for the heroine in his *The Book of Idolatry*. This name is phonetically similar to Adela, the maid in his novels, and also phonetically similar to the word "idol."[1] The forbidden, out of reach woman is an obvious symbol for the Oedipal mother. In fact, Schulz's first drawings were of horses and wagons. He was correct to describe these drawings as "full of weight and arcane symbolism" (Chmurzyński, 1995, p. 36), for they nicely depict the primal scene fantasy in which a child witnesses his parents during sex. This theme was one that he pursued throughout his life, as many drawings depict a driver (himself or a look-alike) with a couple—the female often naked—seated in a carriage behind

---

[1] Adela, the fictionalized version of Rachela, a maid in Schulz's home, was the only person who had power over Schulz's father. Schulz once confessed that a domineering and punitive nanny was responsible for his adult masochistic desires (Ficowski, 2003, p. 40).

him. Schulz bends over, sometimes sneaks a peek, and often seizes the reins in an attempt to control his passions. The extremely high hat he wears symbolizes the excitement he feels. Once again, he is separated from the action, left to imagine what is taking place behind him. At times naked men replace the horses as they pull the women behind them.

With Bianca in "Spring" and these Oedipal tableaux, Schulz's desire for women never reaches fulfillment. In his drawings men approach women but never obtain what they want. Besides the drawings in his *The Book of Idolatry*, Schulz produced many drawings of people seated around a table. He is often one of these people, squeezed between others. At times he is placed between two luscious, naked women. At others, the table seats a number of pious Jews. Sometimes, he brings these two themes together, and the religious elders are seated with the young women. Occasionally it is he who is naked, emaciated, holding his head up with his hand, revealing a painful inward yearning. Significantly, there is never food on the table and the plates remain empty, indicating that drives—both hunger and sex— cannot be satisfied. As in his *The Book of Idolatry*, these drawings are split with the table creating a dividing line between the upper part of the drawing and the lower section. Here Schulz shows the civilized congregat- ing around a table while the table cloth barely conceals what lies below: genitals, feet, shoes, dogs, and hunched over males—the animal body that is forever at odds with the bound and social self (see Plate 40). Beneath the table are hunger and lust, fear and desperation; above the table are the masks of propriety. Importantly, the dog is positioned directly under or near Schulz in these drawings, indicating the affinity he felt with this ani- mal. The story "Nimrod," about a dog the family adopts, reveals Schulz's identification with what he called a "crumb of life," "scrap of life," and "meager life" who "could not rid himself of the feeling of loneliness and homelessness" (Schulz, 1989, pp. 41–42): "My heart was filled with sympa- thy for that manifestation of the eternity of life, with loving tender curios- ity that was identical with self-revelation" (p. 42). Nimrod stays close to Adela's feet in an attitude of acceptance and submission.

Schulz described the unfeasibility of his desire in terms of a standoff: "We feel threatened by possibilities, shaken by the nearness of fulfillment, pale and faint with the delightful rigidity of realization. And that is as far as it goes" (Schulz, 1989, *The Street of Crocodiles*, p. 71). Women represent forbidden, and therefore unattainable, pleasure. In this regard, Schulz recalls Marcel Proust, one of his favorite authors, who famously and painfully longed for his mother's affections in *A La Recherche du Temps Perdu* (*Remembrance of Things Past*); yet even Proust obtained more gratification than Schulz.

Schulz seemed to realize that the only way he was able to seduce was through his art. Words and drawings replace physical contact (Jarzębski, 2009). *Cinnamon Shops* began as stories he sent in his letters to Deborah Vogel, a woman he even wished to marry at one time and a philosopher and author in her own right. The two never married, and their relationship remained primarily within the bounds of their letters. Unlike the women in his drawings, who are unappreciative of his work, Vogel enthusiastically encouraged Schulz to write.

Schulz never married, though he was once engaged to Jósefina Szelińska, a woman he felt "enslaves me and obligates me" (Ficowski, 1988, p. 138). "She, my fiancée, represents my participation in life; only by her mediation am I a human being and not just a lemur or gnome" (Ficowski, 1988, p. 135). Yet Szelińska broke off the engagement because she thought Schulz too impractical, especially with regard to moving out of Drohobycz and planning a wedding. Again and again the self-castration dream Schulz had as a child replayed itself in the patterns of his life, while his brush, and especially his pen, remained truly enchanted.

THE MESSIAH: HOPE FOR THE HOPELESS

During his lifetime, Schulz alternately competed with and felt abandoned by God, but he never relinquished his search for the ever-elusive divinity. In "Spring," he likened a stamp album to the story of creation: "I opened it, and the glamour of colorful worlds, of becalmed spaces, spread before me" (Schulz, 1989, p. 154). The "world immeasurable in its creation" (p. 153) is divulged to Schulz and he, in turn, reveals it to us. God walks through the pages and Schulz cannot help but speak to Him: "You reached into your pocket and showed me, like a handful of marbles, the possibilities that your world contained ... You wanted to dazzle me, Oh God, to seduce me, perhaps to boast, for even You have moments of vanity when you succumb to self-congratulation. Oh, how I love these moments!" (p. 154).

Schulz's dialogue with God seems to have taken on new dimensions toward the end of his life. His final book, titled *The Messiah*, was lost, and all we know about it are its opening lines: "Mother awakened me in the morning, saying, 'Joseph, the Messiah is near; people have seen him in Sambor'" (Ficowski, 2003, p. 157).[1] In 1939, he wrote, "At the moment I am drawn to increasingly inexpressible themes. Paradox, the tension between their vagueness and their evanescence and their universal claim, their aspiration to represent 'everything' is the most powerful creative stimulus" (Ficowski, 2003, pp. 146–147). This tantalizing excerpt suggests that, despite his doubt and the relentless honesty of his probing imagination, Schulz remained driven to pursue that ineffable and ephemeral realm where the beauty and nobility of life would finally meld with its absurdity and arbitrariness in inconceivable unity—for what is a Messiah if not the incarnation of that promise? How much sadder then is the tragedy of what

---

[1] Sambor is a town near Drohobycz that also had a sizable Jewish population before the war.

he witnessed toward the end of his life, so ruthlessly cut short by a psychopath's bullet?

Schulz's preoccupation with Jewish themes in his final years is most evident in his drawings, most probably illustrations for his lost manuscript. Many depict gatherings of Orthodox Hasidic Jews, crowds of bearded men wearing skullcaps, fur hats, or prayer shawls and congregating around a well (the one Joseph was thrown into?) or a table (the Passover table?). Unlike Schulz's *The Book of Idolatry*, where women take center stage, this is a man's world. Pious men stand huddled in passageways or remain seated beside one another. One speaks and the others lean forward to hear what he has to say. Their eyes are downcast and their demeanor sad as they engage in what appears to be serious conversation. Were these men discussing Jewish texts? Were they imagining what the world would be like once the Messiah appeared? Or were they disputing the fate of Jews in Drohobycz?

The fact that most of the Jewish men in these drawings are elderly is significant. Besides the fact that some of them resemble Schulz's father, they also belong to a generation that was on its way out. In his story, "The Book," Schulz describes them as

> little gray old men, whose indistinct faces, corroded by life, seemed covered by cobwebs—faces with watery, immobile eyes slowly leaking away, emaciated faces as discolored and innocent as the cracked and weathered bark of trees, and now like bark smelling only of rain and sky. (Schulz, 1989, p. 123)

Just as these men were ravaged by life and quickly disappearing from it, so too the Jews of Drohobycz were rapidly vanishing.[1] When Schulz wrote of the tailors' dummies, he could well have been speaking of the plight of the Jews in Eastern Europe.

> Can you imagine the pain, the dull imprisoned suffering, hewn into the matter of that dummy which does not know why it must be what it is, why it must remain in that forcibly imposed form which is no more than a parody? Do you understand the power of form, of expression, of pretense, the arbitrary tyranny imposed on a helpless block, and ruling it like its own, tyrannical despotic soul? (Schulz, 1989, "Tailors' Dummies," p. 34)

---

[1] In 1938, there were approximately 17,000 Jews in Drohobycz. Germans invaded Poland in 1939, and they occupied Drohobycz on June 30, 1941. By the time the Nazis were driven out of the town, only 400 Jews remained ("Brief History of the Jews of Drohobycz and Boryslaw," compiled by William Fern, May 3–5, 1985. Drohobycz-Boryslaw Reunion, Pines Hotel, South Fallsburg, New York).

In a 1934 letter in answer to a classmate's query about what was depressing him at the time, Schulz wrote, "The sadness of life, fear of the future, some dark conviction that everything is headed for a tragic end, a decadent *Weltschmerz* or devil knows what" (Ficowski, 1988, p. 77). It is true that Schulz had always been keenly aware of the fragility of life, with its "endless possibilities for mistakes" (Schulz, 1989, "Visitation," p. 12) long before the war years. Yet how prescient his statement seems in light of the horror that darkened the world 7 years later.

Bruno Schulz plumbed the depths of his creativity in search of *The Messiah*, his final manuscript that would tower above all others. It is a great loss to literature that this work disappeared during the Nazi occupation. Still, what he left behind has inspired writers like Phillip Roth in "The Prague Orgy," Cynthia Ozick in *The Messiah of Stockholm*, and David Grossman in *See Under Love*. His legacy will continue to astonish readers for a long time to come.

References

Abbott, A. (2009, October 15). Psychology: A reality check [Editorial]. *Nature*, *461*, 847.

Adorno, T. (1974). *Minima moralia: Reflections from a damaged life*. London: New Left Books.

Adorno, T. (1992). Engagement (R. Tiedmann, Ed. & S. W. Nicholson, Trans.). In *Notes to literature* (pp. 76–94). New York: Columbia University Press. (Original work published 1962)

Agassi, M. (1997). M. H. T.: Looking as a test or the test of looking: Michal Heiman and the examination of the subject life of the image. In M. Heiman, *Michal Heiman Test* (pp. 1–33). Givatayim, Israel: Eli Meir.

Alexander, F., & French, T. (1974). *Psychoanalytic principles and application*. Lincoln, NE: Nebraska University Press.

Andreason, N. C. (1987). Creativity and mental illness: Prevalence rates in writers and their first-degree relatives. *American Journal of Psychiatry*, *144*(10), 1288–1292.

Andreason, N. C., & Glick, I. D. (1988). Bipolar affective disorder and creativity: Implications and clinical management. *Comprehensive Psychiatry*, *29*(3), 207–217.

Anton, U., & Fuchs, W., Eds. (1996). So I don't write about heroes: An interview with Philip Dick. *SF Eye* (14, Spring) pp. 37–46.

Anzieu, D. (1986). *Freud's self-analysis* (P. Graham, Trans.). London: Hogarth Press.

Arieti, S. (1976). *Creativity: The magic synthesis*. New York: Basic Books.

Arlow, J. (1980). The revenge motive in the primal scene. *Journal of the American Psychoanalytic Association*, *28*, 519–541.

Auster, P. (1982). *The invention of solitude*. New York: Penguin Books.

Baker, T. B., McFall, R., & Shoham, V. (2008). Current status and future prospects of clinical psychology: Toward a scientifically principled approach to mental and behavioral health care. *Psychological Science in the Public Interest*, *9*(2), 67–103.

Balint, M. (1968). *The basic fault*. London: Tavistock.

Banaji, M. R., & Greenwald, A. G. (1994). Implicit stereotyping and prejudice. In M. P. Zanna & J. M. Olsen (Eds.), *The psychology of prejudice: The Ontario symposium* (Vol. 7, pp. 55–76). Hillsdale, NJ: Lawrence Erlbaum Associates.

Bargh, J. A. (1994). The four horsemen of automaticity: Awareness, intention, effi-ciency, and control in social cognition. In R. S. Wyer, Jr., & T. K. Srull (Eds.), *Handbook of social cognition* (2nd ed., pp. 1–40). Hillsdale, NJ: Lawrence Erlbaum Associates.

Bargh, J. A., & Chartran, T. L. (1999). The unbearable automaticity of being. *American Psychologist, 54,* 462–479.

Barreras del Rio, P., & Perrault, J. (1988). *Ana Mendieta: A retrospective.* New York: The New York Museum of Contemporary Art.

Bauby, J.-D. (1997). *The diving bell and the butterfly: A memoir of life in death* (J. Leggart, Trans.). New York: Vintage Books.

Baudelaire, C. (1974). Envirez-vous. *Yale French Studies, 50,* pp. 5–7.

Baudelaire, C. (1975). *My heart laid bare, and other prose writings.* New York: Haskell House Publishers.

Baudelaire, C. (1982). *Les fleurs du mal* (R. Howard, Trans.). Boston: Godine.

Baudelaire, C. (1995). *The painter of modern life and other essays* (J. Mayne, Ed. & Trans.). London: Phaidon Press. (Original work published 1964)

Baudelaire, C. (1998). *Artificial paradises: Baudelaire's masterpiece on hashish.* New York: Citadel. (Original work published 1860)

Becker, E. (1973). *The denial of death.* New York: Free Press.

Beebe, B. (2000). Co-constructing mother-infant distress: The microsynchrony of maternal impingement and infant avoidance in the face-to-face encounter. *Psychoanalytic Inquiry, 20*(3), 421–440.

Beebe, B. (2003). Brief mother-infant treatment: Psychoanalytically informed video feedback. *Infant Mental Health Journal, 24,* 24–52.

Beebe, B., & Lachmann, F. M. (2002). *Infant research and adult treatment: Co-constructing interactions.* Hillsdale, NJ: Analytic Press.

Beebe, B., & Stern, D. (1977). Engagement-disengagement and early object expe-riences. In M. Freedman & S. Grand (Eds.), *Communicative structures and psychic structures* (pp. 35–55). New York: Plenum.

Begley, S. (2009, October 2). Ignoring the evidence: Why do psychologists reject sci-ence? *Newsweek,* p. 30.

Bell, C. (1925, April). Dr. Freud on art. *The Dial,* pp. 280–281.

Bellak, L. (1973). Adaptive regression in the service of the ego. In L. Bellak, H. Gediman, & M. Hurvich (Eds.) *Ego functions in schizophrenics, neurotics, and normals: A systematic study of conceptual, diagnostic, and therapeutic aspects.* (pp. 180–190). New York: Wiley. (Oiriginal work published 1954)

Benyakar, M., & Knafo, D. (2004). Disruption: Individual and collective threats. In D. Knafo (Ed.), *Living with terror, working with trauma: A clinician's hand-book* (pp. 83–110). Lanham, MD: Jason Aronson.

Bion, W. R. (1978, July 10). *A seminar held in Paris.* Retrieved from http://www. psychoanalysis.org.uk/bion78.htm

Bion, W. R. (1984). Attacks on linking. In *Second thoughts: Selected papers on psy-cho-analysis* (pp. 93–109). New York: Jason Aronson. (Original work pub-lished 1959)

Blocker, J. (1999). *Where is Ana Mendieta?* Durham, NC: Duke University Press.

Bloom, H. (2002). *Genius: A mosaic of one hundred exemplary creative minds.* New York: Warner Books.

Blos, P. (1962). *On adolescence.* Glencoe, IL: Free Press.

Blos, P. (1967). Second individuation of adolescence. *The Psychoanalytic Study of the Child*, 22, 162–186.

Blum, H. (1979). On the concept and consequences of the primal scene. *Psychoanalytic Quarterly*, 48, 27–47.

Blum, H. (1994). The conceptual development of regression. *The Psychoanalytic Study of the Child*, 49, 60–76.

Blum, H. (1998). Ego psychology and contemporary structural theory. *International Psychoanalysis Newsletter*, 7(2), 31–36.

Bohm-Duchen, M. (1995). Fifty years on. In *After Auschwitz: Responses to the Holocaust in contemporary art* (pp. 103–145). Sunderland, UK: Northern Center for Contemporary Art.

Bollas, C. (1989). *Forces of destiny: Psychoanalysis and the human idiom*. London: Free Association.

Bollas, C. (2009). *The infinite question*. London: Routledge.

Boulanger, G. (2007). *Wounded by reality: Understanding and treating adult onset trauma*. Mahwah, NJ: Analytic Press.

Bowlby, J. (1969). *Attachment*. New York: Basic Books.

Bowlby, J. (1979). Psychoanalysis as art and science. *International Review of Psychoanalysis*, 6, 3–14.

Breton, A. (1972). Manifesto of surrealism. In *Manifestoes of surrealism* (R. Seaver & H. R. Lane, Trans.) (pp. 1–48). Ann Arbor, MI: University of Michigan Press. (Original work published 1924)

Brett, G. (2004). One energy. In O. M. Viso (Ed.), *Ana Mendieta, earth body: Sculpture and performance, 1972–1985*. Washington, DC: Hirshhorn Museum and Sculpture Garden, Smithsonian Institute with Hatje Cantz, pp. 181–204.

Breuer, J., & Freud, S. (1955). Studies on hysteria. In J. Strachey (Ed. & Trans.), *The standard edition of the complete psychological works of Sigmund Freud* (Vol. 2). London: Hogarth Press. (Original work published 1893–1895)

Bromberg, P. M. (1998). *Standing in the spaces: Essays on clinical process, trauma, and dissociation*. Hillsdale, NJ: Analytic Press.

Bucci, W. (2011). The interplay of subsymbolic and symbolic processes in psychoanalytic treatment: It takes two to tango—but who knows the steps, who's the leader? The choreography of the psychoanalytic interchange. *Psychoanalytic Dialogues*, 21, 45–54.

Buchholz, E. S. (1997). *The call of solitude: Aloneness in a world of attachment*. New York: Simon and Schuster.

Burke, N. (1997). InVisible worlds: On women and solitude. *Gender and Psychoanalysis*, 2(3), 327–341.

Burroughs, W. S. (1964). *Nova express*. New York: Grove Press.

Burroughs, W. S. & Odier, D. (1989). *The job: Interviews with William S. Burroughs*. London: Penguin Books.

Burroughs, W. S. & Ulin, D. (2009). *Naked lunch*. New York: Grove Press.

Bush, M. (1969). Psychoanalytic and scientific creativity—with special reference to regression in the service of the ego. *Journal of the American Psychoanalytic Association*, 17, 136–189.

Byron, G. G. (1886). *Childe Harold's pilgrimage*. Boston: Ticknor and Company. (Original work published 1812–1818)

Cacioppo, J. T., & Patrick, W. (2008). *Loneliness: Human nature and the need for social connection*. New York: W. W. Norton & Co.

Capote, T. (1987). *Answered prayers: The unfinished novel*. New York: Random House.

Caruso, F. C. (Producer), & Lynch, D. (Writer & Director). (1986). *Blue Velvet* [Motion picture]. USA: MGM.

Chasseguet-Smirgel, J. (1985). *The ego ideal: A psychoanalytic essay on the malady of the ideal*. New York: W. W. Norton & Co.

Chasseguet-Smirgel, J. (1986). *Sexuality and mind: The role of the father and the mother in the psyche*. New York: New York University Press.

Cheever, S. (1989). *Home before dark*. Boston: Houghton Mifflin.

Chipp, H. (1968). *Theories of art*. Berkeley: University of California Press.

Chmurzyński, W. (Ed.). (1995). *Bruno Schulz 1892–1942* [English supplement of catalogue memoirs of the exhibition]. Warsaw: Muzeum Literatury.

Clearwater, B. (1993). *Ana Mendieta: A book of works*. Miami Beach, FL: Grassfield Press.

Cocteau, J. (1957). *Opium*. (M. Crosland & S. Road, Trans.). London: Librairie Stock.

Coleridge, S. T. (1899). Kubla Khan. In T. F. Huntington (Ed.), *Coleridge's Ancient Mariner, Kubla Khan and Christabel* (pp. 35–37). New York: The MacMillan Company.

Comini, A. (1973). *Schiele in prison*. Greenwich, CT: New York Graphic Society.

Comini, A. (1974). *Egon Schiele's portraits*. Berkeley, CA: University of California Press.

Dali, S. (1964). *Salvador Dali: Diary of a genius* (R. Howard, Trans.). London: Picador.

Davies, J. M. & Frawley, M. G. (1992). Dissociative processes and transference-counter-transference paradigms in the psychoanalytically oriented treatment of adult survivors of childhood sexual abuse. *Psychoanalytic Dialogues, 2*, 5–36.

Dawson, J. (1997). *Logical dilemmas: The life and work of Kurt Gödel*. Wellesley, MA: AK Peters.

de Gelder, B., de Haan, E., & Heywood, C. (2002). *Out of mind: Varieties of unconscious processes*. New York: Oxford University Press.

De Nicholas, A. (1998). *Meditations through the Rg Veda: Four dimensional man*. York Beach, ME: Weiser Books.

De Quincy, T. (1950). *Confessions of an English opium-eater*. New York: Heritage Press. (Original work published 1821)

DeLong, G. R. (1990). Lithium treatment and bipolar disorders in childhood. *North Carolina Medical Journal, 51*, 152–154.

Derrida, J. (2003). The rhetoric of drugs. In A. Alexander, & M. Roberts (Eds.), *High culture: Reflections on addiction and modernity* (pp. 19–44). Albany, NY: State University of New York Press.

Dillard, A. (1974). *Pilgrim at Tinker Creek*. New York: Harper.

Director, L. (2002). The value of relational psychoanalysis in the treatment of chronic drug and alcohol use. *Psychoanalytic Dialogues, 12*(4), 551–579.

Dobisz, J. (2004). *The wisdom of solitude: A Zen retreat in the woods*. New York: Harper San Francisco.

Donn, L. (1988). *Freud and Jung: Years of friendship, years of loss*. New York: Scribner.

Douglas, C. (1996). Precious and splendid fossils. In *Beyond reason: Art and psychosis*. (pp. 35–47). Berkeley, CA: University of California Press.

Eagle, M. (1981). Interests as object relations. *Psychoanalysis and Contemporary Thought, 4*, 527–565.

Eagle, M. (2011). *From classical to contemporary psychoanalysis: A critique and integration*. New York: Routledge.

Edelheit, H. (1967). Discussion of A. J. Lubin: The influence of the Russian Orthodox Church on Freud's Wolf-Man. *Psychoanalytic Forum, 2*, 165–166.

Ehrenzweig, A. (1967). *The hidden order of art*. Berkeley, CA: University of California Press.

Eigen, M. (2009). *Flames from the unconscious: Trauma, madness, and faith*. London: Karnac.

Eisenstadt, M., Haynal, A., Rentchnick, P., & De Senarclens, P. (1989). *Parental loss and achievement*. Madison, CT: International Universities Press.

Eliot, T. S. (1963). Burnt Norton. In *Collected Poems: 1909–1962* (pp. 189–195). London: Faber and Faber.

Erikson, E. (1974). Womanhood and inner space. In J. Strouse (Ed.), *Women and analysis* (pp. 291–319). New York: Viking Press. (Original work published 1968)

Esman, A. (1973). The primal scene: A review and a reconsideration. *The Psychoanalytic Study of the Child, 7*, 173–215.

Evans, D. (1996). *An introductory dictionary of Lacanian psychoanalysis*. New York: Routledge.

Fairbairn, R. (1952). The repression and the return of the bad objects (with special reference to war neurosis). In *Psychoanalytic studies of personality* (pp. 59–81). London: Routledge and Kegan Paul. (Original work published 1943)

Fenichel, O. (1939). Problems of psychoanalytic technique. *Psychoanalytic Quarterly, 8*, 438–470.

Felstiner, M. L. (1994). *To paint her life: Charlotte Salomon in the Nazi era*. New York: HarperCollins.

Ferro, A. (2006). *Psychoanalysis as therapy and storytelling*. (P. Slotkin, Trans.) London: Routledge. (Original work published in 1999)

Feuerstein, G. (2001). *The Yoga tradition: Its history, literature, philosophy, and practice*. Prescott, AZ: Hohm Press.

Ficowski, J. (Ed.). (1988). *Letters and drawings of Bruno Schulz* (W. Arndt, Trans.). New York: Harper & Row.

Ficowski, J. (2003). *Regions of the great heresy: A biographical portrait* (T. Robertson, Ed. & Trans.). New York: Norton.

Fitzgerald, F. S. (1994). *A life in letters*. M. J. Bruccoli & J. Baughman (Ed.). New York: Macmillan Publishing Company.

Fleming, W. (1968). *Arts and ideas* (3rd ed.). New York: Holt, Rinehart & Winston.

Freud, A. (1967). Comments on psychic trauma. In S. S. Furst (Ed.), *Psychic trauma* (pp. 235–245). New York: Basic Books.

Freud, A. (1970). The role of regression in mental development. In *Research at the Hampstead child-therapy clinic and other papers 1956–1965* (pp. 407–418). London: Hogarth. (Original work published 1963)

Freud, S. (1953a). Fragment of an analysis of a case of hysteria. In J. Strachey (Ed. & Trans.), *The standard edition of the complete psychological works of Sigmund Freud* (Vol. 7, pp. 7–122). London: Hogarth Press. (Original work published 1905)

Freud, S. (1953b). The interpretation of dreams. In J. Strachey (Ed. & Trans.), *The standard edition of the complete psychological works of Sigmund Freud* (Vols. 4–5). London: Hogarth Press. (Original work published 1900)

Freud, S. (1953c). Three essays on the theory of sexuality. In J. Strachey (Ed. & Trans.), *The standard edition of the complete psychological works of Sigmund Freud* (Vol. 7, pp. 125–244). London: Hogarth Press. (Original work published 1905)

Freud, S. (1955). Beyond the pleasure principle. In J. Strachey (Ed. & Trans.), *The standard edition of the complete psychological works of Sigmund Freud* (Vol. 18, pp. 7–64). London: Hogarth Press. (Original work published 1920)

Freud, S. (1957a). Leonardo da Vinci and a memory of his childhood. In J. Strachey (Ed. & Trans.), *The standard edition of the complete psychological works of Sigmund Freud* (Vol. 11, pp. 59–137). London: Hogarth Press. (Original work published 1910)

Freud, S. (1957b). Mourning and melancholia. In J. Strachey (Ed. & Trans.), *The standard edition of the complete psychological works of Sigmund Freud* (Vol. 14, pp. 237–258). London: Hogarth Press. (Original work published 1917)

Freud, S. (1957c). Thoughts for the times on war and death. In J. Strachey (Ed. & Trans.), *The standard edition of the complete psychological works of Sigmund Freud* (Vol. 14, pp. 275–300). London: Hogarth Press. (Original work published 1915)

Freud, S. (1957d). The unconscious. In J. Strachey (Ed. & Trans.), *The standard edition of the complete psychological works of Sigmund Freud* (Vol. 14, pp. 159–215). London: Hogarth Press. (Original work published 1915)

Freud, S. (1958a). The handling of dream-interpretation. In J. Strachey (Ed. & Trans.), *The standard edition of the complete psychological works of Sigmund Freud* (Vol. 12, pp. 91–108). London: Hogarth Press. (Original work published 1911)

Freud, S. (1958b). On beginning the treatment: Further recommendations on the technique of psycho-analysis. In J. Strachey (Ed. & Trans.), *The standard edition of the complete psychological works of Sigmund Freud* (Vol. 12, pp. 123–144). London: Hogarth Press. (Original work published 1912)

Freud, S. (1958c). Recommendations to physicians practicing psycho-analysis. In J. Strachey (Ed. & Trans.), *The standard edition of the complete psychological works of Sigmund Freud* (Vol. 12, pp. 109–120). London: Hogarth Press. (Original work published 1912)

Freud, S. (1958d). The theme of the three caskets. In J. Strachey (Ed. & Trans.), *The standard edition of the complete psychological works of Sigmund Freud* (Vol. 12, pp. 289–301). London: Hogarth Press. (Original work published 1913)

Freud, S. (1959a). An autobiographical study. In J. Strachey (Ed. & Trans.), *The standard edition of the complete psychological works of Sigmund Freud* (Vol. 20, pp. 7–70). London: Hogarth Press. (Original work published 1925)

Freud, S. (1959b). Creative writers and day-dreaming. In J. Strachey (Ed. & Trans.), *The standard edition of the complete psychological works of Sigmund Freud* (Vol. 9, pp. 143–153). London: Hogarth Press. (Original work published 1908)

Freud, S. (1960). Jokes and their relation to the unconscious. In J. Strachey (Ed. & Trans.), *The standard edition of the complete psychological works of Sigmund Freud* (Vol. 8, pp. 9–236). London Press: Hogarth, 1960. (Original work published 1905)

Freud, S. (1961a). Civilization and its discontents. In J. Strachey (Ed. & Trans.), *The standard edition of the complete psychological works of Sigmund Freud* (Vol. 21, pp. 64–145). London: Hogarth Press. (Original work published 1930)

Freud, S. (1961b). Female sexuality. In J. Strachey (Ed. & Trans.), *The standard edition of the complete psychological works of Sigmund Freud* (Vol. 21, pp. 225–243). London: Hogarth Press. (Original work published 1931)

Freud, S. (1961c). Negation. In J. Strachey (Ed. & Trans.), *The standard edition of the complete psychological works of Sigmund Freud* (Vol. 19, 235–239). London: Hogarth Press. (Original work published 1925)

Freud, S. (1961d). Remarks on the theory and practice of dream-interpretation. In J. Strachey (Ed. & Trans.), *The standard edition of the complete psychological works of Sigmund Freud* (Vol. 19, pp. 109–121). London: Hogarth Press. (Original work published 1923)

Freud, S. (1961e). Some psychical consequences of the anatomical distinction between the sexes. In J. Strachey (Ed. & Trans.), *The standard edition of the complete psychological works of Sigmund Freud* (Vol. 19, pp. 248–258). London: Hogarth Press. (Original work published 1925)

Freud, S. (1962a). The aetiology of hysteria. In J. Strachey (Ed. & Trans.), *The standard edition of the complete psychological works of Sigmund Freud* (Vol. 3, pp. 191–221). London: Hogarth Press. (Original work published 1896)

Freud, S. (1962b). A psychical mechanism of forgetfulness. In J. Strachey (Ed. & Trans.), *The standard edition of the complete works of Sigmund Freud* (Vol. 3, pp. 287–297). London: Hogarth Press. (Original work published 1898)

Freud, S. (1963). The paths to the formation of symptoms. In J. Strachey (Ed. & Trans.), *The standard edition of the complete psychological works of Sigmund Freud* (Vol. 16, pp. 358–377). London: Hogarth Press. (Original work published 1917)

Freud, S. (1964). Lecture 29: Revision of the theory of dreams (from New introductory lectures on psycho-analysis). In J. Strachey (Ed. & Trans.), *The standard edition of the complete psychological works of Sigmund Freud* (Vol. 22, pp. 7–30). London: Hogarth Press. (Original work published 1933)

Freud, S. (1966). Extracts from the Fliess papers. In J. Strachey (Ed. & Trans.), *The standard edition of the complete psychological works of Sigmund Freud* (Vol. 1, pp. 173–280). London: Hogarth Press. (Original work published 1892–1899)

Freund, C. P. (2002, October 6). The art of terror. *The San Francisco Chronicle.* Retrieved from http://articles.sfgate.com/2002-10-06/opinion/17566858_1_ damien-hirst-karlheinz-stockhausen-new-Zealand-s-first

Fromm, E. (1941). *Escape from freedom.* New York: Holt, Rineheart & Winston.

Fromm-Reichmann, F. (1959). Loneliness. *Psychiatry, 22,* 1–15.

Frost, M., & Lynch, D. (Executive producers). (1990). *Twin peaks* [Television series]. USA: American Broadcasting Company.

Fry, R. (1924). *The artist and psychoanalysis.* London: Writers and Readers.

Fuller, P. (1980). *Art and psychoanalysis.* London: Writers and Readers.

Fusco, C. (1992). Traces of Ana Mendieta. *Poliester, 4,* 61.

Galler, F. (1981). The two faces of regression. *Psychoanalytic Inquiry, 1,* 133–154.

Gardner, H. (1982). *Art, mind, and brain: A cognitive approach to creativity.* New York: Basic Books.

Gay, P. (1988). *Freud: A life for our time*. New York: Norton.

Gedo, J. (1983). *Portraits of the artist: Psychoanalysis of creativity and its vicissitudes*. New York: Guilford Press.

Gedo, J. (1996). *The artist and the emotional world: Creativity and personality*. New York: Columbia University Press.

Geleerd, E. (1964). Adolescence and adaptive regression. *Bulletin of the Menninger Clinic, 28*, 302–308.

Gilbert, S., & Gubar, S. (1979). *The madwoman in the attic: The woman writer and the nineteenth-century literary imagination*. New Haven, CT: Yale University Press.

Gilligan, C. (1982). *In a different voice: Psychological theory and women's development*. Cambridge, MA: Harvard University Press.

Gilot, F. (2001). A painter's perspective. In K. H. Pfenninger & V. Shubik (Eds.), *The origins of creativity* (pp. 163–176). New York: Oxford University Press.

Goodwin, D. W. (1988). *Alcohol and the writer*. Kansas City, MO: Andrews and McMeel.

Goodwin, F. G., & Jamison, K. R. (1990). *Manic-depressive illness*. New York: Oxford University Press.

Green, A. (1986a). The dead mother. In *On private madness* (pp. 142–173). London: Hogarth Press.

Green, A. (1986b). *On private madness*. Madison, CT: International Universities Press.

Green, A. (1987). The analyst, symbolization and absence in the analytic setting. In *On private madness* (pp. 30–59). New York: International Universities Press.

Greenacre, P. (1971a). The childhood of the artist. In *Emotional growth* (Vol. 2, pp. 479–504). New York: International Universities Press. (Original work published 1957)

Greenacre, P. (1971b). Early physical determinants in the development of the sense of identity. In *Emotional growth* (Vol. 1, pp. 113–127). New York: International Universities Press. (Original work published 1958)

Greenberg, J., & Mitchell, S. (1983). *Object relations in psychoanalytic theory*. Cambridge, MA: Harvard University Press.

Greenwald, A. G. (1992). New look 3: Unconscious cognition reclaimed. *American Psychologist, 47*, 766–779.

Grinstein, A. (1980). *Sigmund Freud's dreams*. New York: International Universities Press.

Grossman, D. (1998, December). My writing process. Paper presented at Psychoanalysis and art—A dialogue. Suzanne Delal Center, Tel-Aviv, Israel.

Grumbach, D. (1995). *Fifty days of solitude*. Boston: Beacon Press.

Gustafson, R., & Källmén, H. (1989a). The effect of alcohol intoxication on primary and secondary processes in male social drinkers. *British Journal of Addiction, 84*, 1507–1513.

Gustafson, R., & Källmén, H. (1989b). Alcohol effects on cognitive personality style in women with special reference to primary and secondary process. *Alcoholism: Clinical and Experimental Research, 13*, 644–648.

Hajcak, F. C. (1976). *The effects of alcohol on creativity* (Dissertation). Ann Arbor, MI: UMI, Dissertation Services.

Hanly, C. (1990). The concept of truth in psychoanalysis. *International Journal of Psychoanalysis, 71*, 375–383.

Hartmann, R. P. (1974). *Malerei aus bereichen des unbewussten: Künstler experimentieren unter LSD*. Cologne: Dumont.

Hassin, R., Uleman, J., & Bargh, J. (Eds.) (2005). *The new unconscious*. New York: Oxford University Press.

Heilbrun, C. (1997). *The last gift of time: Life beyond sixty*. New York: Ballantine.

Heiman, M. (1998). *Michal Heiman Test 2 (M. H. T.)*. Givatayim, Israel: Eli Meir.

Herrera, H. (1983). *Frida: A biography of Frida Kahlo*. New York: Harper Colophon Books.

Herrera, H. (1991). *Frida Kahlo: The paintings*. New York: HarperCollins.

Herzberg, J. (1981). *Charlotte: Life or theater: An autobiographical play by Charlotte Salomon* (L. Venewitz, Trans.). New York: Viking.

Herzberg, J. A. (1998). *Ana Mendieta: The Iowa years: A critical study, 1969–1977* (Doctoral dissertation). City University of New York.

Herzberg, J. A. (2004). Ana Mendieta's Iowa years, 1970–1980. In O. M. Viso (Ed.), *Ana Mendieta, earth body: Sculpture and performance, 1972–1985*. Washington, DC: Hirshhorn Museum and Sculpture Garden, Smithsonian Institute with Hatje Cantz, pp. 137–180.

Higgins, E. T. (1989). Knowledge accessibility and activation: Subjectivity and suffering from unconscious sources. In J. S. Uleman & J. A. Bargh (Eds.), *Unintended thought* (pp. 75–123). New York: Guilford Press.

Hirsch, N. (1931). *Genius and creative intelligence*. New York: Philosophical Library.

Hoffman, I. Z. (2009). Doublethinking our way to "scientific" legitimacy: The dissection of human experience. *Journal of the American Psychoanalytic Association*, 57(5), 1043–1069.

Horsfield, K., Miller, B., Garcia-Ferraz, N. (Writers & Directors). (1987). *Ana Mendieta: Fuego de tierra* [Motion picture]. USA

Huxley, A. (1956). *The doors of perception & heaven and hell*. New York: HarperCollins Publishers Inc.

Ikonen, P., & Rechardt, E. (1984). On the universal nature of the primal scene fantasies. *International Journal of Psychoanalysis*, 65, 63–72.

Irigaray, L. (1985). *This sex which is not one* (C. Porter, Trans.). Ithaca, NY: Cornell University Press. (Original work published in 1977)

Jacobson, E. (1964). Early infantile preoedipal and oedipal phases. In *The self and the object world* (pp. 3–86). New York: International Universities Press.

James, W. (1890). *The principles of psychology: Volume II*. New York: Henry Holt and Company.

Jamison, K. R. (1989). Mood disorders and patterns of creativity in British writers and artists. *Psychiatry*, 52, 125–134.

Jamison, K. R. (1993). *Touched by fire: Manic-depressive illness and the artistic temperament*. New York: Free Press.

Janet, P. (1976). *Psychological healing: A historical and clinical study* (2 vols.) (E. & C. Paul, Trans.). New York: Arno Press. (Original work published 1919)

Jarzębski, J. (2009). Bruno Schulz and seductive discourse. In D. de Bruyn & K. van Heuckelom (Eds.), *(Un)masking Bruno Schulz: New combinations, further fragmentations, ultimate reintegrations* (pp. 327–338). Amsterdam: Rodopi.

Jones, E. (1953). *The life and work of Sigmund Freud*. New York: Basic Books.

Jung, C. G. (1952). Psychology and literature. In B. Ghiselin (Ed.), *The creative process* (pp. 217–232). New York: New American Library.

Jung, C. G. (1961). *Memories, dreams, reflections*. New York: Vintage.

Jung, C. G. (1964). *Civilization in transition* (R. F. C. Hull, Trans.). New York: Pantheon Books. (Original work published in 1933)

Jung, C. G. (1971). On the relation of analytical psychology to poetry. In J. Campbell (Ed.), *The portable Jung* (R. F. C. Hull, Trans.) (pp. 301–322). New York: Penguin Books. (Original work published 1922)

Jung, C. G. (1985). The significance of the father in the destiny of the individual. In A. Samuel (Ed.), *The father: Contemporary Jungian perspectives* (pp. 229–247). New York: New York University Press. (Original work published 1909)

Jung, C. G. (2009). *The red book* (S. Shamdasani, Ed.). New York: Norton.

Kafka, F. (1973). *Letters to Felice* (E. Heller & H. Born, Eds.; J. Stern & E. Duckworth, Trans.). New York: Shocken Books.

Kakutani, M. (2010, October 26). A writing stone: Chapter and verse. *New York Times*, pp. C1, C6.

Kalin, R., McClelland, D. C., & Kahn, M. (1965). The effects of male social drinking on fantasy. *Journal of Personality and Social Psychology, 1*, 441–452.

Kallir, J. (1990). *Egon Schiele: The complete works*. New York: Abrams.

Kallir [-Nirenstein], O. (1966). *Egon Schiele: Oeuvre catalogue of the paintings*. New York-Vienna: Crown Publishers and Paul Zsolnay Verlag.

Kandel, E. R. (1999). Biology and the future of psychoanalysis: A new intellectual framework for psychiatry revisited. *The American Journal of Psychiatry, 156*(4), 505–524.

Karper, K. (1994). *Where God begins to be: A woman's journey into solitude*. Grand Rapids, MI: Eerdmans.

Katz, R. (1990). *Naked by the window: The fatal marriage of Carl Andre and Ana Mendieta*. New York: Atlantic Monthly Press.

Katz-Freiman, T. (1996). *A matter of distance. Desert cliché: Israel now—local images, 10*. [Exhibit catalog]. Miami Beach, FL: The Israeli Forum of Art Museums and Bass Museum of Art.

Kenton, S. (1960). The playboy panel: Narcotics and the jazz musicians. *Playboy, 7*(11), 35–48, 117–118, 126–127.

Kernberg, O. (1994). The erotic in film and mass psychology. *Bulletin of the Menninger Clinic, 58*(1): 88–108.

Khantzian, E. (1995). Self-regulation vulnerabilities in substance abusers: Treatment implications. In S. Dowling (Ed.), *The psychology and treatment of addictive behavior* (pp. 65–100). Madison, CT: International Universities Press.

Kihlstrom, J. (1987). The cognitive unconscious. *Science, 237*(1), 445–452.

Kihlstrom, J. F., Barnhardt, T. M., & Tataryn, D. J. (1992). The psychological unconscious: Found, lost, and regained. *American Psychologist, 47*(6), 788–791.

Klein, G. (1976). *Psychoanalytic theory*. New York: International Universities Press.

Klein, M. (1975). On the sense of loneliness. In *Melanie Klein: Envy and gratitude and other works 1946–1963: The writings of Melanie Klein* (Vol. 3, pp. 300–313). New York: Delta. (Original work published 1963)

Klein, M. (1979a). Infantile anxiety situations reflected in a work of art and the creative impulse. In *Melanie Klein: Love, guilt and reparation and other works 1921–1945* (pp. 210–218). New York: Delta Books. (Original work published 1929)

Klein, M. (1979b). Mourning and its relation to manic depressive states. In *Melanie Klein: Love, guilt and reparation and other works 1921-1945: The writings of Melanie Klein* (Vol. 1, pp. 344–369). London: Hogarth Press. (Original work published 1940)

Klein, M. (1984). Notes on schizoid mechanisms. In *Melanie Klein: Envy and gratitude and other works 1946–1963: The Writings of Melanie Klein* (Vol. 3, pp. 1–24). New York: Delta. (Original work published 1946)

Klibansky, R., Saxl, F., & Panovsky, E. (1964). *Saturn and melancholy: Studies in the history of natural philosophy, religion and art*. London: Nelson.

Knafo, D. (1991). David Lynch's darker passions. *Academy Forum, 35*(1, 2), 5–7.

Knafo, D. (1993). *Egon Schiele: A self in creation: A psychoanalytic study of the artist's self-portraits*. Rutherford, NJ: Fairleigh Dickinson University Press.

Knafo, D. (1996). In her own image: Self-representation in the art of Frida Kahlo and Ana Mendieta. *Art Criticism, 11*(2), 1–19.

Knafo, D. (1998). Transitional space in the treatment of immigrants. *Israel Journal of Psychiatry, 35*, 48–55.

Knafo, D. (1999). Anti-Semitism in the clinical setting: Transference and countertransference dimensions. *Journal of the American Psychoanalytic Association, 47*(1), 35–63.

Knafo, D. (2002). Revisiting Ernst Kris' concept "regression in the service of the ego." *Psychoanalytic Psychology, 19*(1), 24–49.

Knafo, D. (2006). Now you see it, now you don't: A case study of castration and "omnisexuality." In D. Knafo & K. Feiner, *Unconscious fantasies and the relational world* (pp. 143–169). Hillsdale, NJ: Analytic Press.

Knafo, D. (2009a). Freud's memory erased. *Psychoanalytic Psychology, 26*(2), 171–190.

Knafo, D. (2009b). *In her own image: Women's self-representation in twentieth-century art*. Rutherford, NJ: Fairleigh Dickinson University Press.

Knafo, D., & Feiner, K. (1996). The primal scene: Variations on a theme. *Journal of the American Psychoanalytic Association, 44*(2), 549–569.

Knafo, D., & Feiner, K. (2006). Not in the family: Family romance fantasies and enactments in psychoanalysis. In D. Knafo & K. Feiner, *Unconscious fantasies and the relational world* (pp. 69–96). Hillsdale, NJ: Analytic Press.

Koch, P. (1994). *Solitude: A philosophical encounter*. Chicago, IL: Open Court.

Kohut, H. (1971). *The analysis of the self*. New York: International Universities Press.

Kohut, H. (1977). *The restoration of the self*. New York: International Universities Press.

Koller, A. (1990). *The stations of solitude*. New York: William Morrow & Co.

Koski-Jännes, A. (1985). Alcohol and literary creativity—The Finnish experience. *Journal of Creative Behavior, 19*, 120–136.

Kraeplin, E. (1921). *Manic-depressive insanity and paranoia*. Manchester: NH : Ayer Co. Pub.

Krafft-Ebbing, R. von. (1936). *Psychopathia Sexualis* (12th ed.) (F. J. Rebman, Trans.). Brooklyn, NY: Physicians and Surgeons Book Co. (Original work published in 1922)

Kris, E. (1936). The psychology of caricature. In *Psychoanalytic explorations in art* (pp. 173–188). New York: International Universities Press.

Kris, E. (1952). *Psychoanalytic explorations in art.* New York: International Universities Press.

Krystal, H. (1982). Alexithymia and the effectiveness of psychoanalytic treatment. *International Journal of Psychoanalytic Psychotherapy, 9,* 353–388.

Krystal, H. (1995). Disorders of emotional development in addictive behavior. In S. Dowling (Ed.), *The psychology and treatment of addictive behavior* (pp. 65–100). Madison, CT: International Universities Press.

Kuspit, D. (1993). The pathology and health of art: Gauguin's self-experience. In *Signs of psyche in modern and postmodern art* (pp. 3–17). Cambridge, MA: Cambridge University Press.

Lacan, J. (2004). *Écrits: A selection* (B. Fink, Trans.). New York: Norton. (Original work published 1953)

Lacan, J. (1977). The mirror stage as formative of the function of the I as revealed in psychoanalytic experience. In *Écrits* (A. Sheridan, Trans.) (pp. 1–7). New York: Norton. (Original work published 1949)

Lacan, J. (1959). *Le Désir et son interpretation, le séminaire, Livre VI.* Unpublished manuscript.

La Charité, V. A. (1977). *Henri Michaux.* Farmington Hills, MI: Twayne Publishers.

LaPlanche, J., & Pontalis, J.-B. (1973). *The language of psycho-analysis* (D. Nicholson-Smith, Trans.). New York: Norton.

Laub, D., & Podell, D. (1995). Art and trauma. *International Journal of Psychoanalysis, 76,* 991–1005.

LeDoux, J. E. (1996). *The emotional brain: The mysterious underpinnings of emotional life.* New York: Simon and Schuster.

Leonard, L. S. (1989). *Witness to the fire: Creativity and the veil of addiction.* Boston: Shambala.

Leopold, R. (1972). *Egon Schiele: Paintings, watercolors, drawings* (A. Lieven, Trans.). London: Phaidon.

Lichtenstein, H. (1977). *The dilemma of human identity.* New York: Jason Aronson.

Lifton, R. J. (1987). *The future of immortality and other essays for a nuclear age.* New York: Basic Books.

Loewald, H. (1974). Psychoanalysis as an art and the fantasy character of the psychoanalytic situation. In *Papers on psychoanalysis: Hans Loewald* (pp. 352–371). New Haven, CT: Yale University Press. (Original work published 1960)

Loewald, H. (1980). On the therapeutic action of psychoanalysis. In *Papers on psychoanalysis* (pp. 2201–2256). New Haven, CT: Yale University Press. (Original work published 1960)

Loewald, H. (1981). Regression: Some general considerations. *Psychoanalytic Quarterly, 50,* 22–43.

Lowell, R. (1988). *Robert Lowell, interviews and memoirs.* J. Meyers (Ed.). Ann Arbor, MI: The University of Michigan Press.

Lowry, M. (1996). *La mordida.* P.A. McCarthy (Ed.). Athens, GA: University of Georgia Press.

Ludwig, A. M. (1994). Mental illness and creative activity in female writers. *American Journal of Psychiatry, 151*(11), 1650–1656.

Malin, J., & Boynton, V. (2003). *Herspace: Women, writing, and solitude.* New York: Haworth Press.

Markoff, J. (2005). What the dormouse said: How the sixties counterculture shaped the personal computer industry. New York: Viking.

Martindale, C. (1998). Creativity and the brain. *Psychology and the Arts*, pp. 5–9.

Martindale, C. (1999). Biological bases of creativity. In R. Sternberg (Ed.), *Handbook of creativity* (pp. 137–152). Cambridge, U.K.: Cambridge University Press.

McDougall, J. (1980). Masturbation and the hermaphroditic ideal. In *Plea for a measure of abnormality* (pp. 141–168). Madison, CT: International Universities Press.

Mehlman, P. (2005, November 15). Zuckerman juiced. *New York Times*. Retrieved from http://www.nytimes.com/2005/11/14/opinion/14mehlma.html

Mendieta, H. (1996). Personal writings: Art and politics. In G. Moure. (Ed.) *Ana Medieta*. Barcelona: Ediciones Polígrafa, pp. 167–219.

Mereweather, C. (1996). From inscription to dissolution: An essay on expenditure in the work of Ana Mendieta. In G. Moure (Ed.), *Ana Mendieta* (pp. 83–134). Barcelona: Ediciones Polígrafa.

Miller, L. (1992/1993). Alone in the temple: A personal essay on solitude and the woman poet. *Kansas Quarterly, 24/25*(4/1), 200–214.

Mills, S. (2002). *Epicurean simplicity*. Washington, DC: Island Press.

Milner, M. (Joanna Field). (1957). *On not being able to paint*. Los Angeles: J. P. Tarcher, Inc.

Milosz, C. (1983). *The witness of poetry*. Cambridge, MA: Harvard University Press.

Mitchell, S. A. (1988). *Relational concepts in psychoanalysis: An integration*. Cambridge, MA: Harvard University Press.

Mitchell, S. A., & Aron, L. (1999). *Relational psychoanalysis: The emergence of a tradition*. Hillsdale, NJ: Analytic Press.

Modell, A. (1993). *The private self*. Cambridge, MA: Harvard University Press.

Moffat, M. J., & Paynter, C. (1974). *Revelations: Diaries of women*. New York: Random House.

Montane, D. (1991, September 15). The rise and fall of TropicAna. *Miami Herald Tropic*, pp. 8–21.

Montano, L. (1988). An interview with Ana Mendieta. *Sulfur, 22, 67*.

Myers, F. (1907). *Human personality and its survival of bodily death*. New York: Longmans, Green, & Co.

Myers, W. (1973). Split self-representation and the primal scene. *Psychoanalytic Quarterly, 42*, 525–538.

Nass, M. (1984). The development of creative imagination in composers. *International Review of Psychoanalysis, 11*, 481–491.

Nebehay, C. (1979). *Egon Schiele: Leben, briefe, gedichte* [Egon Schiele: Life, correspondence, poetry]. Salzburg: Residenz Verlag.

Nin, A. (1974). *The diary of Anaïs Nin: 1947–1955*. G. Stuhlmann (Ed.). San Diego, CA: Harcourt Brace Jovanovich, Publishers.

Nochlin, L. (1988). Why have there been no great women artists? In *Women, art, and power and other essays* (pp. 145–178). New York: Harper and Row. (Original work published 1971)

Norlander, T. (1999). Inebriation and inspiration? A review of the research on alcohol and creativity. *Journal of Creative Behavior, 33*(1), 22–44.

Noy, P. (1969). A revision of psychoanalytic theory of the primary process. *International Journal of Psychoanalysis, 50*, 155–178.

O'Connor, F. (1985). The psychodynamics of the frontal self-portrait. In M. M. Gedo (Ed.), *Psychoanalytic perspectives on art* (pp. 169–221). Hillsdale, NJ: Analytic Press.

Ogden, T. (1994a). Projective identification and the subjugating third. In *Subjects of analysis* (pp. 97–106). Northvale, NJ: Jason Aronson.

Ogden, T. (1994b). The analytic third: Working with intersubjective clinical facts. In *Subjects of analysis* (pp. 61–69). Northvale, NJ: Jason Aronson.

Ogden, T. (1997). *Reverie and interpretation: Sensing something human.* London: Karnac.

Olsen, T. (1965). *Silences.* New York: Delacorte Press.

Orenstein, G. F. (1994). Recovering her story: Feminist artists reclaim the great goddess. In N. Broude & M. Garrard (Eds.), *The power of feminist art: The American of the 1970s, history and impact* (pp. 174–189). New York: Abrams.

Oz, A. (1988, December 11). Interview with the author. *Haaretz*, pp. 16–18.

Paz, O. (1983). *Alternating current.* (H. Lane, Trans.). New York: Arcade Publishing.

Pederson-Krag, G. (1949). Detective stories and the primal scene. *Psychoanalytic Quarterly, 8,* 207–214.

Phillips, A. (1993). On risk and solitude. In *On kissing, tickling and being bored: Psychoanalytic essays on the unexamined life* (pp. 27–41). Cambridge, MA: Harvard University Press.

Pierce, C. S., & Jastrow, J. (1884). On small differences in sensation. *Memoirs of the National Academy of Science, 3,* 75–83.

Plant, S. (1999). *Writing on drugs.* New York: Farrar, Straus & Giroux.

Poe, E. A. (1992). *The collected tales and poems of Edgar Allen Poe: Modern Library Edition.* New York: Random House, Inc.

Poland, W. (2000). The analyst's witnessing of otherness. *Journal of the American Psychoanalytic Association, 48*(1), 17–35.

Pollock, G. (1975). On mourning, immortality and utopia. *Journal of the American Psychoanalytic Association, 23,* 334–362.

Quinodoz, J.-M. (1996). The sense of solitude in the psychoanalytic encounter. *International Journal of Psychoanalysis, 77,* 481–497.

Rank, O. (1924). *The trauma of birth.* New York: Dover.

Rank, O. (1932). *Art and artist.* New York: Agathon.

Rank, O. (1971). *The double* (J. H. Tucker, Ed. & Trans.). New York: New American Library. (Original work published 1914)

Rauch, H., & Suro, F. (1992). Ana Mendieta's primal scream. *Americas, 45*(4), 44.

Rauch, L. (2000). The poet syndrome: Opiates, psychosis and creativity. *Journal of Psychoactive Drugs, 32*(3), 343–350.

Reik, T. (1948). *Listening with the third ear: The inner experience of a psychoanalyst.* New York: Grove Press.

Richards, R. L., Kinney, D. K., Lunde, I., & Benet, M. (1988). Creativity in manic-depressives, cyclothymes, and their normal first-degree relatives: A preliminary report. *Journal of Abnormal Psychology, 97,* 281–288.

Rickman, J. (1940). On the nature of ugliness and the creative impulses. *International Journal of Psychoanalysis, 21,* 297–298.

Rilke, R. M. (1992). *Letters to a young poet* (J. M. Burnham, Trans.). San Rafael, CA: New World Library. (Original work published 1934)

Ringstrom, P. (2011). Principles of improvisation: A model of therapeutic play in relational psychoanalysis. In L. Aron & A. Harris (Eds.), *Relational Psychoanalysis* Vol. V. (pp. 447–474). New York: Analytic Press.

Roessler, A. (1948). *Erinnerungen an Egon Schiele* [In memoriam: Egon Schiele] (2nd ed.). Vienna: Verlag der Buchandlung.

Rose, G. (1980). Psychoanalysis, creativity, and literature: A French-American inquiry. *Psychoanalytic Quarterly, 49,* 161–167.

Rose, G. (1995). *Necessary illusions: Art as "witness."* New York: International Universities Press.

Rothenberg, A. (1990). *Creativity and madness: New findings and old stereotypes.* Baltimore: Johns Hopkins University Press.

Said, E. (2000). *Reflections on exile.* Cambridge, MA: Harvard University Press.

Salomon, C. (1981). *Charlotte: Life or theatre? An autobiographical play* (L. Vennewitz, Trans.). New York: Viking Press.

Salomon, D. (1997). *Utopia parkway: The life and work of Joseph Cornell.* New York: Farrar, Straus & Giroux.

Salomon, N. (2006). On the impossibility of Charlotte Salomon in the classroom. In M. Steinberg & M. Bohm-Duchen (Eds.), *Reading Charlotte Salomon* (pp. 212–222). Ithaca, NY: Cornell University Press.

Sandler, J., & Sandler, A. M. (1994). Theoretical and technical comments on regression and anti-regression. *International Journal of Psychoanalysis, 75,* 431–439.

Sarton, M. (1973). *Journal of a solitude.* New York: Norton.

Schafer, R. (1958). Regression in the service of the ego: The relevance of a psychoanalytic concept of personality assessment. In G. Lindzey (Ed.), *Assessment of human motives* (pp. 119–148). New York: Rinehart.

Schafer, R. (1992). *Retelling a life.* New York: Basic Books.

Schiele, E. (1988). *I, eternal child: Paintings and poems* (A. Hollo, Trans.). New York: Grove Press.

Schildkraut, J. J., Hirshfeld, A. J., & Murphy, J. M. (1994). Mind and mood in modern art, II: Depressive disorders, spirituality, and early deaths in the abstract expressionist artists of the New York School. *American Journal of Psychiatry, 151*(4), 482–489.

Schöndle, A. (1991). Cinnamon shops by Bruno Schulz: The apology of tandeta. *The Polish Review, 36*(2), 127–144.

Schulz, B. (1920–1922). *The book of idolatry* (J. Ficowski, Ed., & B. Piotrowska, Trans.). Warsaw: Interpress.

Schulz, B. (1989). *The complete fiction of Bruno Schulz* (C. Wieniewska, Trans.). New York: Walker & Co.

Searles, H. F. (1965). The effort to drive the other person crazy: An element in the aetiology and psychotherapy of schizophrenia. In *Collected papers on schizophrenia and related subjects* (pp. 254–283). New York: International Universities Press. (Original work published 1959)

Segal, H. (1964). *Introduction to the work of Melanie Klein* (2nd ed.). New York: Basic Books.

Segal, H. (1991). Art and the depressive position. In *Dream, phantasy and art* (pp. 85–100). London: Routledge.

Sexton, A. (1981). *Anne Sexton: The complete poems.* Boston: Houghton Mifflin Company.

Shedler, J. (2010). The efficacy of psychodynamic psychotherapy. *American Psychologist, 63*(2), 98–109.

Shengold, L. (1974). The metaphor of the mirror. *Journal of the American Psychoanalytic Association, 22*, 97–115.

Sinclair, U. (1956). *The cup of fury.* Great Neck, NY: Channel Press.

Silverman, L. H. (1983). The subliminal psychodynamic method: Overview and comprehensive listing of studies. In J. Masling (Ed.), *Empirical studies of psychoanalytic theory* (Vol. 1, pp. 69–103). Hillsdale, NJ: Lawrence Erlbaum Associates.

Simonton, D. K. (1999). *Origins of genius: Darwinian perspectives on creativity.* New York: Oxford University Press.

Smith, C., & Kuwayama. (1997). Interview with Agnes Martin in Taos. Retrieved from http://www.youtube.com/watch/v=_JFYmo50A

Sontag, S. (2003). *Regarding the pain of others.* New York: Farrar, Straus and Giroux.

Spence, D. (1982). *Narrative truth, historical truth.* New York: Norton.

Spero, N. (1992). Tracing Ana Mendieta. *Artforum, 30*, 75–77.

Spitz, R. (1965). *The first year of life.* New York: International Universities Press.

Steiner, G. (1967). *Language and silence: Essays on language, literature, and the inhuman.* New York: Atheneum.

Stern, D. B. (1989). The analyst's unformulated experience of the patient. *Contemporary Psychoanalysis, 19*, 71–99.

Stern, D. N. (1985). *The interpersonal world of the infant: A view from psychoanalysis and developmental psychology.* New York: Basic Books.

Stern, D. N. (1995). *The motherhood constellation: A unified view of parent-infant psychotherapy.* New York: Basic Books.

Stevenson, R. L. (1909). *The strange case of Dr. Jekyll and Mr. Hyde.* New York: Current Literature Publishing Company.

Stevenson, R. L. (2002). *The strange case of Dr. Jekyll and Mr. Hyde and other tales.* London: Penguin Group. (Original work published 1886)

Stiles, K. (1992). Survival ethos and destruction art. *Discourse: Journal for Theoretical Studies in Media and Culture, 14*, 74–102.

Storr, A. (1976). *The dynamics of creation.* Harmondsworth, England: Penguin Books.

Storr, A. (1988). *Solitude: A return to the self.* New York: Ballantine.

Taylor, J. (1983). *Dream work: Techniques for discovering the creative power in dreams.* Mahwah, NJ: Paulist Press.

Ten Berge, J. (1999). Breakdown or breakthrough? A history of European research into drugs and creativity. *Journal of Creative Behavior, 33*, 257–276.

Ten Berge, J. (2002). Jekyll and Hyde revisited: Paradoxes in the appreciation of drug experiences and their effects on creativity. *Journal of Psychoactive Drugs, 34*(3), 249–262.

Thevoz, M. (1991). L'alibi artistique: Pourquoi les psychotropes sont-ils plus prolifiqes en narcodollars qu'en oeuvres d'art. *Psychotropes, 6*(3), 73–76.

Thoreau, H. D. (2009). *Walden and civil disobedience.* Ann Arbor, MI: Borders Classics.

Tuttman, S. (1979). Regession: Is it necessary or desirable? *Journal of the American Academy of Psychoanalysis, 7*, 221–230.

van Alphen, E. (1997). *Caught by history: Holocaust effects in contemporary art, literature, and theory.* Stanford, CA: Stanford University Press.

van Alphen, E. (2006). Giving voice: Charlotte Salomon and Charlotte Delbo. In M. Steinberg & M. Bohm-Duchen (Eds.), *Reading Charlotte Salomon* (pp. 114–125). Ithaca, NY: Cornell University Press.

van der Kolk, B. A. (1997). The psychobiology of post-traumatic stress disorder. *Journal of Clinical Psychiatry, 58*, 16–24.

Van Gogh, V. (1937). *Dear Theo: The autobiography of Vincent Van Gogh* (I. Stone, Ed.). New York: New American Library.

Velmanns, M. (1991). Is human information processing conscious? *Behavioral and Brain Sciences, 14*, 651–726.

Viso, O. M. (2004). *Ana Mendieta, earth body: Sculpture and performance, 1972–1985.* Washington, DC: Hirshhorn Museum and Sculpture Garden, Smithsonian Institute with Hatje Cantz.

von Sacher-Masoch, L. (2008). *Venus in furs* (F. Savage, Trans.). London: Bookkake.

Vonnegut, K. (1982). *Deadeye Dick*. New York: Delacorte.

Walcott, D. (2007). The schooner flight. In D. Walcott & E. Baugh (Eds.), *Selected poems* (pp. 127–136). New York: Farrar, Straus and Giroux.

Wallace, D. F. (1997). David Lynch keeps his head. In *A supposedly fun thing I'll never do again* (pp. 146–213). Boston: Little Brown & Co.

Wegner, D. (2002). *The illusion of conscious will*. Cambridge, MA: MIT Press.

Wegrocki, H. J. (1946). Masochistic motives in the literary and graphic art of Bruno Schulz. *Psychoanalytic Review, 33*, 154–164.

Wehr, G. (1988). *Jung: A biography*. Boston: Shambala.

Weinberger, J., & Hardaway, R. (1990). Separating science from myth in subliminal psychodynamic activation. *Clinical Psychology Review, 10*(6), 727–756.

Weiss, A. (2003). Baudelaire, Artaud and the aesthetics of intoxication. In A. Alexander & M. Roberts (Eds.), *High culture: Reflections on addiction and modernity* (pp. 157–172). Albany, NY: State University of NY Press.

Weissman, P. (1971). The artist and his objects. *International Journal of Psychoanalysis, 52*, 401–406.

Whitford, F. (1981). *Egon Schiele*. New York: Oxford University Press.

Wiesel, E. (1976). *Messengers of God: Biblical portraits and legends* (M. Wiesel, Trans.). New York: Random House.

Wilson, T. D. (2002). *Strangers to ourselves: Discovering the adaptive unconscious.* Cambridge, MA: Harvard University Press.

Winnicott, D. W. (1968). The capacity to be alone. In *The maturational processes and the facilitating environment* (pp. 29–36). New York: International Universities Press. (Original work published 1958)

Winnicott, D. W. (1971a). Creativity and its origins. In *Playing and reality* (pp. 65–85). London: Tavistock.

Winnicott, D. W. (1971b). Mirror-role of mother and family in child development. In *Playing and reality* (pp. 111–118). London: Tavistock.

Winnicott, D. W. (1975). Transitional objects and transitional phenomena. In *Through pediatrics to psycho-analysis* (pp. 229–242). New York: Basic Books. (Original work published 1951)

Winnicott, D. W. (1988). *Human nature*. London: Free Association.

Zweig, S. (1963). *The world of yesterday*. Lincoln: University of Nebraska Press. (Original work published 1943)

Index